W9-DDI-415

CCNA:
Cisco Certified
Network Associate

Exam Notes

CCNA™:
Cisco® Certified
Network Associate®
Exam Notes™

Todd Lammle
Sean Odom

San Francisco • Paris • Düsseldorf • Soest • London

SYBEX

Associate Publisher: Neil Edde
Contracts and Licensing Manager: Kristine O'Callaghan
Acquisitions and Developmental Editor: Jeff Kellum
Editor: Pete Gaughan
Production Editor: Elizabeth Campbell
Technical Editor: Matthew Luallen
Book Designer: Bill Gibson
Graphic Illustrator: Tony Jonick
Electronic Publishing Specialist: Judy Fung
Proofreaders: Laurie O'Connell, Nancy Riddiough
Indexer: Lynnzee Elze
Cover Designer: Archer Designs
Cover Illustrator/Photographer: Tony Stone Images

Library of Congress Card Number: 00-109138
ISBN: 0-7821-2648-0

Manufactured in the United States of America

10 9 8 7 6 5 4 3 2 1

*This book is dedicated to Erin,
the most wonderful woman in the world.*

—Sean Odom

Acknowledgments

I would like to thank the wonderful staff at Sybex for all their support and help throughout this book process. I also want to personally thank Sean Odom for being so dependable.

—Todd Lammle

First, I want to thank my family for all the hours they lived without me during the writing process, especially Erin. I need to thank Todd Lammle for bringing me into this project and giving me the opportunity to get a CCNA book under my belt. I would also like to thank those behind the scenes at Sybex, including Elizabeth Campbell and Pete Gaughan, and Jeff Kellum for signing me not only for this book, but for my first as well! Jeff has no idea how he changes lives as an acquisitions editor, especially mine. I also thank the technical editor, Matthew Luallen, and Hanson Nottingham for his valuable input.

—Sean Odom

Sybex would like to thank electronic publishing specialist Judy Fung, proofreaders Laurie O'Connell and Nancy Riddiough, and indexer Lynnzee Elze for their valuable contributions to this book.

Contents

Introduction

This book is intended to start you out on an exciting new path toward obtaining your CCNA certification. It reaches beyond popular certifications like the MCSE and CNE to provide you with an indispensable factor in understanding today's network—insight into the Cisco world of internetworking and network design.

If you've purchased this book, you are probably chasing one of the Cisco professional certifications: CCNA/CCNP, CCDA/CCDP, or CCIE. All of these are great goals, and they are also great career builders. Glance through any newspaper and you'll find employment opportunities for people with these certifications—these ads are there because finding qualified network administrators is a challenge in today's market. The certification means you know something about the product, but more importantly, it means you have the ability, determination, and focus to learn—the greatest skills any employee can have!

You've probably also heard all the rumors about how hard the Cisco tests are—believe us, the rumors are true! Cisco has designed a series of exams that truly challenge your knowledge of their products. Each test not only covers the materials presented in a particular class, it also covers the prerequisite knowledge for that course.

Is This Book for You?

This book focuses on the exam objectives for the Cisco Certified Network Associate (CCNA). It will teach you how to install LAN, WAN, and dial-in networks using Cisco products. Each chapter begins with a list of the CCNA test objectives; be sure to read over them before working through the chapter.

The Sybex Exam Notes books were designed to be succinct, portable exam review guides. They can be used either in conjunction with a more complete study program—supplemented by books, CBT courseware, or practice in a classroom/lab environment—or as an exam review for those who don't feel the need for more extensive test preparation. It isn't our goal to "give the answers away," but rather to identify those topics on which you can expect to be tested and to provide sufficient coverage of these topics.

Perhaps you've been working with Cisco internetworking technologies for years now. The thought of paying lots of money for a specialized Cisco exam preparation course probably doesn't sound too appealing. What can they teach you that you don't already know, right? Be careful, though. Many experienced network administrators, even CCIEs, have walked confidently into test centers only to walk sheepishly out of them after failing a Cisco exam. As they discovered, there's the Cisco of the real world and the Cisco of the Cisco certification exams. It's our goal with the Exam Notes books to show you where the two converge and where they diverge. After you've finished reading through this book, you should have a clear idea of how your understanding of the technologies involved matches up with the expectations of the Cisco test makers.

Or perhaps you're relatively new to the world of Cisco internetworking, drawn to it by the promise of challenging work and higher salaries. You've just waded through an 1,800-page Cisco CCNA study guide or taken a class at a local training center. Lots of information to keep track of, isn't it? Well, by organizing the Exam Notes books according to the Cisco exam objectives and by breaking up the information into concise, manageable pieces, we've created what we think is the handiest exam review guide available. Throw it in your briefcase and carry it to work with you. As you read through the book, you'll be able to quickly identify those areas you know best and those that require more in-depth review.

NOTE The goal of the Exam Notes series is to help Cisco certification candidates familiarize themselves with the subjects on which they can expect to be tested in the certification exams. The CCNA exam objectives can be found at www.cisco.com/warp/public/10/wwtraining/ certprog/testing/pdf/ccna_507.pdf. You'll notice that the objectives are vague. For complete, in-depth coverage of the technologies and topics involved in Cisco networking, we recommend the *CCNA: Cisco Certified Network Associate Study Guide,* from Sybex.

How Is This Book Organized?

As mentioned previously, this book is organized according to the official exam objectives list prepared by Cisco for the CCNA exam. Within each chapter, the individual exam objectives are addressed in turn. Each objective section is further divided according to the type of information presented. Those sections are titled:

- Critical Information
- Necessary Procedures
- Exam Essentials
- Key Terms and Concepts
- Sample Questions

Critical Information

This section presents the greatest level of detail on information that is relevant to the objective. This is the place to start if you're unfamiliar with or uncertain about the technical issues related to the objective.

Necessary Procedures

Here you'll find instructions for procedures that require a lab computer to be completed. From configuring IP addressing to establishing serial point-to-point connections, the information in these sections addresses the hands-on requirements for the CCNA exam.

NOTE Not every objective has a hands-on procedure associated with it. For such objectives, the Necessary Procedures section has been left out.

Exam Essentials

In this section, we've put together a concise list of the most crucial topics of subject areas that you'll need to comprehend fully prior to taking the Cisco exam. This section can help you identify those topics that might require more study on your part.

Key Terms and Concepts

Here we've compiled a mini-glossary of the most important terms and concepts related to the specific objective. You'll understand what all those technical words mean within the context of the related subject matter.

Sample Questions

For each exam objective, we've included a selection of questions similar to those you'll encounter on the actual Cisco exam. Answers and explanations are provided so you can gain some insight into the test-taking process.

How Do You Become a CCNA?

With their certification program, Cisco has created a stepping-stone approach to CCIE (Cisco Certified Internetwork Expert) certification. You can become a CCNA by passing one written exam.

Why Become a CCNA?

Cisco has created a certification process, not unlike that of Microsoft or Novell, to give administrators a set of skills and prospective employers an authenticated way to measure those skills. Becoming a CCNA can be the initial step of a successful journey toward a new or refreshed, highly rewarding, and sustainable career.

As you study for the CCNA exam, we can't stress this enough: It's critical that you have some hands-on experience with Cisco routers. If you can get your hands on some 2500 series routers, you're set!

NOTE   One way to get the hands-on router experience you'll need in the real world is to attend one of the seminars offered by Globalnet Training Solutions, Inc. (http://www.lammle.com), taught by this book's authors, Todd Lammle and Sean Odom. Each student has three routers and a switch to configure throughout the six-day seminar. Each seminar teaches the students what they need to know to pass his or her CCNA and CCDA exams!

NOTE   You can also purchase the CCNA Virtual Lab e-Trainer, which is a simulated lab environment complete with three routers and one switch. (A more robust version can be downloaded from www.routersim.com.)

Where Do You Take the Exams?

You may take the exams at any one of the more than 800 Sylvan Prometric Authorized Testing Centers around the world. For the location of a testing center near you, call 800-204-3926. Outside the United States and Canada, contact your local Sylvan Prometric Registration Center. To register for a Cisco exam:

1. Determine the number of the exam you want to take. (The CCNA exam number is 640-507.)

2. Register with the Sylvan Prometric Registration Center nearest you. You will need to pay in advance for the exam. At the time of this writing, registration costs $100 per exam, and the test must be taken within one year of payment. You can sign up for an exam up to six weeks in advance or as late as the day you wish to take it. If

something comes up and you need to cancel or reschedule your exam appointment, contact Sylvan Prometric at least 24 hours in advance.

3. When you schedule the exam, you'll be provided with instructions regarding all appointment and cancellation procedures, the ID requirements, and information about the testing center location.

NOTE Cisco recently announced that exams will also be administered at Virtual University Enterprises. Cisco expects the exams to be available December 2000. Visit www.vue.com or www.cisco.com/warp/public/10/wwtraining/certprog/testing/register.htm for more information.

What the Cisco CCNA Certification Exam Measures

The CCNA program was not only created to provide a solid introduction to the Cisco internetworking operating system (IOS) and to Cisco hardware, but also to internetworking in general, making it helpful to you in areas not exclusively Cisco's. It's hard to say at this point in the certification process, but it's not unrealistic to imagine that future network managers—even those without Cisco equipment—could easily require Cisco certifications of their job applicants.

To meet the CCNA certification skill level, you must be able to understand or perform the following:

- Install and support simple routed LAN, routed WAN, and switched LAN networks. The exam assumes basic networking understanding.

- Determine whether a hub, Ethernet switch, or router would be more appropriately used.

- Use Cisco software to identify addresses, protocols, and connectivity status in a network that contains multiple interconnected Cisco devices.

- Interconnect Cisco switches and routers using specified network design requirements.

- Configure Cisco switches and routers to support a specified list of protocols and technologies.

- Configure access lists to control access to network devices or segments and general network traffic.

- Verify that Cisco switches and routers, and their configured network services and protocols, operate correctly in a given network specification.

Tips for Taking Your Cisco CCNA Exam

The CCNA test contains around 65 questions, which are to be answered in 90 minutes. Now, Cisco allows you to schedule and take your exam on the same day. You are also now able to take more than one exam per day.

Many questions on the exam will have potential answers that at first glance look identical—especially the syntax questions! Remember to read through the choices carefully, because a "close" answer won't cut it. If you choose an answer in which the commands are in the wrong order or there is even one measly character missing, you'll get the question wrong. So to practice, take the sample quizzes at the end of each objective section in this book over and over, until they feel natural to you.

Also, never forget that the right answer is the Cisco answer. In many cases, more than one answer will appear to be the answer, but the *correct* answer is the one Cisco recommends.

Here are some general tips for exam success:

- Arrive early at the exam center so you can relax and review your study materials—particularly IP tables and lists of exam-related information.

- Read the questions *carefully*. Don't jump to conclusions. Make sure you're clear on *exactly* what the question is asking.

- Don't leave any unanswered questions. These will be counted against you.

- When answering multiple-choice questions you're not sure about, use a process of elimination to get rid of the obviously incorrect answers first. Doing this will greatly improve your odds should you need to make an "educated guess."

Once you have completed an exam, you'll be given immediate online notification of your pass or fail status, plus a printed Examination Score Report indicating whether you passed or failed, along with your exam results by section. (The test administrator will give you the printed score report.) Test scores are automatically forwarded to Cisco within five working days after you take the test, so you don't need to send your score to them. If you pass the exam, you'll receive confirmation from Cisco, typically within two to four weeks.

How to Contact the Authors

Todd Lammle can be reached at todd@lammle.com.

Sean Odom can be reached at sodom@rcsis.com.

How to Contact the Publisher

Sybex welcomes reader feedback on all of their titles. Visit the Sybex Web site at http://www.sybex.com for book updates and additional certification information. You'll also find online forms to submit comments or suggestions regarding this or any other Sybex book.

Chapter

1

Bridging/Switching

CISCO EXAM OBJECTIVES COVERED IN THIS CHAPTER:

his first chapter will introduce you to VLANs and how to configure VLANs on Cisco switches using static VLAN number assignments. Understanding frame tagging within a VLAN will also be discussed.

When there is more than one path through the network, data can come back to the original source. In this situation, Spanning-Tree Protocol (STP) is used in Layer 2 switched networks to prevent these network loops, and to block ports that can allow data to return, causing a loop. We will discuss the basics of STP and how to use STP in a Layer 2 switched internetwork.

Cisco switches can operate in three different LAN switch modes: store-and-forward, cut-through, and FragmentFree. This chapter will discuss all three methods.

The chapter will end with a discussion of the Point-to-Point Protocol (PPP). PPP is used to connect either asynchronous serial or synchronous serial links. Configuration of PPP, as well as PPP authentication, will be discussed.

Switches were placed in networks to replace bridges and hubs in flat-topology networks (where there is no segmentation of broadcast or collision domains). As networks grow, so does the amount of broadcast traffic. Not all broadcasts are bad; they are a necessity in today's networking protocols, to allow the location of certain devices to be known throughout the network segment. But when devices on the same network segment number in the hundreds, the result of all these devices sending broadcasts as well as data traffic can slow the network and the devices to a crawl.

Excessive broadcasts reduce the bandwidth available to end users and require every node on the network to process every frame, regardless of whether it is the intended recipient of the data. The processor in each machine is responsible for doing this task, taking away from the processing power needed for the end-user applications.

As more and more broadcasts enter your network, the network can actually grind to a halt. This situation is known as a *broadcast storm*. Broadcast storms occur when broadcasts throughout the LAN use up all available bandwidth, bringing the network completely to a stop. Switches use VLANs to segment the network into smaller broadcast and collision domains. Let's look at the two different types of VLANs, both static and dynamic.

NOTE   Token Ring, Fast Ethernet, Gigabit Ethernet, and Fiber Distributed Data Interface (FDDI) are also interfaces that can be found on Cisco switches.

Static VLANs

If you want to allow different ports on a switch to be part of different subnetworks, you need to create virtual LANs within the switch. A virtual local area network (VLAN) is a logical grouping of network users and resources connected to defined ports on the switch. A VLAN looks like, and is treated like, its own subnet. By using virtual LANs, you're no longer confined to physical locations. VLANs can be created by location, function, department—even by the application or protocol used—regardless of where the resources or users are located.

VLANs are created by an administrator to break up broadcast domains in a Layer 2 switch. The administrator then assigns switch ports to the VLAN. This objective will discuss how VLAN assignments are created and configured on Cisco switches.

Critical Information

The two types of VLAN assignments are static and dynamic. A static VLAN is the typical means of creating a VLAN. The switch port to which you assign a VLAN association maintains that association until an administrator changes the port assignment. This type of VLAN configuration is easy to set up and monitor, working well in a network where the movement of users within the network is controlled. Using network management software to configure the ports can be helpful but is not mandatory.

Dynamic VLANs determine a node's VLAN assignment automatically. Using intelligent management software, you can enable hardware (MAC) addresses, protocols, or even applications to create dynamic VLANs. For example, suppose MAC addresses have been entered into a centralized VLAN management application. If a node is then attached to an unassigned switch port, the VLAN management database can look up the hardware address and assign and configure the switch port to the correct VLAN. This can make management and configuration easier for the administrator. If a user moves, the switch will automatically assign them to the correct VLAN. However, more administration is needed initially to set up the database.

Cisco administrators can use the VLAN Management Policy Server (VMPS) service to set up a database of MAC addresses that can be used for dynamic addressing of VLANs. VMPS is a MAC address–to–VLAN mapping database.

Necessary Procedures

To configure VLANs on a switched internetwork, you need to follow the steps listed below:

- Configure the VLANs.
- Assign switch ports to VLANs.

- Identify the VLANs.

- Verify the configuration.

NOTE See Appendix B of the *CCNA: Cisco Certified Network Associate Study Guide* (Sybex, 2000) for more information on configuring VLANs, including such topics as how to configure trunk ports, clearing VLANs from trunk lines, verifying trunk lines, and configuring ISL routing.

Configuring VLANs

Configuring VLANs is the easy part of the job. It's actually understanding what users you want in each VLAN that is time-consuming. Once you have decided the number of VLANs you want to create and the users that will be members of each, you can create your VLAN.

To configure VLANs on the 1900 series switch, choose **K** from the initial user interface menu to get into IOS configuration. Even though you can create VLANs with the menu system available with the 1900 switch, we will only show you how to configure VLANs with the 1900 switch CLI. This is because it is the Cisco IOS, and also because the CCNA exam objectives only cover the CLI method of configuration on the 1900 switch.

The following switch output is the console display when connecting to a 1900 switch. Press **K** to enter the CLI mode:

```
1 user(s) now active on Management Console.

        User Interface Menu

    [M] Menus
    [K] Command Line
    [I] IP Configuration

Enter Selection:  K
```

```
CLI session with the switch is open.
To end the CLI session, enter [Exit].
```

Enter global configuration mode using the enable command and then config t (short for configure terminal). To configure VLANs on an IOS-based switch, use the vlan *[vlan#]* name *[vlan_name]* command. The following demonstrates how to configure VLANs on the switch by creating three VLANs for three different departments:

```
>en
#config t
Enter configuration commands, one per line.
   End with CNTL/Z
(config)#hostname 1900EN
1900EN(config)#vlan 2 name sales
1900EN(config)#vlan 3 name marketing
1900EN(config)#vlan 4 name mis
1900EN(config)#exit
```

After you create the VLANs that you want, you can use the show vlan command to see the configured VLANs. However, notice that by default all ports on the switch are in VLAN 1. To change the VLAN associated with a port, you need to go to each interface and tell it what VLAN to be a part of.

NOTE Remember that a created VLAN is unused until it is mapped to a switch port or ports, and that all ports are always in VLAN 1 unless set otherwise.

Once the VLANs are created, verify your configuration with the show vlan command (**sh vlan** for short). For instance:

```
1900EN#sh vlan
```

```
VLAN Name                 Status      Ports
----------------------------------------
1    default              Enabled     1-12, AUI, A, B
2    sales                Enabled
3    marketing            Enabled
4    mis                  Enabled
1002 fddi-default         Suspended
1003 token-ring-defau     Suspended
1004 fddinet-default      Suspended
1005 trnet-default        Suspended
----------------------------------------
[output cut]
```

Now that we can see the three VLANs created, we can now assign switch ports to a VLAN. Normally, each port can only be part of one VLAN. Trunking is used to overcome the one-VLAN rule and make a port available to one or more VLANs at a time

Assigning Switch Ports to VLANs

You can configure each port to be in a VLAN by using the vlan-membership command. You can only configure VLANs one port at a time. There is no command to assign more than one port to a VLAN at a time with the 1900 switch.

Remember that you can configure either static memberships or dynamic memberships on a port. This book and the Cisco CCNA exam objectives only cover static VLAN memberships.

NOTE   VLAN Membership Policy Server (VMPS) is the server implemented in order to maintain a database of MAC addresses associated with an identified VLAN for use with dynamic VLAN assignments.

In the following example, we configure interface 2 to VLAN 2, interface 4 to VLAN 3, and interface 5 to VLAN 4:

```
1900EN#config t
Enter configuration commands, one per line.
End with CNTL/Z
1900EN(config)#int e0/2
1900EN(config-if)#vlan-membership ?
  dynamic  Set VLAN membership type as dynamic
  static   Set VLAN membership type as static
1900EN(config-if)#vlan-membership static ?
  <1-1005>  ISL VLAN index
1900EN(config-if)#vlan-membership static 2
1900EN(config-if)#int e0/4
1900EN(config-if)#vlan-membership static 3
1900EN(config-if)#int e0/5
1900EN(config-if)#vlan-membership static 4
1900EN(config-if)#exit
1900EN(config)#exit
```

Now, type **sh vlan** again to see the ports assigned to each VLAN:

```
1900EN#sh vlan
```

VLAN	Name	Status	Ports
1	default	Enabled	1, 3, 6-12, AUI, A, B
2	sales	Enabled	2
3	marketing	Enabled	4
4	mis	Enabled	5
1002	fddi-default	Suspended	
1003	token-ring-defau	Suspended	
1004	fddinet-default	Suspended	
1005	trnet-default	Suspended	

```
[ouput cut]
```

NOTE   You could also just type **show vlan <#>** to gather information about only one VLAN at a time. Another command you can use to see the ports assigned to a VLAN is **show vlan-membership**.

Identifying VLANs

VLANs can span multiple connected switches. Switches in this switch fabric must keep track of frames and which VLAN they belong to. Frame tagging performs this function. Switches can then direct frames to the appropriate port.

There are two different types of links in a switched environment:

Access Link   A link that is only part of one VLAN and is referred to as the native VLAN of the port. Any device attached to an access link is unaware of a VLAN membership. This device just assumes it is part of a broadcast domain, with no understanding of the physical network. Switches remove any VLAN information from the frame before it is sent to an access link device. Access link devices cannot communicate with devices outside their VLAN unless the packet is routed through a router.

Trunk Link   A link that can carry multiple VLANs. Originally named after the trunks of the telephone system, which carry multiple telephone conversations, trunk links are used to connect switches to other switches, to routers, or even to servers. Trunked links are supported on Fast Ethernet or Gigabit Ethernet only. To identify the VLAN that a frame belongs to with Ethernet technology, Cisco switches support two different identification techniques: Inter-Switch Link (ISL) and 802.1q. Trunk links are used to transport VLANs between devices and can be configured to transport all VLANs or just a few.

NOTE   See Chapter 6 of the *CCNA: Cisco Certified Network Associate Study Guide* (Sybex, 2000) for more information on identifying VLANs.

Verifying the Configuration

The switch in an internetwork needs a way to keep track of users and frames as they travel the switch block. A switch block is a group of switches sharing the same VLAN information. As the frame traverses through each switch from the port of entry to the port of exit, the highway of wires, processors, and ASICs between the ports is referred to as the switch fabric.

VLAN frame identification, or frame tagging, is a relatively new approach that was specifically developed for switched communications. In this approach, a unique user-defined identifier is placed in the header of each frame as it's forwarded throughout the switch fabric. (This identifier is sometimes referred to as a VLAN ID or VLAN color.) The identifier is understood and examined by each switch prior to any broadcasts or transmissions to switch ports of other switches, routers, or end-station devices. When the frame exits the switch fabric, the switch removes the identifier before the frame is transmitted to the target end station.

All this means is that the switch tags a frame with a VLAN identifier that is only used within the switch fabric itself. Before that frame leaves the switch, it removes the VLAN ID, because nothing outside the switch would be able to understand that ID. There is one exception: When you run ISL, the VLAN ID is preserved as it passes over the ISL link.

The following points summarize frame tagging:

- Specifically developed for multi-VLAN, inter-switch communication.
- Places a unique identifier in the header of each frame.
- Identifier is removed before frame exits switch on non-trunk links.
- Functions at the Data Link layer.
- Requires little processing or administrative overhead.
- Inter-Switch Link (ISL) frame tagging is a Cisco proprietary frame tagging method that encapsulates an existing frame with the VLAN information.

Exam Essentials

Understand what a VLAN is.   Virtual LANs are used to break up broadcast domains in a Layer 2 switched internetwork.

Understand how to configure static VLAN assignments.   Static VLAN assignments are created by an administrator configuring each switch port to a VLAN by hand.

Understand frame tagging.   Frame tagging is used to keep track of frames as they traverse a trunked link. Cisco uses the proprietary ISL method of frame tagging on Fast Ethernet and Gigabit Ethernet links.

Key Terms and Concepts

virtual local area network (VLAN)   Network type used to break up broadcast domains in a Layer 2 switched internetwork.

static VLAN   Assignment of a switch port to a VLAN by an administrator.

frame tagging   Method used to identify frame membership in a VLAN as the frame traverses a trunked link.

Inter-Switch Link (ISL)   Cisco proprietary method of frame tagging for Fast Ethernet and Gigabit Ethernet links.

Sample Questions

1. Which of the following is true regarding frame tagging? (Choose all that apply.)

   A. Frame tagging assigns a user-defined ID to each frame.

   B. Frame tagging places a unique identifier in the header of each frame.

C. ISL frame tagging is a Cisco proprietary method that encapsulates an existing frame with the VLAN information.

D. Frame tagging can only be used on Cisco switches.

Answer: A, B, C. Frame tagging can be used on all types of switches; however, ISL is a Cisco proprietary method.

2. Which of the following are two types of Fast Ethernet frame tagging techniques Cisco switches support?

A. TRLS

B. 802.1q

C. ISL

D. 802.2u

Answer: B, C. ISL and 802.1q are Fast Ethernet frame tagging methods. ISL is proprietary to Cisco.

Spantree

Is understanding Spanning-Tree Protocol (STP) important? It used to be very important in the old bridged IBM environments. STP is a great, resilient protocol that runs in the background and keeps your network loop-free.

NOTE   STP is enabled by default on the Cisco 1900 and 2820 series switches.

After routing was introduced and administrators began replacing bridges with routers, STP was not used anymore. However, with the invention of the switch, its purpose in life was resurrected! In this section, we'll talk about the main purpose of STP, which is to stop network loops from occurring on your Layer 2 network (bridges or switches). STP is constantly monitoring the network to find all links and make sure that loops do not occur by shutting down redundant links.

Critical Information

STP finds all links in the network and shuts down redundant links to stop any network loops from occurring. It does this by electing a root bridge that will decide on the network topology. There can only be one root bridge in any given network. The root bridge ports are called designated ports, and designated ports operate in what is called forwarding state. Forwarding state ports send and receive traffic.

If you have other switches in your network, as shown in Figure 1.1, then these are nonroot bridges. However, the port that has the lowest cost to the root bridge is called a root port and sends and receives traffic. The cost is determined by the bandwidth of a link.

FIGURE 1.1: Spanning-tree operations

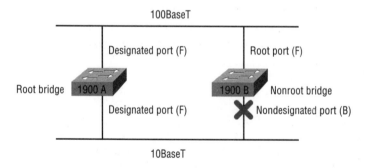

Ports that are determined to have the lowest cost path to the root bridge are also called designated ports and, like root bridge ports, operate in forwarding state (noted as *F* in the illustration). Other ports on the bridge are considered nondesignated and will not send or receive traffic. This is called blocking mode (noted as *B* in the illustration).

Selecting the Root Bridge

Switches or bridges running STP exchange information with bridge protocol data units (BPDUs). BPDUs are used to send configuration messages using multicast frames, carrying the bridge ID of each device to other devices.

The bridge ID is used to determine the root bridge in the network and to determine the root port. The bridge ID is eight bytes long and includes the priority and MAC address of the device. The default priority on all devices running the IEEE STP version is 32768.

To determine the root bridge, the priority of the bridge and the MAC address is combined. If two switches or bridges have the same priority value, then the lower MAC address is used to determine who has the lowest ID.

For example, if two switches both use the default priority of 32768, then the MAC addresses are compared. If switch A's MAC address is 0000.0c00.1111.1111 and switch B's MAC address is 0000.0c00 .2222.2222, then switch A becomes the root bridge.

NOTE For more information on selecting a root bridge, see Chapter 2 of the *CCNA: Cisco Certified Network Associate Study Guide* (Sybex, 2000).

Selecting the Designated Port

To determine the port or ports that will be used to communicate with the root bridge, the path cost is determined. The STP cost is an accumulated total path cost based on the bandwidth of the links. Table 1.1 shows the typical costs associated with the different Ethernet networks. The IEEE 802.1d specification has recently been revised to handle the new higher-speed links; the 1900 switches use the *original* IEEE 802.1d specifications.

TABLE 1.1: Typical Costs of Various Ethernet Networks

Speed	New IEEE Cost	Original IEEE Cost
10 Gbps	2	1
1 Gbps	4	1
100 Mbps	19	10
10 Mbps	100	100

Spanning-Tree Port States

The ports on a bridge or switch running STP can transition through four different states:

Blocking   Won't forward frames, listens to BPDUs. All ports are in blocking state by default when the switch is powered up.

Listening   Listens to BPDUs to make sure no loops occur on the network before passing data frames.

Learning   Learns MAC addresses and builds a filter table, but does not forward frames.

Forwarding   Able to send and receive data on the bridge port.

Typically, switch ports are in either blocking or forwarding state. A forwarding port is a port that has been determined to have the lowest cost to the root bridge. However, if the network has a topology change because of a failed link, or even if the administrator adds a new switch to the network, the ports on a switch will be in listening and learning states.

Blocking ports are used to prevent network loops. Once a switch determines the best path to the root bridge, then all other ports will be in blocking state. Blocked ports still receive BPDUs.

If a switch determines that a blocked port should now be the designated port, it will go to listening state. The port will check all BPDUs heard to make sure that it won't create a loop once the port goes to forwarding state.

Convergence

Convergence occurs when bridges and switches have transitioned to either the forwarding or blocking states. No data is forwarded during this time. Convergence is important to make sure that all devices have the same database.

The problem with convergence is the time it takes for all devices to update. Before data can start to be forwarded, all devices must be updated. The time it usually takes to go from blocking to forwarding state is 50 seconds. It is not recommended to change the default STP timers, but the timers can be adjusted if they need to be. The time it takes to transition a port from listening to the learning state or from learning to forwarding state is called the forward delay.

Spanning-Tree Example

In Figure 1.2, the three switches all have the same priority of 32768. However, notice the MAC address of each switch. By looking at the priority and MAC addresses of each switch, you should be able to determine the root bridge.

FIGURE 1.2: Spanning-tree example

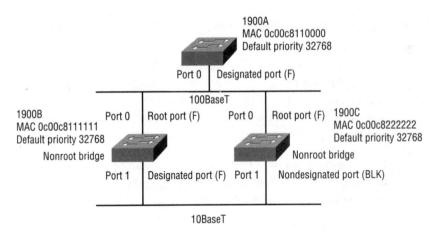

Since 1900A has the lowest MAC address and all three switches use the default priority, then 1900A will be the root bridge.

To determine the root ports on switches 1900B and 1900C, you need to look at the cost of the link connecting the switches. Since the connection from both switches to the root switch is from port 0 using a 100 Mbps link, that port has the best cost and will be the root port for both switches.

To determine the designated ports on the switches, the bridge ID is used. The root bridge always has all ports as designated. However, since both 1900B and 1900C have the same cost to the root bridge, the designated port will be on switch 1900B because it has the lowest bridge ID. Because 1900B has been determined to have the designated port, switch 1900C will put port 1 in blocking state to stop any network loop from occurring. In the next section, let's look at an example of the procedures needed to configure the Cisco Catalyst 1900 series switch.

Necessary Procedures

In this section, we'll take a step-by-step look at verifying the STP configuration, which can be essential to troubleshooting.

Verifying STP Information

To verify if STP is configured and running on a switch, you can use the show spantree (**sh span** for short) command. This will show you information for VLAN 1 only. To see information about other VLANs running STP, use the show spantree [vlan #], as seen here:

```
1900A#sh span
VLAN1 is executing the IEEE compatible
                              Spanning Tree Protocol
    Bridge Identifier has priority 32768,
        address 0030.80CC.7B40
    Configured hello time 2, max age 20,
        forward delay 15
```

```
       Current root has priority 32768, address
            0030.80CC.7B40
       Root port is N/A, cost of root path is 0
       Topology change flag not set,
            detected flag not set
       Topology changes 0,
            last topology change occured 0d00h00m00s ago
       Times:  hold 1, topology change 8960
                hello 2, max age 20, forward delay 15
       Timers: hello 2, topology change 35,
            notification 2
   Port Ethernet 0/1 of VLAN1 is Forwarding
       [output cut]
```

The show spantree command displays the STP information for
VLAN 1. Notice that the bridge ID, MAC address, and timers are displayed. The output "VLAN 1 is executing the IEEE compatible Spanning Tree Protocol" is telling you that STP is running on this VLAN.

NOTE   There are no Necessary Procedures directly related to this objective. Throughout this book, you will see the Necessary Procedures
section only for objectives that involve procedures.

Exam Essentials

Understand how the root bridge is elected.   The root bridge is
determined by the bridge priority and bridge MAC address.

Understand how a designated port is determined.   To determine
the designated ports on the switches, the bridge ID is used. All ports
of the root bridge are always designated ports.

Understand how root ports are determined.   To determine the root
ports on switches, you need to look at the cost of the link connecting
the switches.

Key Terms and Concepts

root bridge   Switch that includes the designated port with the highest priority or the lowest MAC address.

802.1D   IEEE specification for STP.

Spanning-Tree Algorithm (STA)   System used to calculate a loop-free network topology for STP.

Spanning-Tree Protocol (STP)   Protocol that allows data transfer without the existence of a virtual circuit.

Sample Questions

1. Which of the following is a benefit of STP?

A. Prevents loops in bridged or switched networks

B. Allows redundant links

C. Prunes topology to a minimal spanning tree

D. Resilient to topology changes and device failures

E. All of the above

Answer: E. Cisco considers each of these to be benefits of STP.

2. What does STA stand for?

A. Spanning-Tree Algorithm (STA)

B. Spanning Tree Always (STA)

C. Stop-the-Loop Algorithm (STA)

D. Spanning-Topology Algorithm (STA)

Answer: A. Spanning-Tree Algorithm is used by STP to map a bridged network and find the links.

3. What parameters are used to elect the root bridge?

A. MAC address

B. IP address

C. Bridge priority

D. Bridge priority and MAC address

E. Bridge priority and IP address

Answer: D. The root bridge is determined by the bridge priority and MAC address of the bridge.

Switching Modes/Methods

Cisco covers three switching methods in its curriculum, and each of these will be described in this section.

LAN switch modes are used to determine how a frame is handled when it is received on a switch port. You must know your LAN switch types for the CCNA exam.

Critical Information

The latency for packet switching through the switch depends on the chosen switching mode. There are three available options:

- Store-and-forward
- Cut-through
- FragmentFree

Store-and-Forward

Store-and-forward switching is one of two primary types of LAN switching. With this method, the LAN switch copies the entire frame into its onboard buffers and computes the cyclic redundancy check (CRC). The frame is discarded if it contains a CRC error, if it's a runt (less than 64 bytes, including the CRC), or if it's a giant (more than 1518 bytes, including the CRC).

If the frame doesn't contain any errors, the LAN switch looks up the destination address in its forwarding, or switching, table and determines the outgoing interface. It then forwards the frame toward its destination. Because this type of switching copies the entire frame and runs a CRC, latency can vary depending on frame length. This is the mode used by Cisco Catalyst 5000 series switches.

Cut-Through

Cut-through switching is the other main type of LAN switching. In this method, the LAN switch copies only the destination address (the first six bytes following the preamble) into its onboard buffers. It then looks up the destination address in its switching table, determines the outgoing interface, and forwards the frame toward its destination. A cut-through switch reduces latency because it begins to forward the frame as soon as it reads the destination address and determines the outgoing interface. Some switches can be configured to perform cut-through switching on a per-port basis until a user-defined error threshold is reached. At that point, they automatically change over to store-and-forward mode. When the error rate falls below the threshold, the port automatically changes back to cut-through mode.

FragmentFree (Modified Cut-Through)

FragmentFree is a modified form of cut-through switching in which the switch waits for the collision windows, which are 64 bytes long, to pass before forwarding. If a packet has an error, it almost always occurs within the first 64 bytes. FragmentFree mode provides better error checking than the cut-through mode, with almost no increase in latency. The FragmentFree LAN switch type looks into the data field of the frame.

Figure 1.3 shows where the different switching modes take place in the frame.

FIGURE 1.3: Different switching modes within a frame

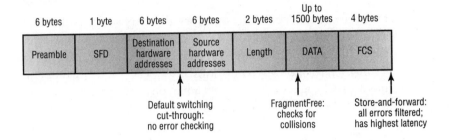

Exam Essentials

Know the difference between cut-through and store-and-forward. The cut-through method of LAN switching has a consistent latency because the switch reads only the first six bytes of the frame after the preamble. Store-and-forward reads the entire frame; therefore, latency varies with frame length.

Remember that FragmentFree is also referred to as "modified cut-through." FragmentFree switching looks into the data field of the frame.

Key Terms and Concepts

cyclic redundancy check (CRC)   Mathematical algorithm used to check for errors when a frame, packet, or segment has been transmitted through a network.

cut-through   LAN switching method that looks only at the destination hardware address in a frame before making forwarding decisions.

FragmentFree   LAN switching method that checks for errors by looking at the first 64 bytes of a frame after it has been received at a switch port.

latency   Time lapse between when a port receives a frame and when it is forwarded to another port.

store-and-forward   LAN switching method that copies the entire frame to onboard buffers and runs a CRC before making forwarding decisions.

Sample Questions

1. Which type of LAN switching method only reads the destination hardware address before forwarding the frame?

   A. Store-and-forward

   B. Port switching

   C. Cut-through

   D. FragmentFree

   Answer: C. Cut-through switching reads only the first six bytes after the preamble in a frame.

2. Which switching method reads the first 64 bytes of a frame before forwarding it?

   A. Port switching

   B. Store-and-forward

   C. Cut-through

   D. FragmentFree

   Answer: D. A FragmentFree switch checks for fragmentation of the frames (collisions) before sending any frames out to any ports. FragmentFree is also known as modified cut-through.

3. Which type of switching method has the highest latency?

A. Store-and-forward

B. Port switching

C. Cut-through

D. FragmentFree

Answer: A. Store-and-forward has the highest latency of any switching method. In addition, latency varies for each frame depending on its size.

Point-to-Point Protocol (PPP)

Point-to-Point Protocol (PPP) is a data-link protocol that can be used over either asynchronous serial (dial-up) or synchronous serial (ISDN) media and that uses the Link Control Protocol (LCP) to build and maintain data-link connections.

PPP was created to work with multiple protocols at the Network layer and to replace Serial Line Internet Protocol (SLIP), which could run only IP at the Network layer. This section covers Cisco support for PPP encapsulation as well as authentication.

Critical Information

PPP can be used in asynchronous and synchronous networks. The steps for configuring PPP for synchronous networks on Cisco routers are covered in the "Necessary Procedures" section. Configuring PPP encapsulation on an interface is a fairly straightforward process.

Of course, in order for PPP encapsulation to work, it must be enabled on both interfaces that are connected to a serial line. Once you have PPP encapsulation enabled, you can verify that it's up and running with the show interface command.

The basic purpose of PPP is to transport Layer 3 packets across a Data Link layer point-to-point link. Figure 1.4 shows the protocol stack compared to the OSI reference model.

FIGURE 1.4: Point-to-Point Protocol stack

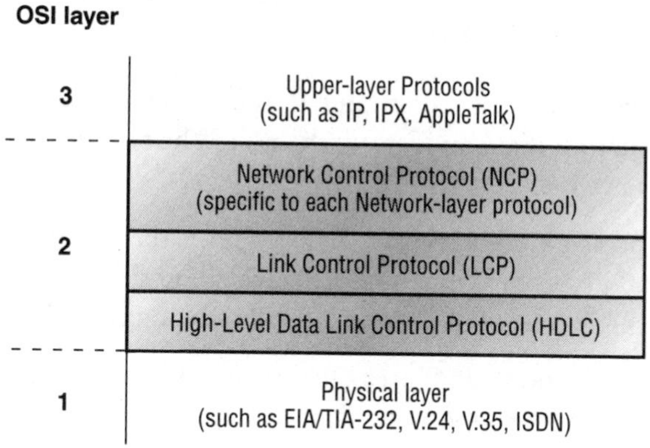

OSI layer

3	Upper-layer Protocols (such as IP, IPX, AppleTalk)
2	Network Control Protocol (NCP) (specific to each Network-layer protocol)
	Link Control Protocol (LCP)
	High-Level Data Link Control Protocol (HDLC)
1	Physical layer (such as EIA/TIA-232, V.24, V.35, ISDN)

PPP contains four main components:

EIA/TIA-232-C   A Physical-layer international standard for serial communication.

High-Level Data Link Control Protocol (HDLC)   A method for encapsulating datagrams over serial links.

Link Control Protocol (LCP)   A method of establishing, configuring, maintaining, and terminating the point-to-point connection.

Network Control Protocol (NCP)   A method of establishing and configuring different Network-layer protocols. PPP is designed to allow the simultaneous use of multiple Network-layer protocols. Some examples of protocols here are Internet Protocol Control Protocol (IPCP) and Internetwork Packet Exchange Control Protocol (IPXCP).

It is important to understand that the PPP protocol stack is specified at the Physical and Data Link layers only. NCP is used to allow communication of multiple Network-layer protocols by encapsulating the protocols across a PPP data link.

TIP You must know your PPP protocols!

LCP Configuration Options

Link Control Protocol (LCP) offers PPP encapsulation different options, including the following:

Authentication This option tells the calling side of the link to send information that can identify the user. The two methods you need know are PAP and CHAP.

Compression This is used to increase the throughput of PPP connections. PPP decompresses the data frame on the receiving end. Cisco uses the Stacker and Predictor compression methods.

Error Detection PPP uses Quality and Magic Number options to ensure a reliable, loop-free data link.

Multilink Starting in IOS version 11.1, multilink is supported on PPP links with Cisco routers. This splits the load for PPP over two or more parallel circuits. The grouping of these multiple links from one location to another is referred to as a bundle.

PPP Session Establishment

PPP can be used with authentication. This means that routers communicating must provide information to identify the link as a valid communication link. When PPP connections are started, the links go through three phases of session establishment:

Link-Establishment Phase LCP packets are sent by each PPP device to configure and test the link. The LCP packets contain a field called Configuration Option that allows each device to see the size of the data, compression, and authentication. If no Configuration Option field is present, then the default configurations are used.

Authentication Phase If configured, either CHAP or PAP can be used to authenticate a link. Authentication takes place before Network-layer protocol information is read.

Network-Layer Protocol Phase   PPP uses NCP to allow multiple Network-layer protocols to be encapsulated and sent over a PPP data link.

PPP Authentication Methods

There are two methods of authentication that can be used with PPP links, either Password Authentication Protocol (PAP) or Challenge Authentication Protocol (CHAP).

Password Authentication Protocol (PAP)   This is the less secure of the two methods. Passwords are sent in clear text, and PAP is only performed upon the initial link establishment. When the PPP link is first established, the remote node sends the username and password back to the sending router until authentication is acknowledged. That's it.

Challenge Authentication Protocol (CHAP)   This is used at the initial startup of a link and at periodic checkups to make sure the router is still communicating with the same host. After PPP finishes its initial phase, the local router sends a challenge request to the remote device. The remote device sends a value calculated using a one-way hash function called MD5. The local router checks this hash value to make sure it matches. If the values don't match, the link is immediately terminated.

Necessary Procedures

PPP is used when you need to connect routers from different manufacturers. Authentication can be used with PPP as well.

Configuring PPP on Cisco Routers

Configuring PPP encapsulation on an interface is a fairly straightforward process. To configure it, follow these router commands:

```
Router#config t
Enter configuration commands, one per line. End with
CNTL/Z.
```

```
Router(config)#int s0
Router(config-if)#encapsulation ppp
Router(config-if)#^Z
Router#
```

Of course, PPP encapsulation must be enabled on both interfaces connected to a serial line to work, and there are several additional configuration options available by using the help command.

Configuring PPP Authentication

After you configure your serial interface to support PPP encapsulation, you can then configure authentication using PPP between routers. First, set the hostname of the router if it is not already set. Then set the username and password for the remote router connecting to your router. Here is an example:

```
Router#config t
Enter configuration commands, one per line. End with
CNTL/Z.
Router(config)#hostname RouterA
RouterA(config)#username todd password cisco
```

When using the hostname command, remember that the username is the hostname of the remote router connecting to your router. It is case-sensitive. Also, the password on both routers must be the same. It is a plain-text password and can be seen with a show run command. You can configure the password to be encrypted by using the command service password-config before you set the username and password. You must have a username and password configured for each remote system you are going to connect to. The remote routers must also be configured with usernames and passwords.

After you set the hostname, usernames, and passwords, choose the authentication type, either CHAP or PAP:

```
RouterA#config t
Enter configuration commands, one per line. End with
CNTL/Z.
RouterA(config)#int s0
RouterA(config-if)#ppp authentication chap
```

If both methods are configured, then only the first method is used during link negotiation. If the first method fails, then the second method will be used.

Verifying PPP Encapsulation

Now that we have PPP encapsulation enabled, let's take a look to verify that it's up and running. You can verify the configuration with the show interface command:

```
RouterA#show int s0
Serial0 is up, line protocol is up
  Hardware is HD64570
  Internet address is 172.16.20.1/24
  MTU 1500 bytes, BW 1544 Kbit, DLY 20000 usec,
      rely 255/255, load 1/255
  Encapsulation PPP, loopback not set,
      keepalive set (10 sec)
  LCP Open
  Listen: IPXCP
  Open: IPCP, CDPCP, ATCP
  Last input 00:00:05, output 00:00:05,
      output hang never
  Last clearing of "show interface" counters never
  Input queue: 0/75/0 (size/max/drops);
      Total output drops: 0
  Queueing strategy: weighted fair
  Output queue: 0/1000/64/0
      (size/max total/threshold/drops)
    Conversations 0/2/256
      (active/max active/max total)
    Reserved Conversations 0/0
      (allocated/max allocated)
  5 minute input rate 0 bits/sec, 0 packets/sec
  5 minute output rate 0 bits/sec, 0 packets/sec
      670 packets input, 31845 bytes, 0 no buffer
      Received 596 broadcasts, 0 runts, 0 giants,
```

```
        0 throttles
    0 input errors, 0 CRC, 0 frame, 0 overrun,
        0 ignored, 0 abort
    707 packets output, 31553 bytes, 0 underruns
    0 output errors, 0 collisions,
        18 interface resets
    0 output buffer failures,
        0 output buffers swapped out
  21 carrier transitions
      DCD=up DSR=up DTR=up RTS=up CTS=up
RouterA#
```

Notice that the fifth line lists encapsulation as PPP, and the sixth line tells us that LCP is open. Remember that LCP's job is to build and maintain connections. The eighth line tells us that IPCP, CDPCP, and ATCP are open. This shows the IP, CDP, and AppleTalk support from NCP. The seventh line reports that we are listening for IPXCP.

NOTE   You can verify the PPP authentication configuration by using the debug ppp authentication command.

Exam Essentials

Remember how the PPP protocols fit within the OSI layers.   PPP uses NCP at the LLC sublayer of the Data Link layer, LCP and HDLC at the MAC sublayer of the OSI Reference Model.

Key Terms and Concepts

Point-to-Point Protocol (PPP)   A data encapsulation method that uses the Physical, Data Link, and Network layer specifications of the OSI model. PPP provides synchronous and asynchronous circuits.

Link Control Protocol (LCP) Used to provide session setup, authentication, dynamic addressing, compression, and multilink.

Network Control Protocol (NCP) Used to provide multiple Network-layer protocols to run over the same PPP link.

Sample Questions

1. What PPP layer is used to provide multiple Network-layer support?

A. LCP

B. MCP

C. NCP

D. HDLC

Answer: C. Network Control Protocol (NCP) is actually a family of protocols, one for each Network-layer protocol that is supported by PPP.

2. What protocol does PPP use to support authentication?

A. LCP

B. MCP

C. NCP

D. HDLC

Answer: A. PPP uses Link Control Protocol (LCP) to support authentication.

Chapter

2

OSI Reference Model and Layered Communication

his chapter will discuss the OSI Reference Model and how it helps application developers create applications to run on a network. The big picture of the OSI model is that it allows applications to run on a network and communicate with disparate systems. All objectives in this chapter relate to the OSI model.

Encapsulating the data in the different protocol stacks related to the OSI model must be completely understood before attempting the CCNA exam. The information you need to know will be presented in detail in this chapter.

Layer Definitions

The OSI (Open Standards Interconnect) Reference Model was created in the late 1970s to help facilitate data transfer between network nodes. One of the greatest functions of the OSI specifications is help in data transfer between disparate hosts. This means that you could transfer data between a Unix host and a PC, for example.

You must have a fundamental understanding of the different layers of the OSI model, and this first objective will lay the groundwork you need.

Critical Information

The OSI model is not physical; rather, it is a set of guidelines that application developers can use when creating and implementing applications to run on a network. It also provides a framework for creating and implementing networking standards, devices, and internetworking schemes.

The OSI model is the primary architectural model for networks. It describes how user data and network information are communicated from an application on one computer to an application on another computer through the network media. The OSI Reference Model breaks this approach into layers.

This model is important in that it helps facilitate troubleshooting. There are many reasons why you must understand it (see the section "Model Benefits" later in this chapter), and Cisco thinks this knowledge is especially important for troubleshooting and understanding data conversion in internetworks.

The OSI model has seven different layers, which are divided into two groups. The top three layers define how the applications within the end stations will communicate with each other and with users. The lower four layers define how data is transmitted, end-to-end. Figure 2.1 illustrates the three upper layers and their functions.

FIGURE 2.1: The upper layers of the OSI model

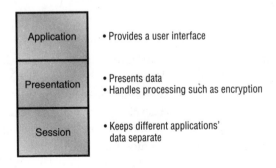

In Figure 2.1, you can see that the user interfaces with the computer at the Application layer, and also that the upper layers are responsible for applications communicating between hosts. Remember that none of the upper layers know anything about networking or network addresses. That is the responsibility of the four bottom layers, which are shown in Figure 2.2.

FIGURE 2.2: The lower, or data flow, layers

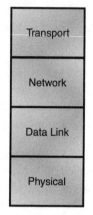

Transport	• Provides reliable or unreliable delivery • Performs error correction before retransmit
Network	• Provides logical addressing, which routers use for path determination
Data Link	• Combines packets into bytes and bytes into frames • Provides access to media using MAC address • Performs error detection, not correction
Physical	• Moves bits between devices • Specifies voltage, wire speed, and pin-out cables

The four bottom layers define how data is transferred through a physical wire, how it moves through switches and routers, and finally how to rebuild a data stream from a transmitting host to a destination host's application.

The OSI Layers

The International Organization for Standardization (ISO) is the Emily Post of the network protocol world. Just like Ms. Post, who wrote the book setting the standards—or protocols—for human social interaction, the ISO developed the OSI Reference Model as the guide and precedent for an open network protocol set. Defining the etiquette of communication models, it remains today the most popular means of comparison for protocol suites. The OSI Reference Model has seven layers, illustrated in Figure 2.3. The diagram also shows the functions defined at each layer. The objective "Layer Functions" describes these layers in detail later in this chapter.

FIGURE 2.3: The OSI layers and their functions

Application	• File, print, message, database, and application services
Presentation	• Data encryption, compression, and translation services
Session	• Dialog control
Transport	• End-to-end connection
Network	• Routing
Data Link	• Framing
Physical	• Physical topology

Exam Essentials

To pass the exam, OSI knowledge is essential. You will not be able to pass the CCNA exam without a complete understanding of the OSI model and how the protocols function within this model.

Understand the different layers and their functions. Just knowing the order of the layers won't suffice. You must have a good understanding of what function each layer provides, including its protocols and specifications. (These are described later in this chapter.)

Key Terms and Concepts

Open Standards Interconnect (OSI) Reference Model Network architectural model developed by the International Organization for Standardization (ISO) and ITU-T in 1977. Their basic purpose was to develop a data communication standard for multivendor interoperability. The OSI model consists of seven layers, each with different specifications.

Sample Questions

1. Which of the following is true regarding the OSI model?

A. Application developers must use the specifications at all layers at all times.

B. The OSI describes how user data and network information are communicated from an application on one computer to an application on another computer through the network media.

C. Application developers must follow the OSI model.

D. It was created by Microsoft to allow user data and network information to be communicated from an application on one computer to an application on another computer through the network media.

Answer: B. The OSI model describes how user data and network information are communicated through the network media. It also segments the complexities of all the rest of the layers.

2. What is the main purpose of the OSI model?

A. To help Microsoft continue to dominate the desktop market

B. To help IBM to dominate the computer market

C. To allow application developers to run applications on disparate systems

D. To allow wireless systems to communicate with fiber technologies

Answer: C. Along with purposes described in Question 1, the OSI Reference Model also allows application developers to run applications on disparate systems.

Encapsulation/De-encapsulation

Data encapsulation is the process in which the information in a protocol is wrapped, or contained, in the data section of another protocol. In the OSI Reference Model, each layer encapsulates the layer immediately above it as the data flows down the protocol stack.

It is imperative to understand the encapsulation method when troubleshooting an internetwork. For example, when running a network analyzer or running troubleshooting commands, you will not be able to find the problem if you do not understand the encapsulation method. Practice running through the conversion steps in your head before taking the CCNA exam.

Critical Information

When a host transmits data across a network to another device, the data is encapsulated with protocol information at each layer of the OSI model. Each layer communicates only with its peer layer on the receiving device.

To communicate and exchange information, each layer uses protocol data units (PDUs). These hold the control information attached to the data at each layer of the model, typically attached to the header of the data field but in some instances in the trailer, or end of the data field.

Each PDU is attached to the data by encapsulating the data at each layer of the OSI model. A specific name is given to each PDU depending on the information each header has. This PDU information is only read by the peer layer on the receiving device; it is then stripped off and the data is handed to the next upper layer.

Figure 2.4 shows the PDUs and how they attach control information to each layer. The diagram shows how the upper-layer user data is converted for transmission on the network. This data stream is handed down to the Transport layer, which sets up a virtual circuit to the receiving device by sending a sync packet. The data stream is then broken up into smaller pieces, a Transport-layer header (PDU) is created, and the header control information is attached to the header of the data field. The result is a segment. Each segment is sequenced so the data stream can be put back together on the receiving side exactly as transmitted.

FIGURE 2.4: Data encapsulation

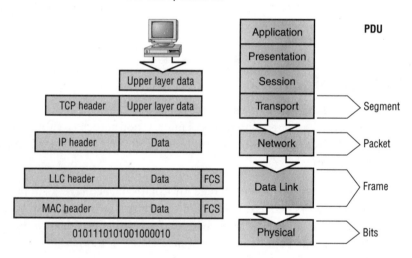

Each segment is then handed to the Network layer for network addressing and routing through an internetwork. Logical addressing is used—for example, IP—to get each segment to the correct network. The Network-layer protocol adds a control header to the segment handed down from the Transport layer, and the entire block is now called a packet or datagram. Remember that the Transport layer and Network layer work together to rebuild a data stream on a receiving host. However, they have no responsibility for placing their PDUs on a local network segment, which is the only way to get the information to a router or host.

The Data Link layer is responsible for taking packets from the Network layer and placing them on the network medium (cable or wireless). The Data Link layer encapsulates each packet in a frame, and the frame's header carries the hardware address of the source and destination local hosts. If the device is on a remote network, then the frame is sent to a router, to be routed through an internetwork. Once it gets to the destination network, a new frame is used to get the packet to the destination host.

To put this frame on the network, it must first be put into a digital signal. Since a frame is really a logical group of bits, the Physical layer is responsible for taking these digits and encapsulating them into a digital signal, which is read by devices on the same local network. The receiving devices will synchronize on the digital signal and extract the ones and zeros from the digital signal. At this point, the devices build the frame, run a cyclic redundancy check (CRC), and check their answer with the answer in the FCS field of the frame. If it matches, the packet is pulled from the frame and the frame is discarded. This process is called de-encapsulation.

The packet is handed to the Network layer, where the address is checked. If the address matches, the segment is pulled from the packet and the packet is discarded. The segment is processed at the Transport layer, which rebuilds the data stream and acknowledges that it received each piece to the transmitting station. It then happily hands the data stream to the upper-layer application.

At a transmitting device, the data encapsulation method is as follows:

1. User information is converted to data for transmission on the network.

2. Data is converted to segments. If you are using a connection-oriented protocol, a reliable connection is established between the transmitting and receiving host. If you are using a protocol such as UDP, the segment is sent unreliable.

3. Segments are converted to packets or datagrams, and the logical address is placed in the header so each packet can be routed through an internetwork.

4. Packets or datagrams are converted to frames for transmission on the local network. Hardware (Ethernet) addresses are used to uniquely identify hosts on a local network segment.

5. Frames are converted to bits, and a digital encoding and clocking scheme is used.

Exam Essentials

Memorize the encapsulation method of each layer. Remember, from the upper layers down, this is the encapsulation method: user data at the Application, Presentation, and Session layers; segments at the Transport layer; packets, or datagrams, at the Network layer; frames at the Data Link layer; and bits at the Physical layer.

Key Terms and Concepts

bits   The Physical layer takes the binary data handed down from the Data Link layer and converts the ones and zeros to a digital signal to be sent out over the physical topology.

frames   These house the packets, or datagrams, handed down from the Network layer to be delivered to a device on a LAN.

packets   Sometimes called datagrams, these house the segments handed down from the Transport layer to be routed through an internetwork.

segments   Defined at the Transport layer, these are parts of a data stream that are handed down from the upper layers to be transmitted to a destination device.

Sample Questions

1. At the Transport layer, user data is converted to:

   A. Packets

B. Frames

C. Segments

D. Bits

Answer: C. The Transport layer breaks data streams into segments and then numbers these segments to be put back together at the destination host. This is called segmentation.

2. At the Data Link layer, packets are converted to:

A. Packets

B. Frames

C. Segments

D. Bits

Answer: B. Frames are used to house a packet or datagram to be delivered on a local LAN.

3. At the Network layer, segments are converted to:

A. Packets

B. Frames

C. Segments

D. Bits

Answer: A. Packets, or datagrams, are defined at the Network layer.

Layer Functions

This objective continues where the first objective left off and describes the OSI layers and their functions in detail. Each of the seven layers will be described in detail.

You must know this information to pass your CCNA exam.

Critical Information

As discussed in the first objective in this chapter (and illustrated back in Figure 2.3), there are seven layers in the OSI Reference Model:

- Application
- Presentation
- Session
- Transport
- Network
- Data Link
- Physical

Application Layer

The Application layer of the OSI model supports the communication components of an application and provides network services to application processes that span beyond the OSI Reference Model specifications.

The Application layer is also responsible for the following:

- Understanding the resources needed to communicate between two devices and establishing their availability
- Synchronizing applications on the server and client
- Agreeing on error control and data integrity of communicating applications
- Providing system-independent processes or program services to end users

Presentation Layer

The Presentation layer is so named because it presents data to the Application layer. It's essentially a translator, making sure that the data sent from one system is readable by the Application layer of the receiving station. The Presentation layer is responsible for code formatting, conversion, and negotiating the data transfer syntax for the Application layer.

A successful data transfer technique is to convert the data into a standard format before transmission. Computers are configured to receive this generically formatted data and then convert the data back into its native format for actual reading (for example, EBCDIC to ASCII). It is important to remember that the Presentation layer is the only layer that can actually change data.

The OSI has protocol standards that define how standard data should be formatted. Tasks such as data compression, decompression, encryption, and decryption are associated with this layer.

Session Layer

The Session layer is responsible for setting up, managing, and then tearing down sessions between Presentation-layer entities. The Session layer also provides dialog control between devices, or nodes. The Session layer coordinates communication between systems, and serves to organize their communication by offering three different modes—simplex, half-duplex, and full-duplex. The Session layer basically keeps different applications' data separate from other applications' data.

Transport Layer

Services located in the Transport layer both segment and reassemble data from upper-layer applications and unite it onto the same data stream. They provide end-to-end data transport services and can establish a logical connection between the sending host and destination host on an internetwork.

Some of you might already be familiar with TCP and UDP (which you will learn about in Chapter 3) and how TCP is a reliable service but UDP is not. Application developers have their choice of the two protocols when working with TCP/IP protocols.

The Transport layer is responsible for providing mechanisms for multiplexing upper-layer application, session establishment, and tear-down of virtual circuits. It also hides details of any network-dependent information from the higher layers by providing transparent data transfer. The use of the term *virtual circuits* here should not confuse you. Cisco uses the phrase as a way of identifying the process here at the Transport layer. This may be confusing to some, because virtual circuits are also used to establish connections over serial links.

Flow Control

Data integrity is ensured at this layer by maintaining flow control and by allowing users the option of requesting reliable data transport between systems. Flow control prevents the problem of a sending host on one side of the connection overflowing the buffers in the receiving host—an event that can result in lost data. Reliable data transport employs a connection-oriented communications session between systems, and the protocols involved ensure that the following will be achieved:

- The segments delivered are acknowledged back to the sender upon their reception.

- Any segments not acknowledged are retransmitted.

- Segments are sequenced back into their proper order upon arrival at their destination.

- A manageable data flow is maintained in order to avoid congestion, overloading, and the loss of any data.

SEE ALSO More information about how the Transport layer creates virtual circuits and reliable sessions is covered under the objective "Connection-Oriented Models" later in this chapter.

Network Layer

The Network layer is responsible for routing through an internetwork and for network addressing. This means that the Network layer is responsible for transporting traffic between devices that are not locally attached. Routers, or Layer 3 devices, are specified at the Network layer and provide the routing services in an internetwork.

When a packet is received on a router interface, the destination IP address is checked. If the packet is not destined for the router, then the router will look up the destination network address in the routing table. Once an exit interface is chosen, the packet will be sent to the interface to be framed and sent out on the local network. If the entry for the destination network is not found in the routing table, the router drops the packet.

Two types of packets are used at the Network layer: data and route updates.

Data Packets   Used to transport user data through the internetwork; protocols used to support data traffic are called routed protocols. Examples of routed protocols are IP and IPX. You'll learn about IP and IPX addressing in Chapter 3.

Route Update Packets   Used to update neighboring routers about networks connected to routers in the internetwork. Protocols that send route update packets are called routing protocols; examples include RIP, EIGRP, and OSPF. Route update packets are used to help build and maintain routing tables on each router.

Routers are used to break up broadcast domains. This means, by default, that broadcasts are not forwarded through a router. This is good. Routers also break up collision domains, but this can also be accomplished through Layer 2 switches. Each interface in a router is a separate network and must be assigned unique network identification numbers. Each host on the network connected to that router must use that same network number.

Some points about routers that you must remember:

- Routers, by default, will not forward any broadcast or multicast packets.

- Routers use the logical address in a Network-layer header to determine the next hop router to forward the packet to.

- Routers can use access lists, created by an administrator, to control security on packets trying to either enter or exit an interface.

- Routers can provide Layer 2 bridging functions if needed, as well as simultaneously routing through the same interface.

- Layer 3 devices (routers in this case) provide connections between virtual LANs (VLANs).

- Routers can provide quality of service (QoS) for specific types of network traffic.

Data Link Layer

The Data Link layer ensures that messages are delivered to the proper device and translates messages from the Network layer into bits for the Physical layer to transmit. It formats the message into data frames and adds a customized header containing the hardware destination and source address. This added information forms a sort of capsule that surrounds the original message in much the same way as engines, navigational devices, and other tools were attached to the lunar modules of the Apollo project. These various pieces of equipment were useful only during certain stages of space flight and were stripped off the module and discarded when their designated stage was complete. Data traveling through networks is much the same. Figure 2.5 shows the Data Link layer with the Ethernet and IEEE specifications.

FIGURE 2.5: The Data Link layer

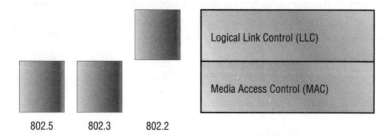

| | | | Logical Link Control (LLC) |
| | | | Media Access Control (MAC) |

802.5   802.3   802.2

You need to understand that routers, which work at the Network layer, do not care about where a host is located, but only where networks are located. They also keep track of the best way to get to a remote network. The Data Link layer is responsible for uniquely identifying each device on a local network.

For a host to send packets to individual hosts and between routers, the Data Link layer uses hardware addressing. Each time a packet is sent between routers, it is framed with control information at the Data Link layer, but that information is stripped off at the receiving router and only the original packet is left completely intact. This framing of the packet continues for each hop until the packet is finally delivered to the receiving host. It is important to understand that the packet was never altered along the route, only encapsulated with the type of control information to be passed upon the different media types.

The IEEE Ethernet Data Link layer has two sublayers:

Media Access Control (MAC) 802.3   This sublayer defines how packets are placed on the media. Contention media access is first-come, first-served media access, where everyone shares the same bandwidth. Physical addressing is defined here as well as logical topologies. Logical topology is the signal path through a physical topology. Line discipline, error notification (not correction), ordered delivery of frames, and optional flow control can also be used at this sublayer.

Logical Link Control (LLC) 802.2   This sublayer is responsible for identifying Network-layer protocols and then encapsulating them. An LLC header is used to tell the Data Link layer what to do with a packet once a frame is received. For example, a host will receive a frame and then look in the LLC header to understand that the packet is destined for the IP protocol at the Network layer. The LLC can also provide flow control and sequencing of control bits.

Switches and Bridges at the Data Link Layer

Switches and bridges both work at the Data Link layer and filter the network by hardware addresses. Layer 2 switching is considered hardware-based bridging because it uses specialized hardware called an application-specific integrated circuit (ASIC). ASICs can run up to gigabit speeds with very low latency.

Bridges and switches read each frame as it passes through the network. The Layer 2 device then puts the source hardware address in a filter table and keeps track of which port it was received on. This tells the switch where that device is located.

After a filter table is built on the Layer 2 device, the device will only forward frames to the segment where the destination hardware address is located. If the destination device is on the same segment as the frame, the Layer 2 device will block the frame from going to any other segments. If the destination is on another segment, the frame is only transmitted to that segment. This is called transparent bridging.

When a frame is received on a Layer 2 device interface and the destination hardware address is unknown to the device, it will forward the frame to all connected segments. If the unknown device answers this forwarding of the frame, then the switch updates the filter table on the location of that device. However, the source address of the transmitting frame may be a broadcast address. The switch will forward all broadcasts or unknown unicasts out every interface, with the exception of the interface of arrival, by default. All devices that the broadcast is forwarded to are considered to be in the same broadcast domain. Layer 2 devices propagate Layer 2 broadcast storms. The only way to stop a broadcast storm from propagating through an internetwork is with a Layer 3 device (router).

The biggest difference between (and benefit of) using switches instead of hubs in your internetwork is that each switch port is its own collision domain. A hub creates one large collision domain. However, switches and bridges do not break up broadcast domains, and instead forward all broadcasts.

Another benefit of LAN switching over hub implementations is that one device on every segment plugged into a switch can transmit at the same time, because each segment is its own collision domain. Hubs allow only one device per network to communicate at a time.

TIP Switches cannot translate between different media types on the same segment.

Physical Layer

The Physical layer has two responsibilities: it sends bits and receives bits. Bits come only in values of 1 or 0—a Morse code with numeric value. The Physical layer communicates directly with the various types of actual communication media. Different kinds of media represent these bit values in different ways. Some use audio tones, while others employ state transitions—changes in voltage from high to low and low to high. Specific protocols are needed for each type of media to describe the proper bit patterns to be used, how data is encoded into media signals, and the various qualities of the physical media's attachment interface.

The Physical layer specifications specify the electrical, mechanical, procedural, and functional requirements for activating, maintaining, and deactivating a physical link between end systems.

At the Physical layer, the interface between the data terminal equipment (DTE) and the data circuit-terminating equipment (DCE) is identified. The DCE is usually located at the service provider, while the DTE is the attached device. The services available to the DTE are most often accessed via a modem or channel service unit/data service unit (CSU/DSU).

The connectors and different physical topologies are defined by the OSI as standards, which allow disparate systems to communicate because of these standard interfaces. The CCNA course and exam is only interested in the Ethernet standards.

Hubs at the Physical Layer

Hubs are really multiple-port repeaters. A repeater receives a digital signal and reamplifies it or regenerates the digital signal, then forwards the digital signal out all active ports without looking at any data. An active hub does the same thing. Any digital signal received from a segment on a hub port is regenerated or reamplified and transmitted out all ports on the hub. This means that all devices plugged into a hub are in the same collision domain as well as in the same broadcast domain. A broadcast domain is defined as all devices on a network segment that hear all broadcasts sent on that segment.

Hubs, like repeaters, do not look at any traffic as it enters and is transmitted out to the other parts of the physical media. Hubs create a physical star network where the hub is a central device and cables extend in all directions, creating the physical star effect. However, Ethernet networks use a logical bus topology. This means that the signal has to run from end to end of the network. Every device connected to the hub, or hubs, must listen if a device transmits.

Exam Essentials

You must know your layers and their functions.   The first objective in this chapter, as well as this objective, described the layers of the OSI and their function. Study these hard.

Understand the different devices used at the various layers.   Routers are defined at the Network layer, bridges and switches at the Data Link layer, and hubs at the Physical layer.

Key Terms and Concepts

bridges   Defined at the Data Link layer, bridges break up collision domains but form one large broadcast domain. To get another broadcast domain, get another bridge.

hardware addressing   Defined at the Data Link layer, hardware addressing is used to uniquely define hosts on a LAN. Hardware addresses are 48 bits long (6 bytes).

logical addressing   Defined at the Network layer, logical addressing is used to define the network address and uniquely define hosts in an internetwork.

routers   Defined at the Network layer, routers break up broadcast domains by default and provide logical addressing of a network.

switches   Defined at the Data Link layer, switches break up collision domains but are one large broadcast domain by default. You can segment broadcast domains by port by assigning them to different virtual LANs, making each VLAN its own broadcast domain.

Sample Questions

1. Which layer is responsible for providing mechanisms for the building and tearing down of virtual circuits?

A. Application

B. Presentation

C. Session

D. Transport

E. Network

F. Data Link

G. Physical

Answer: D. The Transport layer is responsible for virtual circuit connection and termination between hosts. This is sometimes referred to as building and tearing down sessions.

2. Which layer is responsible for negotiating data-transfer syntax?

A. Application

B. Presentation

C. Session

D. Transport

E. Network

F. Data Link

G. Physical

Answer: B. The Presentation layer is responsible for data conversion. This is the only layer that can actually change the data.

3. Which layer is responsible for understanding the resources needed to communicate between two devices and establishing their availability?

A. Application

B. Presentation

C. Session

D. Transport

E. Network

F. Data Link

G. Physical

Answer: A. The Application layer is responsible for understanding the resources needed to communicate between two devices and establishing their availability.

4. What device works at the Data Link layer (Layer 2)?

A. Hub

B. Router

C. Repeater

D. Switch

Answer: D. Switches are used at Layer 2 to break up collision domains.

Connection-Oriented Models

Connectionless and connection-oriented services can be used at almost all layers of the OSI model, and the decision to use them at any given layer is completely up to the application developer.

Understanding the differences will help you troubleshoot an internetwork, configure Cisco routers correctly, and find the correct answers on the CCNA exam. This objective will describe the connection-oriented network service.

Critical Information

When talking about the difference between connection-oriented and connectionless network service, people usually refer to an actual protocol as an example; for instance, IP is connectionless and TCP is connection-oriented. This is true; however, these are just protocols that use the specifications of the Network and Transport layers to set up and deliver data to network devices. They do not actually define the network service.

This objective will discuss the actual connection-oriented service used at the Transport layer. However, remember that connection-oriented services can be used at almost any layer of the OSI model, but that the CCNA exam is concerned with only the connection-oriented service at the Transport layer.

Connection-Oriented Communication

In reliable transport operation, one user first establishes a connection-oriented session with its peer system. Figure 2.6 portrays a typical reliable session taking place between sending and receiving systems. In it, both hosts' application programs begin by notifying their individual operating systems that a connection is about to be initiated. The two operating systems communicate by sending messages over the network confirming that the transfer is approved and that both sides are ready for it to take place. Once the required synchronization is complete, a connection is fully established and data transfer begins.

FIGURE 2.6: Establishing a connection-oriented session

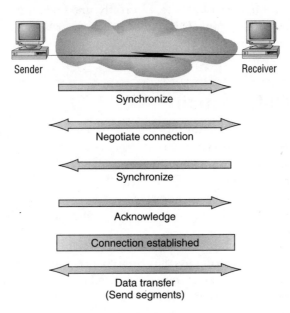

While the information is being transferred between hosts, the two machines periodically check in with each other, communicating through their protocol software, to ensure that all is going well and that the data is being received properly.

The following summarizes the steps in a connection-oriented session pictured in Figure 2.6:

1. The first "connection agreement" segment is a request for synchronization.

2. The second and third segments acknowledge the request and establish connection parameters between hosts.

3. The final segment is also an acknowledgment. It notifies the destination host that the connection agreement is accepted and that the actual connection has been established. Data transfer can now begin.

NOTE Windowing is an important part of the connection-oriented session and is covered in Chapter 3.

The steps of a connection-oriented session are sometimes summarized into the following steps:

1. Call setup, which consists of each segment in Figure 2.6 down to "Connection established."

2. Data transfer: the last segment in Figure 2.6 and step 3 in the previous list.

3. Call termination (not shown in the figure).

Exam Essentials

Understand what makes a reliable session. It is important to understand how a reliable connection is created by using a virtual circuit.

Key Terms and Concepts

connection-oriented Data transfer that requires the establishment of a virtual circuit. Typically called a reliable connection.

connectionless Data transfer that does not use a virtual circuit. Typically described as best-effort delivery of datagrams.

Sample Questions

1. Which of the following describes a connection-oriented session?

   A. User Datagram Protocol (UDP)

   B. Analogous to sending a postcard

C. Data transfer that does not use a virtual circuit

D. Data transfer that requires the establishment of a virtual circuit

Answer: D. A session is set up before any data is transmitted in a connection-oriented session.

2. Which is *not* a phase in a connection-oriented session?

A. Call setup

B. Signal reflection

C. Call termination

D. Data transfer

Answer: B. A connection-oriented session first sets up a call, data transfer takes place, and then the call is terminated. There is no signal reflection, so option B is the correct answer.

Connectionless Models

Connectionless protocols can be used in applications that do not want the overhead associated with setting up a virtual circuit. As mentioned previously, the application developers decided on what type of connection service to use.

Connectionless protocols can be used to save a tremendous overhead over connection-oriented protocols. This objective will give you the basic information regarding connectionless models.

Critical Information

Perhaps the best and most often used analogy for connectionless and connection-oriented communication is the difference between sending a postcard and a registered letter.

A connectionless network service is similar to sending a postcard or letter. You put the correct source and destination host addresses on the postcard and then drop it in the mailbox. Does it get to its destination? You hope so. Since the message on the postcard is probably not a matter of life or death, you don't need an acknowledgment of its receipt. Using this type of delivery saves time and overhead, but at the cost of reliability.

As mentioned previously, the decision about whether to use connectionless service is totally up to the application developer and not up to the end user. Application developers choose this type of service when they need a quick transfer at a specific layer and aren't overly concerned with reliability.

Exam Essentials

Understand the difference between connection-oriented and connectionless services. Connection-oriented protocols must set up a virtual circuit; connectionless protocols do not.

Key Terms and Concepts

connection-oriented Data transfer that requires the establishment of a virtual circuit. Typically called a reliable connection.

connectionless Data transfer that does not use a virtual circuit. Typically described as best-effort delivery of datagrams.

Sample Questions

1. What is a benefit of a connectionless network service?

   A. More bandwidth usage.

   B. Transmitting device must wait until session is set up before transmitting.

   C. Transmitting device does not have to wait until session is set up before transmitting.

D. Reliability.

Answer: C.

2. Which of the following describes a connectionless network service?

A. Transmission Control Protocol (TCP)

B. Analogous to sending a registered letter

C. Data transfer that does not use a virtual circuit

D. Data transfer that requires the establishment of a virtual circuit

Answer: C. A session is not set up before data is sent in a connectionless network service.

Model Benefits

One of the first things to understand is that Cisco presents many different reasons why the industry uses a layered model. Here we will define the reasons that we think are the most important for you to remember for the exam.

You should have a fundamental understanding of the OSI model, including knowing why the industry uses a model and what the benefits are. Knowing this can help you fulfill business requirements in the real world as well as prepare for the CCNA exam.

Critical Information

There are many advantages to using a layered model. Because developers know that another layer will handle functions they're not currently working on, they can confidently focus on just one layer's functions. This promotes specialization. Another benefit is that if changes to protocols are made to one layer, it doesn't necessarily change protocols within the other layers. A third big advantage of using layered models is compatibility. If software developers adhere to the specifications outlined in the reference model, all the protocols written to conform to that model will work together. This is very good. Compatibility creates the foundation for a large number of protocols to be written and used.

Cisco's official reasons for why the industry uses a layered model include the following:

- It clarifies general functions rather than specifics.

- It divides the complexity of networking into more manageable sublayers.

- It uses standard interfaces to enable ease of interoperability.

- It allows developers to change the features of one layer without changing all the code.

- It permits specialization, which helps the industry progress.

- It eases troubleshooting.

Exam Essentials

Use this information, along with the first objective in this chapter (on the seven OSI layers), to see the "big picture" of how Cisco looks at the OSI model.

Remember why developers use layered models.   Ease of troubleshooting, a standard interface, and industry specialization are three good reasons Cisco gives for using a layered model in the networking industry.

Key Terms and Concepts

compatibility This is a key reason for reference models. Application developers can ensure compatibility between disparate systems if they use the specifications of a layered model, such as the OSI Reference Model.

Sample Questions

1. Which of the following are reasons the networking industry uses a layered model? (Choose all that apply.)

   A. Allows gigabit speed between LANs

   B. Allows administrators to make changes in one layer without changing all layers

   C. Speeds up network industry progress by allowing specialization

   D. Facilitates systematic troubleshooting

   Answer: B, C, D. Troubleshooting, specialization, and the ability to change protocols in one layer without changing all the layers are key reasons why the industry uses a layered model.

2. Which of the following are benefits of having layers in a reference model? (Choose all that apply.)

   A. Allows gigabit speeds between LANs

   B. Allows specialization of applications while still maintaining interoperability

   C. Allows databases to update and back up at any time

   D. Allows ease of troubleshooting between internetworks

   Answer: B, D. Specialization and troubleshooting are two reasons why the industry uses a layered model.

Chapter

3

Network Protocols

his chapter will cover some very important information, but it will only provide what you need to know for the CCNA exam.

This book cannot cover TCP/IP addressing in complete detail, so read Chapter 3 of *CCNA: Cisco Certified Network Associate Study Guide* (Sybex, 2000) to make sure you have a fundamental understanding of IP addressing and subnetting.

IPX will be covered; however, this also will be a brief summary of the important points you need to understand for the CCNA exam, and we will assume you have read Chapter 8 in *CCNA: Cisco Certified Network Associate Study Guide* as well.

Windowing is a flow control technique used in the TCP protocol. We will cover the aspects of flow control where Chapter 2 of this book left off.

TCP/IP

The Transmission Control Protocol/Internet Protocol (TCP/IP) suite was created by the Department of Defense (DoD) to ensure data integrity and preserve it, as well as to maintain communications in the event of catastrophes such as war. If designed and implemented correctly, a TCP/IP network can be very dependable and resilient. In this chapter, we'll briefly cover the protocols of TCP/IP, enough to help you understand what you need to study to pass your CCNA exam.

We can't stress this enough: This is just a summary of what is included in *CCNA: Cisco Certified Network Associate Study Guide* (Sybex, 2000).

Critical Information

This section will start off by taking a look at the Department of Defense's version of TCP/IP, and then compare this version and protocols with the OSI Reference Model discussed in Chapter 2. After you have an understanding of the protocols used at the various levels of the DoD model, it will be time to understand IP addressing. This chapter also covers subnetting an IP network address.

IP addressing and subnetting is not difficult, but it is a large subject. Read this section over and over again until you feel you have grasped the topic of IP addressing.

TCP/IP and the DoD Model

The DoD model is a condensed version of the OSI model, comprising four, instead of seven, layers. These layers are:

- The Process/Application layer
- The Host-to-Host layer
- The Internet layer
- The Network Access layer

Figure 3.1 shows a comparison of the four-layer DoD model and the seven-layer OSI model. As you can see, the two are similar in concept, but each has a different number of layers with different names.

FIGURE 3.1: The DoD and OSI models

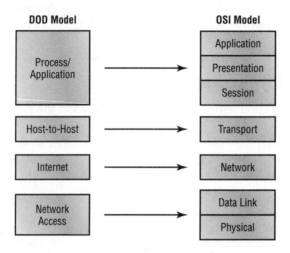

A vast array of protocols combine at the DoD model's Process/Application layer to integrate the various activities and duties spanning the focus of the OSI's corresponding top three (Session, Presentation, and Application) layers. (We'll be looking closely at those protocols in the next part of this chapter.) The Process/Application layer defines protocols for node-to-node application communication and also controls user interface specifications.

The Host-to-Host layer parallels the functions of OSI's Transport layer, defining protocols for setting up the level of transmission service for applications. It tackles issues like creating reliable end-to-end communication and ensuring the error-free delivery of data. It handles packet sequencing and maintains data integrity.

The Internet layer corresponds to the OSI's Network layer, designating the protocols relating to the logical transmission of packets over the entire network. It takes care of host addressing by giving each host an Internet Protocol (IP) address, and it handles the routing of packets among multiple networks. The Internet layer also controls the communication flow between two hosts.

At the bottom of the model, the Network Access layer monitors the data exchange between the host and the network. The equivalent of the Data Link and Physical layers of the OSI model, the Network Access layer oversees hardware addressing and defines protocols for the physical transmission of data.

While the DoD and OSI models are alike in design and concept and have similar functions in similar places, *how* those functions occur are different. Figure 3.2 shows the TCP/IP protocol suite and how its protocols relate to the DoD model layers.

FIGURE 3.2:   The TCP/IP protocol suite

DOD Model

| Process/Application | Telnet | FTP | LPD | SNMP |
| | TFTP | SMTP | NFS | X window |

| Host-to-Host | TCP | | UDP | |

| Internet | ICMP | BootP | ARP | RARP |
| | IP | | | |

| Network Access | Ethernet | Fast Ethernet | Token Ring | FDDI |

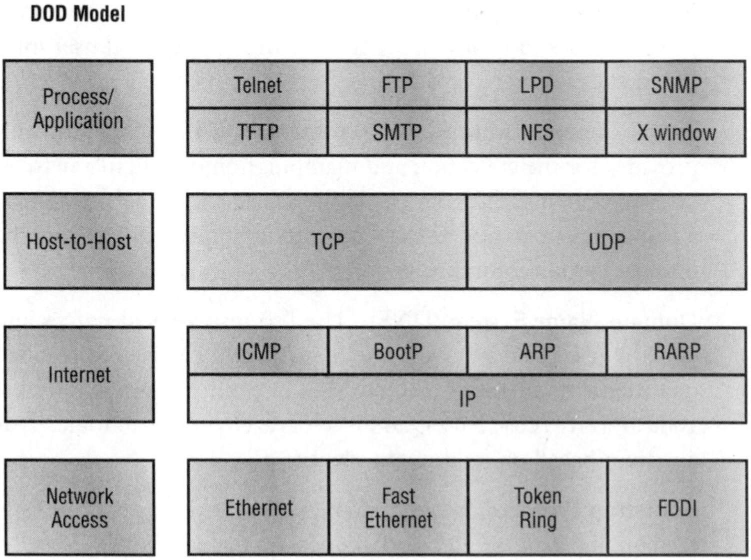

Process/Application-Layer Protocols

In this section, we will talk about the various protocols, applications, and services typically used in IP networks:

Telnet   This protocol's specialty is terminal emulation. It allows a user on a remote client machine, called the Telnet client, to access the resources of another machine, the Telnet server.

File Transfer Protocol (FTP) The protocol that actually lets us transfer files. FTP is a connection-oriented service that uses TCP and can provide login and authentication.

Trivial File Transfer Protocol (TFTP) The stripped-down, stock version of FTP. It uses UDP at the Transport layer and is connectionless.

Network File System (NFS) Designed by Sun Microsystems to provide a file system that can be shared by disparate systems.

Simple Mail Transfer Protocol (SMTP) Answering our ubiquitous call to e-mail, SMTP uses a spooled, or queued, method of mail delivery

Line Printer Daemon (LPD) Designed for printer sharing.

X Window Designed for client-server operations, X Window (or just X) defines a protocol for the writing of graphical user interface–based client/server applications.

Simple Network Management Protocol (SNMP) The protocol that provides for the collection and manipulation of valuable network information. It gathers data by polling the devices on the network from a management station at fixed or random intervals, requiring them to disclose certain information.

Domain Name System (DNS) Used to resolve host names and specifically used to resolve Internet names. DNS is used to resolve fully qualified domain names (FQDNs)—for example, `www.lammle.com` or `todd.lammle.com`. An FQDN is a hierarchy that can logically locate a system based on its domain identifier.

Bootstrap Protocol (BootP) When a diskless workstation is powered on, it broadcasts a BootP request on the network. A BootP server hears the request and looks up the client's MAC address in its BootP file. If it finds an appropriate entry, it responds by telling the machine its IP address and the file that it should boot from.

Dynamic Host Configuration Protocol (DHCP) Used to give IP addresses to hosts.

Host-to-Host–Layer Protocols

The Host-to-Host layer's main purpose is to shield the upper-layer applications from the complexities of the network. The two protocols at this layer are the Transmission Control Protocol (TCP) and User Datagram Protocol (UDP).

Transmission Control Protocol (TCP)

The Transmission Control Protocol (TCP) takes large blocks of information from an application and breaks them into segments. It numbers and sequences each segment so that the destination's TCP can put the segments back into the order that the application intended. After these segments are sent, TCP (on the transmitting host) waits for an acknowledgment of the receiving end's TCP virtual circuit session, retransmitting those that aren't acknowledged.

Before a transmitting host starts to send segments down the model, the sender's TCP contacts the destination's TCP in order to establish a connection. What is created is known as a virtual circuit. This type of communication is called connection-oriented. During this initial handshake, the two TCP layers also agree on the amount of information that's going to be sent before the recipient's TCP sends back an acknowledgment. With everything agreed upon in advance, the path is paved for reliable communication to take place.

TCP is a full-duplex, connection-oriented, reliable, accurate protocol, and establishing all these terms and conditions, in addition to checking for errors, is no small task. TCP is very complicated and, not surprisingly, very costly in terms of network overhead.

User Datagram Protocol (UDP)

Application developers can use the User Datagram Protocol (UDP) in place of TCP. UDP is the scaled-down economy model and is considered a thin protocol.

UDP also doesn't offer all the bells and whistles of TCP, but it does do a fabulous job of transporting information that doesn't require reliable delivery—and does it using far fewer network resources.

NOTE UDP is covered thoroughly in RFC 768.

A circumstance calling for UDP instead of TCP is when the matter of reliability is already accomplished at the Process/Application layer. For example, NFS handles its own reliability issues, making the use of TCP both impractical and redundant. However, the application developer decides whether to use UDP or TCP, not the user who wants to transfer data faster.

UDP receives upper-layer blocks of information and breaks them into segments. Like TCP, each UDP segment is given a number for reassembly into the intended block at the destination. However, UDP does *not* sequence the segments and does not care in which order the segments arrive at the destination; it leaves sequencing up to the application to order the segments. At least it numbers them. But after that, UDP sends the segments off and forgets about them. It doesn't follow through, check up on them, or even allow for an acknowledgment of safe arrival—complete abandonment. Because of this, it's referred to as an *unreliable* protocol. This does not mean that UDP is ineffective, only that it doesn't handle issues of reliability. A USP header contains only the Source Port, Destination Port, Length, and the Checksum fields.

Further, UDP doesn't create a virtual circuit, nor does it contact the destination before delivering information to it. It is, therefore, also considered a connectionless protocol. Since UDP assumes that the application will use its own reliability method, it doesn't use any. This gives an application developer a choice when running the Internet Protocol stack: TCP for reliability or UDP for faster transfers.

Internet-Layer Protocols

There are two main reasons for the Internet layer's existence: routing, and providing a single network interface to the upper layers.

None of the protocols on layers above or below have any functions relating to routing; this complex and important task is the job of the

Internet layer. The second reason for the Internet layer is to provide a single network interface to the upper-layer protocols. Without this layer, application programmers would need to write "hooks" into every one of their applications for each different Network Access protocol. This would not only be a pain in the neck, but it would lead to different versions of each application—one for Ethernet, another one for Token Ring, and so on. To prevent this, IP provides one single network interface for the upper-layer protocols. That accomplished, it's then the job of IP and the various Network Access protocols to get along and work together.

All network roads don't lead to Rome—they lead to IP. And all the other protocols at this layer, as well as all those at the upper layers, use it. Never forget that. All paths through the model go through IP. The following sections describe the protocols at the Internet layer.

The protocols that work at the Internet layer are these:

Internet Protocol (IP)   Responsible for logical network addressing and routing through an internetwork.

Internet Control Message Protocol (ICMP)   Used to provide a messaging service for IP (covered in depth in Chapter 4).

Address Resolution Protocol (ARP)   Used to resolve an known IP address to an Ethernet address.

Reverse Address Resolution Protocol (RARP)   Used to resolve a known Ethernet address to an IP address.

IP Addressing

One of the most important topics in any discussion of TCP/IP is IP addressing. An IP address is a numeric identifier assigned to each machine on an IP network. It designates the location of a device on the network. An IP address is a software address, not a hardware address—the latter is hard-coded on a network interface card (NIC) and used for finding hosts on a local network. IP addressing was designed to allow a host on one network to communicate with a host on a different network, regardless of the type of LANs the hosts are participating in.

SEE ALSO Please read Chapter 3 in *CCNA: Cisco Certified Network Associate Study Guide* (Sybex, 2000) for a complete discussion of IP addressing.

Hierarchical IP Addressing Scheme

An IP address is made up of 32 bits of information. These bits are divided into four sections, referred to as *octets* or bytes, each containing 1 byte (8 bits). You can depict an IP address using one of three methods:

- Dotted-decimal, as in 172.16.30.56

- Binary, as in 10101100.00010000.00011110.00111000

- Hexadecimal, as in 82 39 1E 38

The 32-bit IP address is a structured or hierarchical address, as opposed to a flat, or nonhierarchical, address. Although either type of addressing scheme could have been used, the hierarchical variety was chosen for a good reason.

The advantage of this scheme is that it can handle a large number of addresses, namely, almost 4.3 billion (a 32-bit address space with two possible values for each position—either 0 or 1—gives you 2^{32}, or approximately 4.3 billion). The disadvantage of the flat addressing scheme, and the reason it's not used for IP addressing, relates to routing. If every address were unique, all routers on the Internet would need to store the address of each and every machine on the Internet. This would make efficient routing impossible, even if only a fraction of the possible addresses were used.

The solution to this dilemma is to use a two- or three-level, hierarchical addressing scheme that is structured by network and host, or by network, subnet, and host.

Network Addressing

The network address uniquely identifies each network. Every machine on the same network shares that network address as part of its IP address. In the IP address 172.16.30.56, for example, 172.16 is the network address.

The node address is assigned to, and uniquely identifies, each machine on a network. This part of the address must be unique because it identifies a particular machine—an individual—as opposed to a network, which is a group. This number can also be referred to as a host address. In the sample IP address 172.16.30.56, 30.56 is the node address.

The designers of the Internet decided to create classes of networks based on network size. For the small number of networks possessing a very large number of nodes, they created the rank of Class A network. At the other extreme is the Class C network, which is reserved for the numerous networks with a small number of nodes. The class distinction for networks between very large and very small is predictably called the Class B network.

Subdividing an IP address into a network and node address is determined by the class designation of one's network. Figure 3.3 provides a summary of the three classes of networks, plus the D and E class addresses not used in production networks.

FIGURE 3.3: Summary of the five classes of network addresses

	8 bits	8 bits	8 bits	8 bits
Class A:	Network	Host	Host	Host
Class B:	Network	Network	Host	Host
Class C:	Network	Network	Network	Host
Class D:	Multicast			
Class E:	Research			

Some IP addresses are reserved for special purposes, and network administrators shouldn't assign these addresses to nodes. Table 3.1 lists the members of this exclusive little club and why they're included in it.

TABLE 3.1: Reserved IP Addresses

Address	Function
Network address of all 0s	Interpreted to mean "this network or segment."
Network address of all 1s	Interpreted to mean "all networks."
Network 127.0.0.1	Reserved for loopback tests. Designates the local node and allows that node to send a test packet to itself without generating network traffic.
Node address of all 0s	Interpreted to mean "this node."
Node address of all 1s	Interpreted to mean "all nodes" on the specified network; for example, 128.2.255.255 means "all nodes" on Class B network 128.2.
Entire IP address set to all 0s	Used by Cisco routers to designate the default route.
Entire IP address set to all 1s (same as 255.255.255.255)	Broadcast to all nodes on the current network; sometimes called an "all 1s broadcast."

Class A Network Addresses

In a Class A network address, the first byte is assigned to the network address, and the three remaining bytes are used for the node addresses. The Class A format is *net.node.node.node.* For example, in the IP address 49.22.102.70, the network address is 49 and 22.102.70 is the node address. Every machine on this particular network would have the distinctive network address of 49.

Class A network addresses are one byte long, with the first bit of that byte reserved and the seven remaining bits available for manipulation. As a result, the maximum number of Class A networks that can be created is 128. Why? Because each of the 7 bit positions can either be a zero or a one, thus 2^7 or 128.

To complicate matters further, the network address of all 0s (00000000) is reserved to designate the default route (see Table 3.1). Additionally, the address 127, which is reserved for diagnostics, can't be used either, which means that you can only use the numbers 1 to 126 to designate Class A network addresses. This means the actual number of usable Class A network addresses is 128 minus 2, or 126. Got it?

Each Class A network address has 3 bytes (24 bit positions) for the node address of a machine. Thus, there are 2^{24}—or 16,777,216—unique combinations and, therefore, precisely that many possible unique node addresses for each Class A network. Because the two address patterns of all zeros and all ones are reserved, the actual maximum usable number of nodes for a Class A network is 2^{24} minus 2, which equals 16,777,214.

CLASS A VALID HOST IDS

Here is an example of how to figure out the valid host IDs in a Class A network address:

10.0.0.0	All host bits turned off is the network address.
10.255.255.255	All host bits turned on is the broadcast address.

The valid hosts are the numbers between the network address and the broadcast address: 10.0.0.1 through 10.255.255.254. Notice that 0s and 255s are valid host IDs. All you need to remember when trying to find valid host addresses is that the host bits cannot *all* be turned off or on at the same time.

Class B Network Addresses

In a Class B network address, the first two bytes are assigned to the network address, and the remaining two bytes are used for node addresses. The format is *net.net.node.node*. For example, in the IP address 172.16.30.56, the network address is 172.16 and the node address is 30.56.

With a network address being 2 bytes of 8 bits each, there would be 2^{16} unique combinations. But the Internet designers decided that all Class B network addresses should start with the binary digits 1 then 0. This leaves 14 bit positions to manipulate and therefore 16,384 (that is, 2^{14}) unique Class B network addresses.

A Class B network address uses two bytes for node addresses. This is 2^{16} minus the two reserved patterns (all zeros and all ones), for a total of 65,534 possible node addresses for each Class B network.

CLASS B VALID HOST IDS

Here is an example of how to find the valid hosts in a class B network:

172.16.0.0	All host bits turned off is the network address.
172.16.255.255	All host bits turned on is the broadcast address.

The valid hosts would be the numbers between the network address and the broadcast address: 172.16.0.1 through 172.16.255.254.

Class C Network Addresses

The first three bytes of a Class C network address are dedicated to the network portion of the address, with only one measly byte remaining for the node address. The format is *net.net.net.node*. Using the example IP address 192.168.100.102, the network address is 192.168.100, and the node address is 102.

In a Class C network address, the first 3 bit positions are always the binary 110. The calculation is such: 3 bytes, or 24 bits, minus 3 reserved positions, which leaves 21 positions. There are therefore 2^{21} or 2,097,152 possible Class C networks.

Each unique Class C network has one byte to use for node addresses. This leads to 2^8, or 256, minus the two reserved patterns of all zeros and all ones, for a total of 254 node addresses for each Class C network.

CLASS C VALID HOST IDS

Here is an example of how to find a valid host ID in a class C network:

192.168.100.0	All host bits turned off is the network address.
192.168.100.1	The first host.
192.168.100.254	The last host.
192.168.100.255	All host bits turned on is the broadcast address.

The valid hosts would be the numbers between the network address and the broadcast address: 192.168.100.1 through 192.168.100.254.

Subnetting

In the previous section, you learned how to define and find the valid host ranges used in a Class A, a Class B, and a Class C network address by turning the host bits all off and then all on. However, in the above section you were defining one network. What happens if you wanted to take one network address and create six networks from it? You would have to perform what is called subnetting, which allows you to take one larger network and break it up into many smaller networks.

NOTE   Although it's possible to subnet Class A, we don't cover it here as it's not relevant to the CCNA exam. You would need to know that for the CCNP test, though.

Subnet Masks

For the subnet address scheme to work, every machine on the network must know which part of the host address will be used as the subnet address. This is accomplished by assigning a subnet mask to each machine, a 32-bit value that allows the recipient of IP packets to distinguish the network ID portion of the IP address from the host ID portion.

The network administrator creates a 32-bit subnet mask composed of ones and zeros. The ones in the subnet mask represent the positions that refer to the network or subnet addresses. Table 3.2 shows the default subnet masks for Classes A, B, and C.

TABLE 3.2: Default Subnet Mask

Class	Format	Default Subnet Mask
A	net.node.node.node	255.0.0.0
B	net.net.node.node	255.255.0.0
C	net.net.net.node	255.255.255.0

Subnetting Class C Network Addresses

In a Class C network address, only 8 bits are available for defining the hosts. Remember that subnet bits start at the left and go to the right, without skipping bits. This means the subnet masks can be:

```
10000000 = 128
11000000 = 192
11100000 = 224
11110000 = 240
11111000 = 248
11111100 = 252
11111110 = 254
```

Now, the RFCs state that you cannot have only one bit for subnetting, since that would mean that the bit would always be either off or on, which would be illegal. So, the first subnet mask that you can legally use is 192, and the last one is 252, since you need at least two bits for defining hosts.

When you have a subnet mask and you need to determine the number of subnets, valid hosts, and broadcast addresses, all you need to do is answer five simple questions. These questions are:

1. How many subnets does the subnet mask produce?

2. How many valid hosts per subnet?

3. What are the valid subnets?

4. What are the valid hosts in each subnet?

5. What is the broadcast address of each subnet?

Here is how you determine the answers to the five questions:

1. $2^x - 2$ = number of subnets. x is the number of masked bits, or the ones. For example, 11000000 would give $2^2 - 2$. In this example, there are 2 subnets.

2. $2^x - 2$ = number of hosts per subnet. x is the number of unmasked bits, or the zeros. For example, 11000000 produces $2^6 - 2$. In this example, there are 62 hosts per subnet.

3. 256 – subnet mask = base number. For example, 256 – 192 = 64.

4. Valid hosts are the numbers between the subnets, minus "all zeros" and "all ones."

5. Broadcast address is all host bits turned on, which is the number immediately preceding the next subnet.

Now, since this can seem confusing, we need to tell you that it is easier than it looks. Just try a few with us and see for yourself.

This section will give you an opportunity to practice subnetting Class C network addresses using the method we just described. We're going to start with the first Class C subnet mask and work through a few subnets, and when we're done, then we'll show you just how easy this is with Class B networks as well.

PRACTICE EXAMPLE 1: 255.255.255.192

In this example, you will subnet the following :

192.168.10.0   The network address

255.255.255.192   The subnet mask

Now, answer the five questions:

1. **How many subnets?** Since 192 is two bits on (11000000), the answer would be $2^2 - 2 = 2$ subnets. (The "minus 2" is the subnet bits all on or all off, which are not valid by default.)

2. **How many hosts per subnet?** We have 6 hosts bits off (11000000), so the equation would be $2^6 - 2 = 62$ hosts.

3. **What are the valid subnets?** $256 - 192 = 64$, which is the first subnet and our base number or variable. Keep adding the variable to itself until you reach the subnet mask. $64 + 64 = 128$. $128 + 64 = 192$, which is invalid because it is the subnet mask (all subnet bits turned on). Our two valid subnets are then 64 and 128.

4. **What are the valid hosts?** and

5. **What is the broadcast address for each subnet?** These are the numbers between the subnets; however, the number right before the next subnet is all hosts bits turned on and is the broadcast address. The easiest way to find the hosts is to write out the subnet address and the broadcast address. This way the valid hosts are obvious. Table 3.3 shows the 64 and 128 subnets, the valid host ranges of each, and the broadcast address of both subnets.

TABLE 3.3: The 64 and 128 Subnet Ranges

Feature	Subnet One	Subnet Two
Subnet address (do this first)	64	128
First host (perform host addressing last)	65	129
Last host	126	190
Broadcast address (do this second)	127	191

PRACTICE EXAMPLE 2: 255.255.255.224

In this example, you will subnet the following network address and subnet mask:

192.168.10.0   The network address

255.255.255.224   The subnet mask

Ask the five questions:

1. How many subnets? 224 is 11100000, so our equation would be $2^3 - 2 = 6$.

2. How many hosts? $2^5 - 2 = 30$.

3. What are the valid subnets? 256 – 224 = 32. 32 + 32 = 64. 64 + 32 = 96. 96 + 32 = 128. 128 + 32 = 160. 160 + 32 = 192. 192 + 32 = 224, which is invalid as it is our subnet mask (all subnet bits on). Our subnets are: 32, 64, 96, 128, 160, and 192.

4. What are the valid hosts? and

5. What is the broadcast address for each subnet? First, just write out the subnets, then write out the broadcast addresses, which is the number right before the next subnet. Then, finally, fill in the host addresses. The following chart shows all the subnets for the 255.255.255.224 Class C subnet mask.

Subnet Address	32	64	96	128	160	192
First Valid Host	33	65	97	129	161	193
Last Valid Host	62	94	126	158	190	222
Broadcast Address	63	95	127	159	191	223

PRACTICE EXAMPLE 3: 255.255.255.240

Let's practice on another one:

192.168.10.0   The network number

255.255.255.240   The subnet mask

Answer the five questions:

1. 240 is 11110000 in binary. $2^4 - 2 = 14$ subnets.

2. Four host bits, or $2^4 - 2 = 14$ hosts per subnet.

3. $256 - 240 = 16$. $16 + 16 = 32$. $32 + 16 = 48$. $48 + 16 = 64$. $64 + 16 = 80$. $80 + 16 = 96$. $96 + 16 = 112$. $112 + 16 = 128$. $128 + 16 = 144$. $144 + 16 = 160$. $160 + 16 = 176$. $176 + 16 = 192$. $192 + 16 = 208$. $208 + 16 = 224$. $224 + 16 = 240$, which is our subnet mask. So, our valid subnets are 16, 32, 48, 64, 80, 96, 112, 128, 144, 160, 176, 192, 208, and 224.

For questions 4 and 5, the following chart shows the pattern of the subnets and the valid hosts and broadcast addresses for each subnet.

Subnet Address	16	32	48	64	80	96	...	224
First Host	17	33	49	65	81	97	...	225
Last Host	30	46	62	78	94	110	...	238
Broadcast	31	47	63	79	95	111	...	239

SUBNETTING IN YOUR HEAD: CLASS C NETWORK ADDRESSES

It is possible to perform subnetting in your head. Do you believe us? It's relatively easy. Take the following example:

192.168.10.33   The network address

255.255.255.224   The subnet mask

First, determine what subnet and broadcast address the above IP address is a member of. You can do this by performing step three in the five-step process: $256 - 224 = 32$. $32 + 32 = 64$. Bingo. The address falls between the two subnets and must be part of the 192.168.10.32 subnet. The next subnet is 64, so the broadcast address is 63. Remember that the broadcast address of a subnet is always the number right before the next subnet. The valid host range is 33–62. This is getting too easy.

Let's try another one. Here, you will subnet another Class C network address. What subnet and broadcast address is this IP address a member of?

192.168.10.33	The network address
255.255.255.240	The subnet mask

256 − 240 = 16. 16 + 16 = 32. 32 + 16 = 48. Bingo, the host address is between the 32 and 48 subnet. The subnet is 192.168.10.32, and the broadcast address is 47. The valid host range is 33–46.

Subnetting Class B Network Addresses

Since we went through some of the possible Class C subnets, let's take a look at subnetting a Class B network. First, let's look at all the possible Class B subnet masks. Notice that we have a lot more possible subnets than with a Class C network address:

```
255.255.128.0
255.255.192.0
255.255.224.0
255.255.240.0
255.255.248.0
255.255.252.0
255.255.254.0
255.255.255.0
255.255.255.128
255.255.255.192
255.255.255.224
255.255.255.240
255.255.255.248
255.255.255.252
```

The Class B network address has 16 bits available for host addressing. This means we can use up to 14 bits for subnetting, since we must leave at least two bits for host addressing.

The process of subnetting a Class B network is the same as with Class C, except you just have more host bits. Use the same subnet numbers you used with Class C, but add a zero to the network portion and a 255 to the broadcast section in the fourth octet. For example, this chart shows you a host range of two subnets used in a Class B network.

16.0	32.0
16.255	32.255

Just add the valid hosts between the numbers and you're set.

PRACTICE EXAMPLE 1: 255.255.192.0

Here is a Class B example:

172.16.0.0	The network address
255.255.192.0	The subnet mask

1. $2^2 - 2 = 2$ subnets.

2. $2^{14} - 2 = 16,382$ hosts per subnet.

3. $256 - 192 = 64. \ 64 + 64 = 128.$

For questions 4 and 5, the following chart shows the two subnets available and the valid host range and broadcast address of each.

Subnet Address	64.0	128.0
First Host	64.1	128.1
Last Host	127.254	191.254
Broadcast Address	127.255	191.255

Notice we just added the fourth octet's lowest and highest values and came up with the answers. Again, these produce the same answers as a Class C subnet, but we just added the fourth octet.

PRACTICE EXAMPLE 2: 255.255.240.0

Here is another example:

| 172.16.0.0 | The network address |
| 255.255.240.0 | The subnet address |

1. $2^4 - 2 = 14$ subnets.

2. $2^{12} - 2 = 4094$ hosts per subnet.

3. $256 - 240 = 16, 32, 48$, etc., up to 224. Notice that these are the same numbers as a Class C 240 mask.

For questions 4 and 5, the following chart shows the first three subnets, their valid hosts, and broadcast addresses.

Subnet Address	16.0	32.0	48.0
First Host	16.1	32.1	48.1
Last Host	31.254	47.254	63.254
Broadcast Address	31.255	47.255	63.255

PRACTICE EXAMPLE 3: 255.255.255.0

Contrary to popular belief, 255.255.255.0 is not a Class C subnet mask. It is amazing how many people see this mask used in a Class B network and say it is a Class C subnet mask. This is a Class B subnet mask with 8 bits of subnetting; it is considerably different from a Class C mask. Subnetting this address is fairly simple.

1. $2^8 - 2 = 254$ subnets.

2. $2^8 - 2 = 254$ hosts per subnet.

3. $3.256 - 255 = 1, 2, 3$, etc. all the way to 254.

For questions 4 and 5, the following chart shows the first three and the last subnet, the valid hosts, and the broadcast addresses.

Subnet Address	1.0	2.0	3.0	...	254.0
First Host	1.1	2.1	3.1	...	254.1
Last Host	1.254	2.254	3.254	...	254.254
Broadcast Address	1.255	2.255	3.255	...	254.255

PRACTICE EXAMPLE 4: 255.255.255.128

This must be illegal! What type of mask is this? Don't you wish it were illegal? This is one of the hardest subnet masks you can play with! This is actually a good subnet to use in production, as it creates more than 500 subnets with 126 hosts per subnet. That's a nice mixture.

1. $2^9 - 2 = 510$ subnets.

2. $2^7 - 2 = 126$ hosts per subnet.

3. This is the tricky part. $256 - 255 = 1, 2, 3$, etc. for the third octet. However, you need to remember the one subnet bit used in the fourth octet. Remember when we showed you how to figure one subnet bit with a Class C mask? You figure this the same way. Now you know why we showed you the one-bit subnet mask in the Class C section: to make this part easier. You actually get two subnets for each third octet value, hence the 510 subnets. For example, if the third octet was showing subnet 3, the two subnets would actually be 3.0 and 3.128.

For questions 4 and 5, the following chart shows how you can create subnets, valid hosts, and broadcast addresses using the 255.255.255 .128 subnet mask.

Subnet Address	0.128	1.0	1.128	2.0	2.128	3.0	3.128
First Host	0.129	1.1	1.129	2.1	2.129	3.1	3.129
Last Host	0.254	1.126	1.254	2.126	2.254	3.126	3.254
Broadcast Address	0.255	1.127	1.255	2.127	2.255	3.127	3.255

PRACTICE EXAMPLE 5: 255.255.255.192

This one gets just a little tricky. Both the zero subnet and the 192 subnet could be valid in the fourth octet. It just depends on what the third octet is doing.

1. $2^{10} - 2 = 1022$ subnets.

2. $2^6 - 2 = 62$ hosts per subnet.

3. $256 - 192 = 64$ and 128. However, as long as all the subnet bits in the third octet are not all off, then subnet 0 in the fourth octet is valid. Also, as long as all the subnet bits in the third octet are not all on, then 192 is valid in the fourth octet as a subnet.

For questions 4 and 5, the following chart shows the first seven subnet ranges, valid hosts, and broadcast addresses.

Subnet Address	0.64	0.128	0.192	1.0	1.64	1.128	1.192
First Host	0.65	0.129	0.192	1.1	1.65	1.129	1.193
Last Host	0.126	0.190	0.254	1.62	1.126	1.190	1.254
Broadcast Address	0.127	0.192	0.255	1.63	1.127	1.191	1.255

Notice that for each subnet value in the third octet, you get subnets 0, 64, 128, and 192 in the fourth octet. This is true for every subnet in the third octet except 0 and 255. The zero subnet value in the third octet is demonstrated above. Notice, however, for the 1 subnet in the third octet, that the fourth octet has four subnets: 0, 64, 128, and 192.

PRACTICE EXAMPLE 6: 255.255.255.224

This is done the same way as the subnet mask above; we just get more subnets and fewer hosts per subnet available.

1. $2^{11} - 2 = 2046$ subnets.

2. $2^5 - 2 = 30$ hosts per subnet.

3. 256 – 224 = 32, 64, 96, 128, 160, 192. However, as demonstrated above, both the 0 and 224 subnets can be used as long as the third octet does not show a value of 0 or 255. Here is a demonstration of having no subnet bits on in the third octet.

For steps 4 and 5, the following chart shows the first range of subnets.

Subnet Address	0.32	0.64	0.96	0.128	0.160	0.192	0.224
First Host	0.33	0.65	0.96	0.129	0.161	0.193	0.225
Last Host	0.62	0.94	0.126	0.158	0.190	0.222	0.254
Broadcast Address	0.63	0.95	0.127	0.159	0.191	0.223	0.255

Let's take a look when a subnet bit is turned on in the third octet. The next chart shows the range of subnets available in the fourth octet.

Subnet Address	1.0	1.32	1.64	...	1.224
First Host	1.1	1.33	1.65	...	1.225
Last Host	1.30	1.62	1.94	...	1.254
Broadcast Address	1.31	1.63	1.95	...	1.255

And this chart shows the last subnet range.

Subnet Address	255.0	255.32	255.64	...	255.192
First Host	255.1	255.33	255.65	...	255.193
Last Host	255.30	255.62	255.94	...	255.222
Broadcast Address	255.31	255.63	255.95	...	255.223

SUBNETTING IN YOUR HEAD: CLASS B NETWORK ADDRESSES

We know what you are thinking. "Are you nuts?" It's actually easier than writing it out. We'll show you how with the next few quick examples. For each IP address, what subnet and broadcast address is it a member of?

IP Address	Subnet and Broadcast Address Calculation
172.16.10.33, mask 255.255.255.224	256 − 224 = 32. 32 + 32 = 64. Bingo, 33 is between 32 and 64. However, remember that the third octet is considered part of the subnet, so the answer would be the 10.32 subnet. The broadcast is 10.63, since 10.64 is the next subnet.
172.16.90.66, mask 255.255.255.192	256 − 192 = 64. 64 + 64 = 128. The subnet is 172.16.90.64. The broadcast must be 172.16.90.127, since 90.128 is the next subnet.
172.16.50.97, mask 255.255.255.224	256 − 224 = 32, 64, 96, 128. The subnet is 172.16.50.96 and the broadcast must be 172.16.50.127, since 50.128 is the next subnet.
172.16.10.10, mask 255.255.255.192	256 − 192 = 64. This address must be in the 172.16.10.0 subnet, and the broadcast must be 172.16.10.63.
172.16.10.10, mask 255.255.255.224	256 − 224 = 32. The subnet is 172.16.10.0 with a broadcast of 172.16.10.31.

Network Access–Layer Protocols

The Network Access layer combines both the Physical and Data Link layers of the OSI Reference Model. The LAN media access protocols and physical cabling topologies found here at this layer of the DoD model are listed below.

802.2 SNAP	FDDI
802.3 CSMA/CD	Category 1–5
802.5 Token Ring	PPP/SLIP

MAC Addressing	ATM
Ethernet II	Coaxial Cables

Exam Essentials

Understand how to find the valid hosts in a subnet.   The best way to do this is to use the equation 256 minus the subnet mask. For example, if you have a 240 mask, you would use 256 – 240. The result, 16, is your first subnet and your base number, or interval. Keep adding the base number to itself until you reach the value of the subnet mask. The valid hosts are the numbers between the subnets.

Understand how to find a broadcast address in a subnet.   Once you find the valid subnets, you can find the valid hosts, which are the numbers between the subnets minus the broadcast address, which is the last number in the host range. For example, in a 240 mask, the first subnet is 16 and the second subnet is 32. That means the valid hosts are 17 through 30, with 31 being the broadcast address for that subnet.

Remember the specifications of each protocol.   You should know that TCP is a connection-oriented protocol and UDP is a connection-less protocol, for example.

Remember the tools to test for IP connectivity on your Cisco network.   Telnet, ping, and trace can be used to test for IP connectivity.

Know all the protocols used and their functions.   It is important to remember the protocols used at the Network layer and what each one does.

Key Terms and Concepts

Address Resolution Protocol (ARP)   Described at the Internet layer of the DoD model, ARP is used to find a hardware address, given the IP address.

Bootstrap Protocol (BootP)   Described at the Internet layer of the DoD model, BootP is used to give diskless workstations an IP address.

Class A   Address class used to differentiate between a network and node within an IP address, creating very few large networks. The syntax is *net.node.node.node.*

Class B   Address class used to differentiate between a network and node within an IP address. The syntax is *net.net.node.node.*

Class C   Address class used to differentiate between a network and node within an IP address, creating many small networks. The syntax is *net.net.net.node.*

IP address   Network address assigned to a node on a network. Used to send and receive packets or datagrams on an internetwork.

Internet Protocol (IP)   A connectionless protocol described at the Internet layer of the DoD model.

subnetting   The breaking up of an IP network address into smaller networks.

Transmission Control Protocol (TCP)   A connection-oriented protocol specified at the Host-to-Host layer of the DoD model.

User Datagram Protocol (UDP)   A connectionless protocol defined at the Host-to-Host layer of the DoD model.

ping   An acronym for Packet Internet Groper, `ping` is used to test connectivity between IP hosts.

Reverse Address Resolution Protocol (RARP)   Described at the Internet layer of the DoD model, RARP is used to find an IP address, given the hardware address.

Telnet   Terminal emulation program used to create a virtual window to a remote device.

trace   Also called Trace Route, `trace` is used to find the route a packet travels through an internetwork to a remote node.

Sample Questions

1. With an IP address of 172.16.10.16 and a mask of 255.255.255 .128, what are the class of the address, subnet address, and broadcast address?

   A. Class C, 172.16.10.0, 172.16.10.128

   B. Class B, 172.16.10.0, 172.16.10.255

   C. Class B, 172.16.10.0, 172.16.10.127

   D. Class B, 172.16.10.0, 172.16.10.126

   Answer: C. 172.16.10.0 is the subnet number because the fourth octet has a value of 16. That is in the range from 0 to 127, and 128 is the next subnet. Therefore 172.16.10.127 is the broadcast address.

2. If you have a 22-bit subnet mask, how many subnets and hosts per subnet do you have?

   A. 4,194,302 subnets, 2 hosts each

   B. 4,194,302 subnets, 4 hosts each

   C. 8190 subnets, 4096 hosts each

   D. 16,382 subnets, 14 hosts each

   Answer: A. A 22-bit subnet mask added onto the default Class A mask is 255.255.255.252. That only leaves you two host bits, or two hosts per subnet. Remember that the best way to solve these kinds of problems on the CCNA exam is to look only for the number of host bits.

3. If you have an IP address of 192.168.10.42 with a 255.255.255 .224 mask, what are your valid hosts?

   A. 10.1 to 10.254

   B. 10.33 to 10.64

   C. 10.33 to 10.62

   D. 10.33 to 10.63

Answer: C. A 224 subnet mask gives you 6 subnets, each with 30 hosts. The valid subnets are 256 – 224 = 32, 64, 96, etc. The 42 in the last octet is in the 32 subnet. Since 32 is the subnet and 63 is the broadcast for that subnet, the valid hosts are 33 through 62.

4. If you have an IP address of 172.16.30.10 with a 255.255.252.0 subnet mask, what are the class of the address, subnet address, and broadcast address?

   A. Class A, 172.16.28.0, 172.16.31.255

   B. Class B, 172.16.28.0, 172.16.31.127

   C. Class B, 172.16.28.0, 172.16.31.254

   D. Class B, 172.16.28.128, 172.16.31.254

   Answer: C. With a 255.255.252.0 mask, you have six bits for subnets. Your valid subnets are 256 – 252 = 4, 8, 12, 16, 20, 24, 28, 32, 36, etc. The third octet is 30, which is in the 28 subnet range. However, you need the fourth octet for host addressing. So your valid range is 28.1 through 31.254, and 31.255 is the broadcast address. 172.16.28.0 is the subnet address.

5. Which of these terms match the description given here?

   A. TCP: connectionless

   B. UDP: connection-oriented

   C. TCP: uses windowing

   D. UDP: uses acknowledgments

   Answer: C. TCP is a connection-oriented protocol, and UDP is a connectionless protocol. Both reside at the Transport layer. Windowing is used in a connection-oriented session for setting flow-control parameters.

6. Which of the following commands or programs can be used to test IP connectivity?

   A. Telnet

   B. ARP

C. ping

D. trace

Answer: A, C, D. Telnet, ping, and trace are used in IP networks to test for connectivity.

7. Which of the following commands or programs will show output such as the following?

```
1 172.16.20.2 24 msec 24 msec 28 msec
2 172.16.40.2 44 msec 44 msec *
```

A. ping

B. Telnet

C. ARP

D. trace

Answer: D. trace uses TTL time-outs to find the route to a destination host. Each time the TTL hits a router or hop, it sends back an ICMP message.

Novell IPX

Most network administrators have, at some point, encountered Internetwork Packet Exchange (IPX). Novell NetWare used IPX as its default protocol, and NetWare was the most popular network operating system during the late 1980s and early 1990s. As a result, millions of IPX networks have been installed. But Novell is changing things with the release of NetWare 5. TCP/IP is now the default communications protocol instead of IPX, although Novell still supports IPX. After all, considering the multitude of installed IPX clients and servers, it would be pretty impractical to yank the support for it.

You must know your IPX routing protocols when taking the CCNA exam. This objective will give you the critical information you need to pass the exam, as well as to configure IPX on Cisco routers.

Critical Information

IPX doesn't map directly to the OSI model, but its protocols do function in layers. Back when they designed IPX, engineers were more concerned with performance than they were with strict compliance to existing standards or models. Even so, comparisons can be made.

Figure 3.4 illustrates the IPX protocols, layers, and functions relative to those of the OSI model.

FIGURE 3.4: The IPX protocol stack and the OSI model

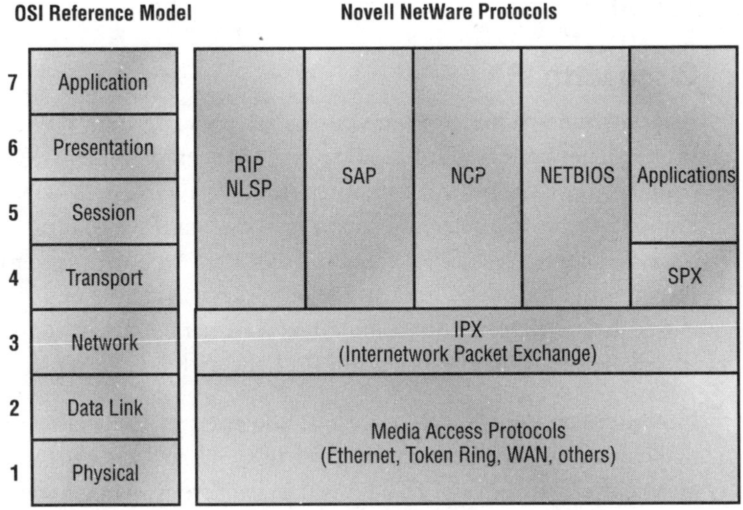

OSI Reference Model   Novell NetWare Protocols

OSI	Layer	Novell NetWare Protocols				
7	Application	RIP NLSP	SAP	NCP	NETBIOS	Applications
6	Presentation					
5	Session					
4	Transport					SPX
3	Network	IPX (Internetwork Packet Exchange)				
2	Data Link	Media Access Protocols (Ethernet, Token Ring, WAN, others)				
1	Physical					

Internetwork Packet Exchange (IPX) Performs functions at Layers 3 and 4 of the OSI model. It controls the assignment of IPX addresses (software addressing) on individual nodes, governs packet delivery across internetworks, and makes routing decisions based on information provided by the routing protocols, RIP or NLSP.

Service Advertising Protocol (SAP)   Used to advertise and request services. Servers use it to advertise the services they offer, and clients use it to locate network services.

Routing Information Protocol (RIP)   A distance-vector routing protocol used to discover IPX routes through internetworks. It employs ticks (1/18 of a second) and hop counts (number of routers between nodes) as metrics for determining preferred routes.

Sequenced Packet Exchange (SPX)   Adds connection-oriented communications to the otherwise connectionless IPX.

NetWare Link Services Protocol (NLSP)   An advanced link-state routing protocol developed by Novell, intended to replace both RIP and SAP.

Cisco with IPX

As you would think, NetWare clients are dependent on servers to locate all network resources. Every NetWare server builds a SAP table comprising all the network resources that it's aware of. When a client requires access to a certain resource, it issues an IPX broadcast called a GetNearestServer (GNS) request to locate a NetWare server that provides that resource. In turn, the servers receiving the GNS request check their SAP tables to locate a NetWare server that matches the specific request; they respond to the client with a GNS reply.

If there are no local NetWare servers, however, the local Cisco router that connects the client's segment to the IPX internetwork can respond to the client's GNS request. This saves the client from having to wait for remote NetWare servers to respond. A second advantage of this arrangement is that precious WAN bandwidth isn't occupied with GNS conversations between clients on a segment with no local NetWare server and remote NetWare servers, as shown in Figure 3.5.

FIGURE 3.5: Remote IPX clients on a serverless network

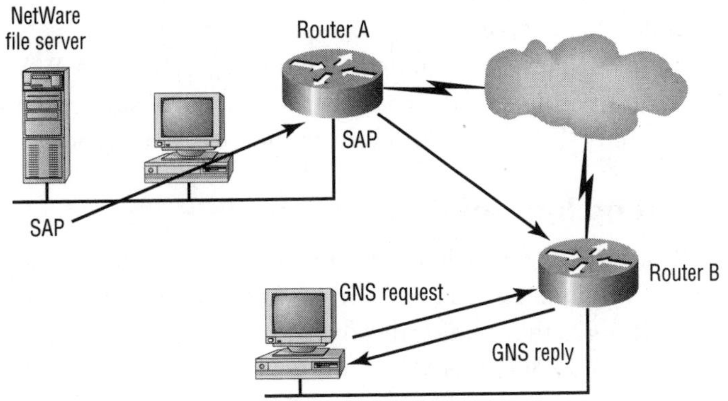

In this figure, you can see client workstations at the remote office site: They require access to server resources at the main office. In this situation, Router A would answer client GNS requests from its SAP table rather than forwarding the request across the WAN to the main office servers. The clients never realize or care that there isn't a NetWare server present on their LAN.

Service Advertising Protocol (SAP)

NetWare servers use SAP to advertise the services they offer by sending out a SAP broadcast every 60 seconds. The broadcast includes all services that the server has learned about from other servers—not just the ones they furnish. All servers receiving the SAP broadcast incorporate the information into their own SAP tables; it then rebroadcasts it in their own SAP updates. Because SAP information is shared among all servers, all servers eventually become aware of all available services and are thereby equipped to respond to client GNS requests. As new services are introduced, they're added to SAP tables on local servers and are rebroadcast until every server knows they exist and where to get them.

So how does a Cisco router fit in here? Well, as far as SAP is concerned, that router acts just like another NetWare server. By default, a SAP broadcast won't cross a Cisco router. A Cisco router catalogs all SAPs heard on any of its IPX-enabled interfaces into its SAP table; it then broadcasts the whole table from each of those interfaces at 60-second intervals, unless you change the settings—just as NetWare servers do. This is an important point, especially with WAN links. The router isolates SAP broadcasts to individual segments and passes along only the summarized information to each segment.

Routing Information Protocol (RIP)

RIP information is exchanged between servers much the same way that SAP information is. Servers build routing tables that contain entries for the networks they're directly connected to, then broadcast this information on to all IPX-enabled interfaces. Other servers on those segments receive those updates and broadcast their RIP tables on their IPX interfaces. Just as SAP information travels from server to server until all servers are enlightened, RIP information is proliferated until all servers and routers know of the internetwork's routes. Like SAP information, RIP information is broadcast at 60-second intervals.

IPX Addressing

IPX addresses use 80 bits, or 10 bytes, of data. As with TCP/IP addresses, they are hierarchical and divided into network and node portions. The first four bytes always represent the network address, and the last six bytes always represent the node address. There's none of that Class A, Class B, or Class C TCP/IP stuff in IPX addressing—the network and node portions of the address are always the same length. After subnet masking, this is sweet indeed!

IPX addresses can be written in several formats. Most often, though, they're written in hex, such as 00007C80.0000.8609.33E9. The first 8 hex digits (00007C80) represent the network portion of the address. It's a common IPX custom when referring to the IPX network to drop leading zeros. Thus, the above network address would be referred to as IPX network 7C80.

The remaining 12 hex digits (0000.8609.33E9) represent the node portion and are commonly divided into three sections of four hex digits each divided by periods. These are the MAC address of the workstation.

Encapsulation

Encapsulation, or framing, is the process of taking packets from upper-layer protocols and building frames to transmit across the network. As you probably recall, frames live at Layer 2 of the OSI model. When you're dealing with IPX, encapsulation is the specific process of taking IPX datagrams (Layer 3) and building frames (Layer 2) for one of the supported media.

Why is this significant? Well, for the very good reason that NetWare supports multiple, incompatible framing methods, and it does so on the same media. For instance, take Ethernet. NetWare has four different frame types to choose from, depending on your needs (see Table 3.4), and each of those frame types is incompatible with the others.

TABLE 3.4: Novell Ethernet Encapsulations

NetWare Frame Type	Features
Ethernet_802.3	Default up to NetWare 3.11
Ethernet_802.2	Default since NetWare 3.12
Ethernet_II	Supports both TCP/IP and IPX
Ethernet_snap	AppleTalk, IPX, and TCP/IP

Sometimes—and only sometimes—you can intentionally have multiple frame types present on the same network. Typically, you'll start working in an environment that already has all frame types configured—usually because the administrator didn't know what to do and just configured all available frame types on all routers and servers, as shown in Figure 3.6.

FIGURE 3.6: Multiple frame types on a single Ethernet segment

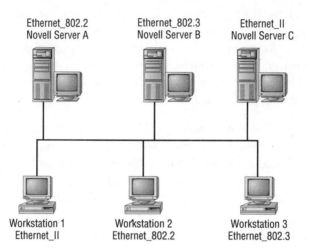

Each frame type in Figure 3.6 has a unique IPX network address. Even though there's a single Ethernet segment, there are three virtual IPX networks and, therefore, three unique IPX network addresses. Each network will be broadcast across the internetwork every 60 seconds.

When configuring a router, you'll need to know both the frame type and the IPX network address information for each segment that you plan to attach that router to. To find this information, ask the network administrator or go to one of the NetWare servers and type **config** at the server console.

Necessary Procedures

To configure IPX routing, use the ipx routing global configuration command. Here is an example:

```
RouterA#config t
RouterA(config)#ipx routing
```

Once you enable IPX routing on the router, RIP and SAP are automatically enabled as well. However, nothing happens until you configure the individual interfaces with IPX addresses.

Enabling IPX on Individual Interfaces

Once you have IPX routing enabled on the router, the next step is to enable IPX on individual interfaces. To enable IPX on an interface, first enter the interface configuration mode then issue the following command:

```
ipx network number [encapsulation encapsulation-type]
↳[secondary]
```

The various parts are defined as follows:

number   The IPX network address.

[encapsulation encapsulation-type]   Optional. Table 3.5 lists the default encapsulation type on various media.

[secondary]   Indicates a secondary encapsulation (frame type) and network address on the same interface.

Here is an example of configuring IPX on a 2500 router named 2500A:

```
2501A#config t
2501A(config)#ipx routing
2501A(config)#int e0
2501A(config-if)#ipx network 10
```

That's all there is to it. Just add the network number, and the rest is done for you. IPX is a very resilient routed protocol because it broadcasts for everything. However, this is also why it causes problems in larger internetworks.

What frame type is now running on Ethernet 0 on 2501A? By default, the frame type is Novell-Ether (802.3). To change the frame type, or to add another frame type, add the encapsulation command to the interface configuration. Table 3.5 lists the different encapsulation (frame types) available with IPX.

To change the IPX frame type on Ethernet 0 of 2501A to SAP (802.2), use the encapsulation command, as shown below:

```
2501A#config t
```

TABLE 3.5: Novell IPX Frame Types

Interface Type	Novell Frame Type	Cisco Keyword
Ethernet	Ethernet_802.3	`novell-ether` (default)
	Ethernet_802.2	`sap`
	Ethernet_II	`arpa`
	Ethernet_snap	`snap`
Token Ring	Token-Ring	`sap` (default)
	Token-Ring_snap	`snap`
FDDI	Fddi_snap	`snap` (default)
	Fddi_802.2	`sap`
	Fddi_raw	`novell-fddi`

```
2501A(config)#int e0
2501A(config-if)#ipx network 10 encapsulation sap
```

This replaces the existing network number and encapsulation with the 802.2 frame type. If you want to add multiple frame types, you need to either use the **secondary** command at the end of the network command line, or create subinterfaces. Both the **secondary** command and subinterfaces are discussed later in this chapter.

To configure a Cisco router into an existing IPX internetwork, you'll need the IPX network address and frame type information from the "config" screen of your NetWare servers for this step. When specifying the encapsulation type on the router, make sure to use the Cisco keyword, *not* the Novell frame type.

Verifying the IPX Routing Tables

To view the IPX routing tables, use the command show ipx route. Like IP, IPX routers only know about directly connected networks by default. However, when you turned on IPX routing in the configuration examples above, IPX RIP was automatically started on all routers.

IPX RIP will find all IPX networks in the internetwork and update all routers' routing tables. Let's take a look at a router running IPX in an internetwork and see the IPX routing table:

```
2621A#sh ipx route
Codes: C - Connected primary network, c - Connected
↳secondary network
[output cut]
5 Total IPX routes. Up to 1 parallel paths and 16
↳hops allowed.
No default route known.
C   10 (NOVELL-ETHER),  Fa0/0
R   20 [07/01] via      10.0000.0c8d.3a7b,   16s, Fa0/0
R   30 [07/02] via      10.0000.0c8d.3a7c,   17s, Fa0/0
R   40 [07/02] via      10.0000.0c8d.3a7c,   17s, Fa0/0
R   50 [13/03] via      10.0000.0c8d.3a7c,   17s, Fa0/0
2621A#
```

The C means a directly connected IPX network, and the Rs are IPX RIP found networks. The [07/01] is the ticks and hops to the remote network.

Adding a Secondary Network

To configure a secondary address on an Ethernet LAN to support multiple frame types, use the ipx network command with the secondary parameter at the end of the command.

Here is an example of adding a secondary network to 2501A's Ethernet connection:

```
2501A#config t
```

```
Enter configuration commands, one per line.  End
⮡with CNTL/Z.
2501A(config)#int e0
2501A(config-if)#ipx network 10a encap sap sec
```

If you don't use the secondary command at the end of the line, the ipx network command will replace the existing entry. (The shortcut commands encap and sec were used here instead of the whole commands encapsulation and secondary.)

The important thing to understand is that each frame type must have a different IPX network number. Notice the 10a in the above example. The 802.3 frame type is using 10, so you cannot configure the 802.2 frame type with that number.

Supporting Multiple Networks with Subinterfaces

To define IPX network numbers to router interfaces that support multiple networks, you can use a subinterface instead of the secondary command. This allows one physical interface to support multiple logical IPX networks. Each subinterface, like a secondary, must have a unique IPX network number and a unique encapsulation type.

To define subinterfaces, use the interface ethernet port.number command. You can use numbers between e0.0 and e0.4292967295— that's a lot of subinterfaces! An example of adding the 802.2 frame type is shown below:

```
2621A(config)#int e0.10
2621A(config-subif)#ipx network 10a encap sap
2621A(config-subif)#^Z
2621A#
```

Monitoring IPX on Cisco Routers

Once you have IPX configured and running, there are several ways to verify and track that your router is communicating correctly. The following commands are important to understand:

show ipx servers   This command is a lot like the display servers command in NetWare—it displays the contents of the SAP table in the Cisco router, so you should see the names of all SAP services here.

show ipx route   This command displays the IPX routing table entries that the router knows about. The router reports networks to which it is directly connected, then reports networks that it has learned of since the router has come online.

show ipx traffic   This command shows the RIP and SAP traffic sent and received on all interfaces of the router.

show ipx interface   This command shows the RIP and SAP information sent and received on each individual interface. Also, it shows the IPX network number and encapsulation for each interface.

show protocol   This command shows the routed protocol addresses for each interface.

debug ipx   This command provides diagnostics for IPX routing.

IPX ping   This command allows you to `ping` IPX router interfaces for diagnostic.

Load Balancing with IPX

If you were to set up parallel IPX paths between routers, the Cisco IOS would not learn about these paths by default. The router will learn a single path to a destination and discard information about alternative, parallel, equal-cost paths. To be able to perform a round-robin load balance over multiple equal cost paths, you need to add the command `ipx maximum-paths [#]` (with # being any number up to 64); this will allow the router to accept the possibility that there might be more than one path to the same destination.

The Cisco IOS will perform per-packet load sharing by default over these parallel lines. Packets will be sent on a round-robin basis between all equal-cost lines, without regard to the destination. However, if you want to ensure that all packets sent to a destination or host will always go over the same line, use the `IPX per-host-load-share` command.

The `ipx maximum-paths` command is shown below. It tells the IPX RIP protocol to perform a round-robin load balance across two equal-cost paths.

```
Router#config t
```

```
Router(config)#ipx maximum-paths 2
Router(config)#^Z
Router#sh ipx route
Codes: C - Connected primary network,    c - Connected
↳[output cut]
5 Total IPX routes. Up to 2 parallel paths and 16
↳hops allowed.
[output cut]
```

The show ipx route command shows that two parallel paths are now supported.

Exam Essentials

Remember the IPX address format.   The syntax for an IPX address is *net.node.node.node*. There are no class distinctions and no other syntax types for IPX addresses.

Remember the output each command gives you.   When practicing the commands on your Cisco router, pay close attention to the output each command displays.

Remember the IPX encapsulation methods used on an Ethernet LAN.   Studying and practicing on a Cisco router will help you remember the different keywords.

Key Terms and Concepts

debug   A command used to display real-time network updates on a console.

Extended Ping   Program that allows you to specify arguments in the ping command. This is useful when you want to ping other protocols besides IP.

Internet Protocol (IP)   A protocol specified at the Internet layer of the Department of Defense (DoD) model. Used to route packets through an internetwork and for network addressing.

Internetwork Packet Exchange (IPX)   A protocol stack developed by Xerox (which they called XNS). Novell copied the protocol and called it IPX. It is used for routing packets through an internetwork and for network addressing.

ping   An acronym for Packet Internet Groper, `ping` is used to test IP connectivity between two IP hosts on an internetwork.

Routing Information Protocol (RIP)   A distance-vector routing protocol that is used to update routing tables dynamically.

Service Advertising Protocol (SAP)   A Novell protocol defined at the Application layer of the OSI model and used to advertise network services on an internetwork.

Sample Questions

1. Which of the following commands displays the IPX address on an interface?

   A. `sh int`

   B. `sh ip int`

   C. `sh ipx int`

   D. `sh proto`

   Answer: C, D. The commands `show ipx interface` and `show protocol` will display the IPX address of a Cisco router interface.

2. Which command displays all the NetWare servers found by your Cisco router?

   A. `show ipx servers`

   B. `display server`

   C. `show servers`

   D. `display routers`

   Answer: A. The command `show ipx servers` is similar to the command `display servers` on a NetWare console.

3. Which command displays the IPX routing table?

A. sh protocol

B. sh ip route

C. show ipx route

D. show route

Answer: C. show ipx route displays the IPX routing table built in a Cisco router. It is important to remember that each protocol has its own routing table.

4. Which statements are true regarding the IPX address 7C89.0000 .3456.1234? (Choose two.)

A. 7C89.0000 is the network number.

B. 3456.1234 is the node number.

C. 7C89 is the network number.

D. 0000.3456.1234 is the node number.

Answer: C, D. The syntax of an IPX address is *net.node.node.node*.

5. Which encapsulation method would you use on a Cisco router interface to configure 802.3?

A. ARPA

B. Ethernet II

C. SAP

D. Novell-Ether

Answer: D. You must remember the Cisco encapsulation methods used on an Ethernet network. 802.3 is the default encapsulation, and Cisco calls it Novell-Ether.

6. Which encapsulation method would you use on a Cisco router interface to configure 802.2?

A. ARPA

B. SNAP

C. SAP

D. Novell-Ether

Answer: C. SAP encapsulation used on Cisco routers is referred to as 802.2.

Windowing

Windowing is a flow control method used in TCP. This flow control is a very efficient method of providing a stable environment for a TCP virtual circuit.

This section will teach you everything you need to know about windowing in TCP in regards for the CCNA exam. However, understanding flow control, the methods involved, and how they are used in a network will provide you with important information you need when working in a production environment.

Critical Information

During a transfer, congestion can occur because a high-speed computer is generating data traffic faster than the network can transfer it, or because many computers are simultaneously sending datagrams through a single gateway or destination. In the latter case, a gateway or destination can become congested even though no single source caused the problem.

When a machine receives a flood of datagrams too quickly for it to process, it stores them in a section in memory called a *buffer*. This buffering action solves the problem only if the datagrams are part of a small burst. However, if the datagram deluge continues, a device's memory will eventually be exhausted, its flood capacity will be exceeded, and it will discard any additional datagrams that arrive.

But, no worries—because of the transport function, network flood control systems work quite well. Instead of dumping resources and allowing data to be lost, the transport can issue a "not ready" indicator, as shown in Figure 3.7, to the sender, or source, of the flood. This mechanism works kind of like a stop light, signaling the sending device to stop transmitting segment traffic to its overwhelmed peer. When the peer receiver has processed the segments already in its memory reservoir, it sends out a "ready" transport indicator. When the machine waiting to transmit the rest of its datagrams receives this "go" indictor, it can then resume its transmission.

FIGURE 3.7: Transmitting segments with flow control

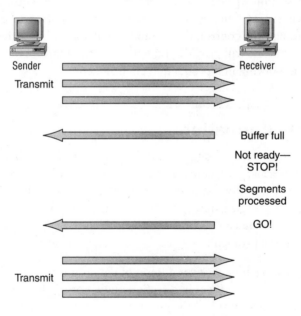

In fundamental, reliable, connection-oriented data transfer, datagrams are delivered to the receiving host in exactly the same sequence they're transmitted; the transmission fails if this order is breached. If any data segments are lost, duplicated, or damaged along the way, this will cause a failure to transmit. The answer to the problem is to have the receiving host acknowledge receiving each and every data segment.

Windowing

Data throughput would be low if the transmitting machine had to wait for an acknowledgment after sending each segment. Since there's time available after the sender transmits the data segment and before it finishes processing acknowledgments from the receiving machine, the sender uses the break to transmit more data. The quantity of data segments the transmitting machine is allowed to send without receiving an acknowledgment for them is called a *window.*

Windowing controls how much information is transferred from one end to the other. While some protocols quantify information by observing the number of packets, TCP/IP measures it by counting the number of bytes. Figure 3.8 illustrates a window size of 1 and a window size of 3. When a window size of 1 is configured, the sending machine waits for an acknowledgment for each data segment it transmits before transmitting another. Configured to a window size of 3, it's allowed to transmit three data segments before an acknowledgment is received. In our simplified example, both the sending and receiving machines are workstations. Reality is rarely that simple, and most often acknowledgments and packets will commingle as they travel over the network and pass through routers. Routing complicates things, but not to worry, you'll learn about applied routing later in the book.

FIGURE 3.8: Windowing

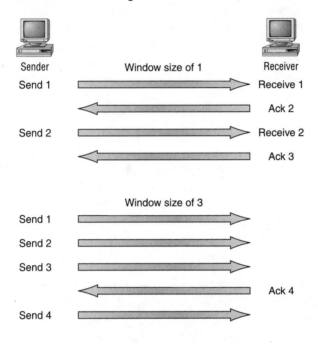

SEE ALSO Please read Chapter 9 in the *CCNA: Cisco Certified Network Associate Study Guide* (Sybex, 2000) for more information on TCP, which operates at the Transport layer.

Acknowledgments

Reliable data delivery ensures the integrity of a stream of data sent from one machine to another through a fully functional data link. It guarantees the data won't be duplicated or lost. The method that achieves this is known as positive acknowledgment with retransmission. This technique requires a receiving machine to communicate with the transmitting source by sending an acknowledgment message back to the sender when it receives data. The sender documents each segment it sends and waits for this acknowledgment before sending the next segment. When it sends a segment, the transmitting machine starts a timer and retransmits if it expires before an acknowledgment for the segment is returned from the receiving end.

In Figure 3.9, the sending machine transmits segments 1, 2, and 3. The receiving node acknowledges it has received them by requesting segment 4. When it receives the acknowledgment, the sender then transmits segments 4, 5, and 6. If segment 5 doesn't make it to the destination, the receiving node acknowledges that event with a request for the segment to be resent. The sending machine will then resend the lost segment and wait for an acknowledgment, which it must receive in order to move on to the transmission of segment 7.

FIGURE 3.9: Transport layer reliable delivery

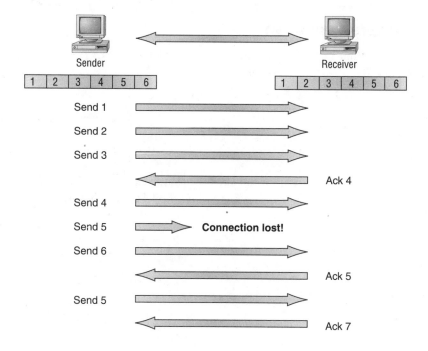

Exam Essentials

Understand that TCP uses windowing. TCP uses windowing as a flow control method.

Key Terms and Concepts

flow control Method implemented on networks to stop a receiving host's buffers from overflowing and dropping data.

windowing Flow control method implemented by TCP.

Sample Question

1. What type of flow control is implemented by TCP?

   A. Buffering

   B. Stop and Go

   C. Windowing

   D. IP

   Answer: C. All of the above, with the exception of IP, are flow control methods. The method used by TCP is windowing.

Chapter

4

Routing

CISCO EXAM OBJECTIVES COVERED IN THIS
CHAPTER:

▶ **IGRP** *(pages 116 – 134)*

▶ **ICMP** *(pages 134 – 139)*

This chapter will focus on routing, specifically IP routing. Interior gateway protocols are used to share information within an autonomous system. This chapter will focus on distance-vector interior protocols.

This is an important chapter to understand both for the exam and when working in a production environment.

Interior Gateway Routing Protocol (IGRP)

Interior gateway protocols (IGPs) are used to dynamically configure routers in an autonomous system (AS). Examples of IGPs are Routing Information Protocol (RIP) and Cisco's Interior Gateway Routing Protocol (IGRP). Exterior gateway protocols (EGPs) are used to communicate between IGPs; one example is Border Gateway Protocol (BGP).

The two IGPs discussed in this book are Routing Information Protocol (RIP) and Interior Gateway Routing Protocol (IGRP), which is a Cisco proprietary dynamic routing protocol. To pass the CCNA exam, you must know the protocols discussed in this objective.

Critical Information

Routing is taking a packet from one device and sending it through the network to another device on a different network. If your network has no routers, then you are not routing. Routers are used to direct and transmit traffic to all the networks in your internetwork. To be able to route packets, a router must have, at a minimum, knowledge of the following:

- Destination address
- Neighbor routers from which it can learn about remote networks
- Possible routes to all remote networks
- The best route to each remote network
- How to maintain and verify routing information

The router learns about remote networks from neighbor routers or from an administrator. The router then builds a routing table that describes how to find the remote networks. If the network is directly connected, then the router already knows how to get to the network. If the networks are not attached, the router must learn how to get to the remote network with either static routing, which means that the administrator must hand-type all network locations into the routing table, or dynamic routing. Dynamic routing is the process of routing protocols running on the router communicating with neighbor routers. The routers then update each other about all the networks they know about. If a change occurs in a network, the dynamic routing protocols automatically inform all routers about the change. If static routing is used, the administrator is responsible for updating all changes by hand into all routers.

Routers can only send packets to remote networks by looking at the routing table and finding out how to get to them. But our configured routers only have information containing directly connected networks in each routing table. What happens when a router receives a packet with a network that is not listed in the routing table? It discards it! It doesn't send a broadcast looking for the remote network—the router just discards the packet. Period.

There are a few different ways to configure the routing tables to include all the networks in our little internetwork so that packets will be forwarded. However, the best way for one network is not necessarily the best way for another. If you understand the different routing types, you will be able to decide what fits best in your business requirements.

The different types of routing we will cover in this objective include:

- Static routing
- Default routing
- Dynamic routing

Static Routing

Static routing is the process of an administrator adding routes in the routing table of each router by hand.

The command used to add a static route to a routing table is:

```
ip route [destination_network] [mask] [next_hop_
address or exitinterface] [administrative_distance]
[permanent]
```

The following list describes each command in the string:

ip route   Command used to create the static route.

destination_network   Network you are placing in the routing table.

mask   Subnet mask being used on the network.

next_hop_address   Address of the next hop router that will receive the packet and forward the packet to the remote network. This is a router interface that is on a directly connected network. You must be able to ping the router interface before you add the route.

exitinterface   Used in place of the next hop address if desired. Must be on a point-to-point link, such as a WAN. This command does not work on a LAN such as Ethernet.

administrative_distance   By default, static routes have an administrative distance of 1. You can change the default value by adding an administrative weight at the end of the command.

permanent   If the interface is shut down or the router cannot communicate to the next hop router, the route is automatically discarded from the routing table. Choosing the permanent option keeps the entry in the routing table no matter what happens.

Default Routing

Default routing, also known as the "gateway of last resort," is used to send packets with a remote destination network not in the routing table to a next hop router. You can only use default routing on stub networks, which means that they have only one exit port out of the network.

To configure a default route, you use wildcards in the network address and mask locations of a static route. Think of a default route as a static route that uses wildcards instead of network and mask information.

The command used to add a default route to a routing table is:

```
ip route 0.0.0.0 0.0.0.0 [next_hop_interface]
```

This command tells the router that any address it doesn't know about, because of a static route or a directly connected network, goes to the next hop router, which should be directly connected.

NOTE   The next hop address is the next_hop_interface connected to the next hop router. This interface must be in the same network as the network configured on the outgoing interface.

Administrative Distances

When configuring routing protocols, you need to be aware of administrative distances. These are used to rate the trustworthiness of routing information received on a router from a neighbor router. An administrative distance is an integer from 0 to 255, where 0 is the most trusted and 255 means no traffic will be passed via this route.

Table 4.1 shows the default administrative distances that a Cisco router will use to decide which route to use to a remote network. In the table, EIGRP (Enhanced Interior Gateway Routing Protocol) and OSPF (Open Shortest Path First) are additional protocols not covered by this objective but that you might encounter in advanced routing problems.

TABLE 4.1: Default Administrative Distances

Route Source	Default Distance
Connected interface	0
Static route	1
EIGRP	90
IGRP	100
OSPF	110
RIP	120
External EIGRP	170
Unknown	255 (this route will never be used)

If a network is directly connected, the router will always use the interface connected to the network and configured to be an interface on the network; the router will always believe its own configuration before that of a static route. If an administrator configures a static route on the router, it will believe that route over any other learned routes obtained from a routing protocol. This means that there can be multiple ways of obtaining a route to a destination network, but the administrative distance decides the route to use. You can change the administrative distance of static routes, but by default, they have a distance of 1.

Dynamic Routing

Dynamic routing is the process of using protocols to find and update routing tables on routers. This is easier than static or default routing, but you use it at the expense of router CPU processes and bandwidth usage on the network links. A routing protocol defines the set of rules used by a router when it communicates between neighbor routers. There are three classes of dynamic routing protocols:

Distance-Vector The distance-vector routing protocols use a distance to a remote network to find the best path. Each time a packet goes through a router, it's called a hop. The route with the least number of hops to the network is determined to be the best route. The vector is the determination of direction to the remote network. Examples of distance-vector routing protocol are RIP and IGRP.

Link-State Typically called shortest path first, the routers each create three separate tables. One of these tables keeps track of directly attached neighbors, one determines the topology of the entire internetwork, and one is used for the routing table. Link-state routers know more about the internetwork than any distance-vector routing protocol. An example of an IP routing protocol that is completely link-state is OSPF.

Hybrid Uses aspects of distance-vector and link-state; for example, EIGRP.

There is no set way of configuring routing protocols for use with every business. This is a task that is performed on a case-by-case basis. However, if you understand how the different routing protocols work, you can make good business decisions.

Distance-Vector Routing Protocols

The distance-vector routing algorithm passes complete routing tables to neighbor routers. The neighbor routers then combine the received routing table with their own routing tables to complete the internetwork map. This is called routing by rumor, as a router receiving an update from a neighbor router believes the information about remote networks without actually finding out for itself.

It is possible to have a network that has multiple links to the same remote network. If that is the case, the administrative distance is first checked. If the administrative distance is the same, a router will have to use other metrics to determine the best path to use to that remote network.

RIP uses only hop count to determine the best path to an internetwork. If RIP finds more than one link to the same remote network with the same hop count, it will automatically perform a round-robin load balance. RIP can perform load-balancing for up to six equal-cost links.

ROUTING LOOPS

Distance-vector routing protocols keep track of any changes to the internetwork by broadcasting periodic routing updates to all active interfaces. This broadcast includes the complete routing table. This works fine, although it takes up CPU processes and link bandwidth. However, if a network outage happens, problems can occur. The slow convergence of distance-vector routing protocols can cause inconsistent routing tables and routing loops. The following are used in distance-vector routing protocols to reduce loop problems:

Split Horizon Reduces incorrect routing information and routing overhead in a distance-vector network by enforcing the rule that information cannot be sent back in the direction from which that information was received.

Route Poisoning with Poison Reverse Sets a downed link to infinity. By poisoning a downed route, neighbor routers are not susceptible to incorrect updates about the downed route. When the neighbor routers received a route poison, they send an update, called a *poison reverse*, back to the router with the downed link. This is to make sure that all routes on the segment have received the poisoned route information.

Hold-Downs Used to prevent regular update messages from reinstating a route that has gone down. Hold-downs help prevent routes from changing too rapidly by allowing time for either the downed route to come back or the network to stabilize somewhat before changing to the next best route. These also tell routers to restrict, for a specific time period, any changes that might affect recently removed routes. This prevents inoperative routers from being prematurely restored to other routers' tables.

Triggered Updates   Hold-downs use triggered updates, which reset the hold-down timer, to let the neighbor routers know of a change in the network. Unlike update messages from neighbor routers, triggered updates create a new routing table that is sent immediately to neighbor routers because a change was detected in the internetwork. There are three instances when triggered updates will reset the hold-down timer:

- The hold-down timer expires.

- The router receives a processing task proportional to the number of links in the internetwork.

- Another update is received indicating the network topology has changed.

ROUTING INFORMATION PROTOCOL (RIP)

Routing Information Protocol (RIP) for IP is a true distance-vector routing protocol. It sends the complete routing table out to all active interfaces every 30 seconds. RIP only uses hop count to determine the best way to a remote network, but it has a maximum allowable hop count of 15, meaning that 16 is deemed unreachable. RIP works well in small networks, but it is inefficient on large networks with slow WAN links or on networks with a large number of routers installed.

RIP version 1 uses only classful routing, which means that all devices in the network must use the same subnet mask. This is because RIP version 1 does not send updates with subnet-mask information in tow. RIP version 2 provides what is called prefix routing and does send subnet-mask information with the route updates; this is called classless routing.

INTERIOR GATEWAY ROUTING PROTOCOL (IGRP)

Interior Gateway Routing Protocol (IGRP) is a Cisco proprietary distance-vector routing protocol. This means that all your routers must be Cisco routers to be able to use IGRP in your network. Cisco created this routing protocol to overcome the problems associated with RIP.

IGRP has a maximum hop count of 255 with a default of 100. This is helpful in larger networks and solves the problem of the 15-hop maximum in a RIP network. IGRP also uses a different metric than RIP. IGRP uses bandwidth and delay of the line by default as a metric for determining the best route to an internetwork; this is called a composite metric. Reliability, load, and maximum transmission unit (MTU) can also be used, although they are not used by default.

Verifying Your Configurations

It is very important to be able to verify your configurations once you have completed them, or at least, once you *think* you have completed them. The following list includes the commands you can use to verify the routed and routing protocols configured on your Cisco routers.

show ip route   Shows the routes the router knows about.

show protocols   Shows the routed protocol information configured on the router.

show ip protocol   Shows the routing protocol information configured on the router.

debug ip rip   Shows routing updates as they are sent and received on the router to the console session.

debug ip igrp events   Summarizes the IGRP routing information that is running on the network.

debug ip igrp transactions   Shows message requests from neighboring routers asking for an update and the broadcasts sent from your router toward those neighbors.

Necessary Procedures

This section will show you how to configure the routing table using:

- Static routing
- Default routing
- Dynamic routing

Configuring Static Routing

The router output below shows the configuration of static routes on a Cisco router. The command is:

```
ip route remote_network mask next_hop
```

Here are some examples:

```
2621A(Config)#ip route 172.16.20.0 255.255.255.0
    172.16.10.2
2621A(Config)#ip route 172.16.30.0 255.255.255.0
    172.16.10.2
2621A(Config)#ip route 172.16.40.0 255.255.255.0
    172.16.10.2
2621A(Config)#ip route 172.16.50.0 255.255.255.0
    172.16.10.2
```

After the router is configured, you can type **show running-config** and **show ip route** to see the static routes. Here is an example:

```
2621A#sh ip route
Codes: C - connected, S - static, I - IGRP, R - RIP,
↳M — [output cut]
Gateway of last resort is not set

       172.16.0.0/24 is subnetted, 5 subnets
S        172.16.50.0 [1/0] via 172.16.10.2
S        172.16.40.0 [1/0] via 172.16.10.2
S        172.16.30.0 [1/0] via 172.16.10.2
S        172.16.20.0 [1/0] via 172.16.10.2
C        172.16.10.0 is directly connected,
↳FastEthernet0/0
2621A#
```

The S is for static routes and C for directly connected routes.

Remember that if the routes don't show up in the routing table, it is because the router cannot communicate to the next hop address you configured. You can use the permanent parameter to keep the route in the routing table even if the next hop device cannot be contacted.

Configuring Default Routing

To configure a default route on a router, use the following command:

ip route 0.0.0.0 0.0.0.0 *next_hop*

Here is an example:

2501C(Config)#**ip route 0.0.0.0 0.0.0.0 172.16.40.1**

If you only configure the default route, you'll see only the directly connected networks, plus an S*, which indicates that this entry is the candidate for a default route:

2501C#**sh ip route**
Codes: C - connected, S - static, I - IGRP, R -
↳RIP, M –
[output cut]
 - IS-IS level-1, L2 - IS-IS level-2, * - candidate
↳efault U - per-user static route, o – ODR

Gateway of last resort is 172.16.40.1 to network
↳0.0.0.0
       172.16.0.0/24 is subnetted, 5 subnets
C   172.16.50.0 is directly connected, Ethernet0
C   172.16.40.0 is directly connected, Serial0
S*   0.0.0.0/0 [1/0] via 172.16.40.1
2501C#

Notice also in the routing table that the gateway of last resort is now set. However, there is one more command you must be aware of when using default routes: the ip classless command.

All Cisco routers are classful routers, which means they expect a default subnet mask on each interface of the router. When a router receives a packet for a destination subnet not in the routing table, it will drop the packet by default. If you are using default routing, you must use the ip classless command because no remote subnets will be in the routing table. The command is shown below:

```
2501C(Config)#ip classless
```

Notice that it is a global configuration mode command. Since version 11.2 of the IOS, the ip classless command has been enabled by default. In a classful network, a router believes that it knows all subnets based on the subnet assigned to the interface's IP address. If a packet is addressed to a host within the classed network space, but the routing table does not have a route to it, the packet will be discarded.

Configuring RIP Routing

To configure RIP routing, just turn on the protocol with the router rip command and tell the RIP routing protocol which networks to advertise. Like this:

```
2621A(config)#router rip
2621A(config-router)#network 172.16.0.0
2621A(config-router)#^Z
2621A#
```

That's it. Two commands, and you're done—sure makes your job a lot easier then when using static routes, doesn't it? However, keep in mind the extra router CPU process and bandwidth that you're consuming.

Verifying the RIP Routing Tables

Each routing table should now have the routers' directly connected routes as well as RIP-injected routes received from neighbor routers.

The router output below shows the contents of a router's routing table:

```
2621A#sh ip route
Codes: C - connected, S - static, I - IGRP, R - RIP,
 M - [output cut]
```

```
Gateway of last resort is not set

     172.16.0.0/24 is subnetted, 5 subnets
R  172.16.50.0 [120/3] via 172.16.10.2, FastEthernet0/0
R  172.16.40.0 [120/2] via 172.16.10.2, FastEthernet0/0
R  172.16.30.0 [120/2] via 172.16.10.2, FastEthernet0/0
R  172.16.20.0 [120/1] via 172.16.10.2, FastEthernet0/0
C  172.16.10.0 is directly connected, FastEthernet0/0
2621A#
```

In the above output, the R means that the networks were added dynamically using the RIP routing protocol. The [120/3] is the administrative distance of the route (120) along with the number of hops to that remote network (3).

Configuring IGRP Routing

The command used to configure IGRP is the same as the one used to configure RIP routing, with one important difference: You use an autonomous system (AS) number. All routers within an autonomous system must use the same AS number, or they will not communicate with routing information. Here is an example of how to turn on IGRP routing, using an AS number of 10:

```
RouterA#config t
RouterA(config)#router igrp 10
RouterA(config-router)#network 172.16.0.0
```

The configuration in the above router commands is as simple as in RIP routing, except that IGRP uses an AS number. This number is used to advertise only to routers that you want to share routing information with.

IGRP can load-balance to six unequal links to a remote network. RIP networks must have the same hop count to be able to load-balance, whereas IGRP uses bandwidth to determine how to load-balance. To load-balance over unequal-cost links, the variance command controls the load-balancing between the best metric and the worst acceptable metric.

Verifying the IGRP Routing Tables

Once the routers are configured, you need to verify the configuration with the show ip route command.

```
2621A#sh ip route
Codes: C - connected, S - static, I - IGRP, R - RIP, M -
[output cut]
        T - traffic engineered route
Gateway of last resort is not set

        172.16.0.0/24 is subnetted, 5 subnets
I       172.16.50.0 [100/160360] via 172.16.10.2,
↳FastEthernet0/0
I       172.16.40.0 [100/160260] via 172.16.10.2,
↳FastEthernet0/0
I       172.16.30.0 [100/158360] via 172.16.10.2,
↳FastEthernet0/0
I       172.16.20.0 [100/158260] via 172.16.10.2,
↳FastEthernet0/0
C       172.16.10.0 is directly connected,
↳FastEthernet0/0
```

The I means IGRP-injected routes. The [100/160360] is the administrative distance of IGRP and the composite metric. The lower the composite metric, the better the route.

Exam Essentials

Understand how RIP works in an internetwork.   RIP uses hop counts to determine the best route to a network. It has an upper hop-count limit of 15.

Go through the commands to add RIP to your router.   To add the RIP routing protocol to your router, go into global configuration mode and type the command **router rip**. You then need to add the number(s) of the network(s) for which your router will advertise.

Know how to view the routing table.   To view routing tables, you can use the commands show ip route or sh ip route rip.

Understand what the routing table shows. You must know how to read a routing table. Make sure you can find the hop count, destination network, and next hop router address.

Remember what an AS is. An autonomous system (AS) is a group of routers that share the same routing information.

Understand the difference between RIP and IGRP. RIP only uses hop counts in determining the best route to a destination network. IGRP can look at bandwidth, load, reliability, MTU, and hop count to find the best route to a destination network.

Know what causes routing loops and how to correct them. You must understand the reasons a routing loop can occur and know all the ways of correcting them.

Understand the differences between the various routing loop solutions. Be able to distinguish between each of these methods: split horizon, poison reverse, and hold-downs, which use triggered updates.

Remember the reasons that hold-downs send triggered updates. There are three instances in which triggered updates will reset the hold-down timer:

- The hold-down timer expires.

- The router receives a processing task proportional to the number of links in the internetwork.

- The hold-down timer receives another update indicating that the network status has changed.

Remember what the arguments are in a static route. To create a static route, use the ip route command followed by the destination network, subnet mask, next hop address, and the metric.

Key Terms and Concepts

bandwidth The transmission capacity of a communications channel, measured in bits per second (bps).

convergence   The time it takes for all routers to update their routing tables to have the same information.

distance-vector   A routing algorithm that typically uses hop counts to find the best path to a network. Some of the newer distance-vector algorithms use other variables such as bandwidth, delay, and line speed. RIP only uses hop count.

hold-downs   A method of stopping routing loops by not sending out updates about networks that have gone down.

Interior Gateway Routing Protocol (IGRP)   A proprietary Cisco distance-vector routing algorithm.

metric   The distance or weight of a link. This value can be used to find the best path to a remote network.

maximum transmission unit (MTU)   The largest packet size that can be sent out of the interface onto the line. If a packet is larger than the MTU of the link, the router will fragment the packet.

route poisoning   Sets a downed link to the maximum number of valid hops or infinity. This is a method of stopping routing loops by not sending an update over an invalid number of hops (16 in RIP) whenever a link outage occurs.

routed protocols   Protocols like IP or IPX, which are used to send packets through an internetwork and deliver user data.

Routing Information Protocol (RIP)   A routing algorithm that uses the distance-vector method of finding the best path to a network (hop count).

routing protocols   Protocols like RIP and IGRP, which are used to send packets between routers to tell each other about networks.

split horizon   A method of stopping routing loops by not sending updates out the same interface through which they were received.

Sample Questions

1. What is the routing metric used by RIP?

A. Distance link

B. MTU

C. Hop count

D. Bandwidth

Answer: C. RIP only uses hop count when determining the best route to a destination network.

2. What does a metric of 16 hops represent in an RIP network?

A. The packet has passed through 16 routers.

B. It is an RIP broadcast.

C. The host is unreachable.

D. The network is unreachable.

Answer: D. Remember, routers know about networks, not hosts! Sixteen hops in an RIP network is considered unreachable.

3. Which commands can you use to see whether your router is receiving RIP updates from other routers? (Choose two.)

A. show ip rip

B. sh ip route

C. debug rip

D. debug ip rip

Answer: B, D. The commands show ip route and debug ip rip will show whether you are receiving updates from neighbor routers.

4. Which of the following parameters does IGRP use in deciding the best route through an internetwork? (Choose all that apply.)

A. Bandwidth

B. Delay

C. Reliability

D. TTL

E. Hop count

F. Load

G. MTU

Answer: A, B, C, E, F, G. When you use the command `sh interface s0`, the third line of output shows the parameters that IGRP uses to decide the best route to a destination network. These are bandwidth, MTU, reliability, hop count, load, and delay.

5. What command can you use to verify the broadcast frequency of IGRP?

A. `sh ip route`

B. `sh ip protocol`

C. `sh ip broadcast`

D. `debug ip igrp`

Answer: B. The only command that will show you the update frequency is `sh ip protocol`.

6. Which of the following statements is true regarding split horizon?

A. A router sets the metric for a downed link to infinity.

B. When routing information is received by an interface, it can't be advertised out that same interface.

C. This prevents regular update messages from reinstating a router that has gone down by not advertising that network.

D. None of the above is true.

Answer: B. When an update is received by a router, it will never send that same information out the interface through which it was received.

7. Which statement describes route poisoning reverse?

A. A router sets the metric for a downed link to infinity and readvertises the link with the maximum hop count.

B. When routing information is received by an interface, it can't be advertised out that same interface.

C. This prevents regular update messages from reinstating a router that has gone down by not advertising that network.

D. None of the above is true.

Answer: A. When a link goes down, a router using RIP will immediately update the routing table with a metric of 16 to indicate that the route is no longer available. Other routers will readvertise that the link is down to make sure all routers know about the downed link.

8. Which of these methods can be used to reset the hold-down timer?

A. Triggered updates

B. Split horizon

C. Reverse poison

D. Hold-downs

Answer: A. Hold-downs use triggered updates to reset the hold-down timer.

Internet Control Message Protocol (ICMP)

Internet Control Message Protocol (ICMP) is one of the protocols used at the Internet layer of the DoD model. ICMP is important to Cisco because it is used for many different things, mainly to send updates to routers about problems with network routes or packets that are undeliverable in the internetwork.

When studying for the CCNA exam, be sure to remember what the protocol ICMP does when IP is configured with Cisco routers.

Critical Information

ICMP works at the Network layer of the OSI Reference Model and is used by IP for many different services. ICMP is a management protocol and messaging service provider for IP. Its messages are carried as IP datagrams. RFC 1256, *ICMP Router Discovery Messages,* is an annex to ICMP, which affords hosts extended capability in discovering routes to gateways.

Periodically, router advertisements are announced over the network, reporting IP addresses for its network interfaces. Hosts listen for these network infomercials to acquire route information. A router solicitation is a request for immediate advertisements and may be sent by a host when it starts up. The following are some common events and messages that ICMP relates to:

Destination Unreachable If a router can't send an IP datagram any further, it uses ICMP to send a message back to the sender advising it of the situation. For example, if a router receives a packet destined for a network that the router doesn't know about, it will send an ICMP "destination unreachable" message back to the sending station.

Buffer Full If a router's memory buffer for receiving incoming datagrams is full, it will use ICMP to send out a "buffer full" message.

Hop Limits Each IP datagram is allotted a certain number of routers that it may go through, called hops. If it reaches its limit of hops before arriving at its destination, the last router to receive that datagram deletes it. The executioner router then uses ICMP to send an obituary message, informing the sending machine of the demise of its datagram.

ping   Packet Internet Groper uses ICMP echo messages to check the physical connectivity of machines on an internetwork.

The following data is from a network analyzer catching an ICMP echo request:

```
Flags:          0x00
  Status:         0x00
  Packet Length:78
  Timestamp:     14:04:25.967000 05/06/1998
Ethernet Header
  Destination:  00:a0:24:6e:0f:a8
  Source:       00:80:c7:a8:f0:3d
  Ether-Type:08-00   IP
IP Header - Internet Protocol Datagram
  Version:              4
  Header Length:        5
  Precedence:           0
  Type of Service:      %000
  Unused:               %00
  Total Length:         60
  Identifier:           56325
  Fragmentation Flags:  %000
  Fragment Offset:      0
  Time To Live:         32
  IP Type:              0x01   ICMP
  Header Checksum:      0x2df0
  Source IP Address:    100.100.100.2
  Dest. IP Address:     100.100.100.1
  No Internet Datagram Options
ICMP - Internet Control Messages Protocol
  ICMP Type:            8  Echo Request
  Code:                 0
  Checksum:             0x395c
```

```
Identifier:           0x0300
Sequence Number:      4352
ICMP Data Area:
abcdefghijklmnop    61 62 63 64 65 66 67 68 69 6a
↳6b 6c 6d
qrstuvwabcdefghi    71 72 73 74 75 76 77 61 62 63
↳64 65 66
```
Frame Check Sequence: 0x00000000

Notice that even though ICMP works at the Network layer, it still uses IP to do the ping request. The Type field in the IP header is 0x01h, which specifies the ICMP protocol.

If you remember reading about the Data Link layer in Chapter 1 and the different frame types, you should be able to look at the above trace and know what type of Ethernet frame this is. The only fields are Destination hardware address, Source hardware address, and Ethernet Type. The only frame that uses a Ethernet Type field is an Ethernet_II frame. (SNAP uses an Ethernet Type field but only within an 802.2 LLC field, which is not present in the frame.)

Exam Essentials

The CCNA test covers all the protocols at the Network (Internet) layer.

Remember what ICMP can do. ICMP sends "destination unreachable" and "buffer full" messages. ICMP can find the number of hops to a destination host.

Remember which programs use ICMP. Packet Internet Groper (ping) uses ICMP echo messages to check the physical connectivity of machines on an internetwork. Trace Route (trace) uses ICMP and TTL (time to live) time-outs to find a packet's destination through an internetwork.

Key Terms and Concepts

Internet Control Message Protocol (ICMP)   Described at the Internet layer of the DoD model, ICMP is used for testing, verification, and notification services.

Sample Questions

1. Which protocol is used to send "destination unreachable" messages to other routers?

   A. IP

   B. RARP

   C. BootP

   D. ICMP

   Answer: D. ICMP sends "destination unreachable" messages to neighboring routers if a problem occurs and packets can't be sent to a remote destination.

2. Which of these use ICMP to test network connectivity? (Choose all that apply.)

   A. Telnet

   B. trace

   C. ping

   D. ARP

   Answer: B, C. Both ping and trace use ICMP messages.

3. Which of these does ICMP help accomplish? (Choose all that apply.)

   A. "Destination unreachable" messages

   B. "Buffer full" messages

C. Hop limits

D. ping

E. ARP

F. trace

Answer: A, B, C, D, F. ICMP is an important protocol at the Network (Internet) layer. It is used to send "destination unreachable" messages, to find the distance to a network (trace), and to send "buffer full" messages, echo requests, and replies.

Chapter

5

WAN Protocols

his chapter will cover the wide area network (WAN) support provided by the Cisco IOS. To pass the CCNA exam, you must know the typical WAN support provided with Cisco router.

ISDN and frame relay will be covered, and you must understand everything that is taught in this chapter. Both the critical information needed to pass the exams, and the necessary procedures that provide the configuration of ISDN and frame relay on Cisco router, will be taught.

High-Level Data-Link Control (HDLC) and asynchronous transfer mode (ATM) will also be discussed.

Integrated Services Digital Network (ISDN)

Integrated Services Digital Network (ISDN) is a very popular type of connectivity, if you can get it. ISDN provides enough bandwidth to allow voice and data transmission at fast speeds, making it very useful for telecommuters. The problem with ISDN is that it is not available everywhere.

Another nice thing about this technology is that it allows digital services over standard telephone cable. However, the reason that it is not available everywhere is that some types of telephone cable cannot support the encoding necessary to transmit large amounts of data.

To pass this portion of the CCNA exam, make sure you understand the purpose of ISDN and its advantages, ISDN protocols, and the reference points used in ISDN.

Critical Information

ISDN is a digital service designed to run over existing telephone networks. Because it can support both data and voice transmissions, ISDN is perfect for the users on your network who telecommute. But ISDN applications require high bandwidth. Typical uses for ISDN include high-speed image applications (such as Group IV facsimile), high-speed file transfer, videoconferencing, and multiple links into the homes of telecommuters.

ISDN is actually a set of communication protocols and standards devised by telephone companies that define the hardware and call-setup schemes for end-to-end digital connectivity. With it they can provide digital services that simultaneously convey data, text, voice, music, graphics, and video to end users, all while using the telephone systems that are already in place. ISDN is referenced by a suite of standards, issued by the International Telecommunication Union Telecommunication Standardization Sector (ITU-T), that encompass the OSI model's Physical, Data Link, and Network layers.

ISDN supports virtually every upper-layer network protocol (IP, IPX, AppleTalk, and so on), and you can choose Point-to-Point Protocol (PPP), High-Level Data-Link Control (HDLC), or Link Access Procedure on the D Channel (LAPD) as your encapsulation protocol.

People in the networking industry tend to use a lot of acronyms and other lingo to describe basic things. The parts of ISDN are no exception. In this section we define some of these terms and the features they describe.

The components we describe are really the nuts and bolts of ISDN, which are very important for you to understand both when you are setting up an ISDN connection and studying for the CCNA exam.

ISDN Protocols

ISDN protocols are defined by the ITU-T. Here are three diverse categories of ISDN protocols whose function is specified by their first letter:

- *E* protocols apply to ISDN on an existing telephone network.

- *I* protocols deal with concepts, terminology, and services.

- *Q* protocols pertain to switching and signaling.

Function Groups

Function groups connecting to the ISDN network are known as terminals. These come in two types:

- TE1 (terminal equipment type 1) devices are Basic Rate Interface (BRI) machines that understand ISDN standards. (BRI will be covered in detail in the next section of this chapter.)

- TE2 (terminal equipment type 2) devices predate ISDN standards. To use a TE2 device, you have to use a terminal adapter (TA) to generate BRI signals for a Cisco router interface.

ISDN Reference Points

ISDN uses four different reference points to define logical interfaces between functional groupings such as TAs and NT (network termination) devices. They are as follows:

- *R* defines the reference point between non-ISDN equipment and a TA.

- *S* defines the reference point between user terminals and an NT2 device.

- *T* defines the reference point between NT1 and NT2 devices.

- *U* defines the reference point between NT1 devices and line-termination equipment in a carrier network. (This type of reference point is only used in North America, where the NT1 function isn't provided by the carrier network.)

NOTE The S and T reference points are generally one in the same.

The NT1 and NT2

The NT1 is a device that resides between the ISDN switch and the Cisco ISDN interface or terminal adapter, both of which are referred to as the terminal endpoints. The NT1 is used to convert two-wire copper loop from the telephone company. This point in the network is called the U-loop. From the U-loop, it converts the two-wire into a four-wire ISDN interface called the S/T bus. Many ISDN TE devices have an NT1 built into the BRI interface.

The NT2 is a device used in older ISDN networks connecting to terminals or other older equipment.

Q.921 and Q.931

In ISDN, the Data Link layer goes by the name of Q.921, which is the ITU standard for ISDN operations at Layer 2 of the OSI Reference Model. One surprising aspect of ISDN is that it has been around since the 1960s. Understanding this and frame relay will help you to understand how LAPD (Link Access Procedure Balanced) uses sequence numbers and delivers ISDN Layer 3 messages on the D channel, without error, from the TE BRI interface to the ISDN switch. Checking and retransmissions are handled at the Data Link layer. LAPD messages are only passed between the TE and ISDN switch, not end-to-end.

Q.931 architecture operating at Layer 3 offers flexibility that allows it to be customized for use in environments such as frame relay SVCs, ATM SVCs, Voice over IP, and digital cellular networks. Q.931 SETUP messages are created by the TE and are then carried in Q.921 LAPD frames to the ISDN switch. The ISDN switch can then route calls over the PSTN (public switched telephone network) to its final destinations based on information in the Q.931 messages.

ISDN Channels

There are two types of channels used in BRI ISDN: B and D. Here's what each one does:

- *B*, or bearer, channels have a 64 Kbps capacity. They can be used for voice or data. Two B channels in a BRI can be combined for a total of 128 Kbps.

- *D*, or data, channels are used for call signaling or clocking. This type of channel has a 16 Kbps capacity.

Cisco's Implementation of ISDN BRI

Basic Rate Interface (BRI) service is very popular in the U.S. because it provides 128 Kbps transmission at a good price. BRI is not the best choice for large, steady data streams, but it works well for bursts of data.

ISDN BRI, also known as 2B+1D, provides two B channels and one D channel. The BRI B-channel service operates at 64 Kbps and carries data, while the BRI D-channel service operates at 16 Kbps and usually carries control and signaling information. The D-channel signaling protocol spans the OSI Reference Model's Physical, Data Link, and Network layers. BRI also provides framing control for a total bit rate of up to 192 Kbps.

When configuring ISDN BRI, you will need to obtain Service Profile Identifiers (SPIDs); you should have one SPID for each B channel or two for BRI. SPIDs can be thought of as the telephone number of each B channel. The ISDN device gives the SPID to the ISDN switch, which then allows the device to access the network for BRI or PRI (Primary Rate Interface) service. If an ISDN device doesn't have an SPID, many ISDN switches won't allow it to place a call on the network.

Necessary Procedures

In order to use ISDN with a Cisco router, you need to purchase either a network termination type 1 (NT1) device or an ISDN modem. If your router has a BRI interface, you're all set. Otherwise, you can use one of your router's serial interfaces—if you can get a hold of a TA (terminal adapter). A router with a BRI interface is called a TE1 (terminal equipment type 1) device; one that requires a TA is called a TE2 device.

ISDN supports virtually every upper-layer network protocol (IP, IPX, AppleTalk, etc.), and you can choose PPP, HDLC, or LAPD as your encapsulation protocol.

NOTE When configuring ISDN, you'll need to know the type of switch that your service provider is using, because each manufacturer has a proprietary protocol for signaling. To see which switches your router will support, use the isdn switch-type ? command in global configuration mode.

For each ISDN BRI interface, you need to specify the SPIDs by using the isdn spid1 and isdn spid2 interface subcommands. Here's an example:

```
RouterA#config t
Enter configuration commands, one per line. End with
⮑CNTL/Z.
RouterA(config)#isdn switch-type basic-dms100
RouterA(config)#int bri0
RouterA(config-if)#encap ppp
RouterA(config-if)#isdn spid1 775456721
RouterA(config-if)#isdn spid2 775456722
```

This configuration assumes that the interfaces on both ends of the link have already been configured with an IP address in the same network. The encapsulation is PPP; ISDN specifies this method, used to establish the digital phone call.

Exam Essentials

Remember the different services that ISDN can run. ISDN can run both voice and data services over existing telephone lines.

Understand the different protocols used in ISDN. The Q protocols specify switching and signaling. E protocols apply to ISDN on an existing telephone network. I protocols deal with concepts, terminology, and services.

Know the difference between a B channel and a D channel. A BRI uses two B channels and one D channel. Each B channel is 64 Kbps; a D channel is 16 Kbps.

Key Terms and Concepts

Basic Rate Interface (BRI)   An ISDN interface composed of two B (bearer) channels and one D (data) channel for circuit-switched communication of voice, video, and data.

Integrated Services Digital Network (ISDN)   A digital communication protocol that permits telephone networks to carry data and voice transmissions at higher speeds than typical analog transmission rates.

International Telecommunication Union Telecommunication Standardization Sector (ITU-T)   Group that creates international standards for internetworks and telecommunications.

Open Standards Interconnect (OSI) Reference Model   Created by the International Organization for Standardization (ISO) to create a layered approach to interoperability between disparate systems.

reference point   Used to define logical interfaces in ISDN.

Sample Questions

1. Which of the following can be transmitted with ISDN?

A. Voice

B. Data

C. Music

D. Video

E. All of the above

Answer: E. ISDN can support all of these types of data and more.

2. Which of the following is a good reason to use ISDN?

A. You need constant data streams.

B. You need to have constant connections to multiple locations.

C. Your network uses off-brand routers.

D. Your network users need high-speed voice and data capability.

Answer: D. Cisco considers ISDN a high-speed connection. Measured against a 28.8K or 56K dial-up connection, this is true.

3. What does an R point define?

A. The reference point between non-ISDN equipment and a TA

B. The reference point between ISDN equipment and a BRI

C. The reference point between ISDN equipment and a PRI

D. The reference point between non-ISDN equipment and an NA1

Answer: A. R points are used when connecting ISDN to a router interface other than a BRI or PRI.

4. When protocols begin with the letter Q, what does that specify?

A. Switching and signaling

B. Existing telephone service

C. Concepts, terminology, and services

D. Quality ISDN service

Answer: A. To read about switching and signaling in ISDN, look for the specifications and protocols that begin with Q.

5. What command can you use to set the ISDN switch type on a BRI interface?

A. switch

B. isdn-switch

C. isdn switch-type

D. switch-type

Answer: C. The command isdn switch-type is used to set the switch type on a BRI interface.

Frame Relay

In this section, we will discuss the terminology used for the various features within a frame relay network. You will learn how two internetwork devices communicate end-to-end through a frame relay cloud by using a DLCI number, DTE, DCE, demarcation (demarc), local loop, and PSE.

It is important to understand the difference between these devices and to know the terms used for them, both when you are working in a production environment and when you are studying for your CCNA exam. In a real network, it will also be helpful if you can visualize how the frame traverses the internetwork; you'll have a better chance of troubleshooting problems.

Critical Information

To understand the terminology used in frame relay networks, first you need to know how the technology works. Figure 5.1 is labeled with the various terms used to describe different parts of a frame relay network.

FIGURE 5.1: Frame relay technology and terms

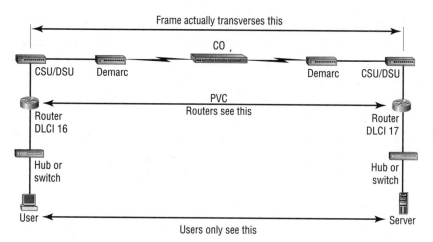

The basic idea behind frame relay is to allow users to communicate between two data terminal equipment (DTE) devices through data circuit-terminating equipment (DCE). The users should not see a difference between connecting to and gathering resources from a local server and a server at a remote site connected with frame relay. Chances are that this connection will be slower than a 100 Mbps Ethernet LAN, but the difference in the connection should be transparent to the user.

Figure 5.1 illustrates everything that must happen in order for two DTE devices to communicate. Here is how the process works:

1. The user's network device sends a frame out on the local network. The hardware address of the router (default gateway) will be in the header of the frame.

2. The router picks up the frame, extracts the packet, and discards the frame. It then looks at the destination IP address within the packet and checks to see if it knows how to get to the destination network by looking in the routing table.

3. The router then forwards the data out the interface that it thinks can find the remote network. (If the router can't find the network in its routing table, it discards the packet.) Since this will be a serial interface encapsulated with frame relay, the router puts the packet onto the frame relay network encapsulated within a frame relay frame. It will add the DLCI (Data Link Connection Identifier) number associated with the serial interface. DLCIs identify the type of virtual circuit—permanent virtual circuit (PVC) or switched virtual circuit (SVC)—to the routers and switches participating in the frame relay network.

4. The channel service unit/data service unit (CSU/DSU) receives the digital signal and encodes it into the type of digital signaling that the switch at the packet switching exchange (PSE) can understand. The PSE receives the digital signal and extracts the ones and zeros from the line. The CSU/DSU is connected to a demarcation point (or "demarc") installed by the service provider, and its location is the service provider's first point of responsibility (the last point on the receiving end). The demarc is typically just an RJ-45 jack installed close to the router and CSU/DSU.

5. The demarc is typically a twisted-pair cable that connects to the local loop. The local loop connects to the closest central office (CO), sometimes called a point of presence (POP). The local loop can connect using various physical media, but twisted-pair or fiber is very common.

6. The CO receives the frame and sends it through the frame relay "cloud" to its destination. This cloud can be dozens of switching offices—or more! The CO looks for DLCI number, which is mapped locally to an IP address in IP networks. It typically can find the DLCI number of the remote device or router by looking up an IP-to-DLCI mapping. Frame relay mappings are usually created statically by the service provider, but they can be created dynamically.

7. Once the frame reaches the switching office closest to the destination office, it is sent through the local loop. The frame gets to the demarc and then to the CSU/DSU. Finally, the router extracts the packet, or datagram, from the frame and puts it in a new LAN frame to be delivered to the destination host. Whew!

The user and the server do not need to know, nor should they know, everything that happens as the frame makes its way across the frame relay network. The remote server should be as easy to use as a locally connected resource.

Necessary Procedures

To prepare you for this portion of the CCNA exam, we will demonstrate how to configure a Cisco router to be used in a frame relay network. We will explain the steps for configuring a router to use the frame relay encapsulation, assigning a DLCI number, and choosing a Local Management Interface (LMI) type. You will also learn how to create a subinterface and why you should use one. We will then finish the configuration by creating a frame relay mapping.

It's important to learn the commands and procedures for configuring a router for use on a frame relay network. Frame relay is used in many internetworks, and Cisco requires you to understand how to configure frame relay if you are going to be a CCNA.

When configuring frame relay on Cisco routers, the first thing you do is specify an encapsulation on serial interfaces. There are only two encapsulation types: Cisco and IETF (Internet Engineering Task Force). Use these commands:

```
RouterA(config)#int s0
RouterA(config-if)#encapsulation frame-relay ?
 ietf Use RFC1490 encapsulation
 <cr>
```

Cisco is the default encapsulation unless you type **ietf**. Use Cisco encapsulation when you are connecting two Cisco devices. Use IETF encapsulation when you are connecting a Cisco device to a non-Cisco device using frame relay.

Data Link Connection Identifiers

As discussed in previous sections, frame relay virtual circuits are identified by Data Link Connection Identifiers (DLCIs). Because many virtual circuits can be terminated on a multipoint frame relay interface, many DLCIs are affiliated with one interface. For the IP devices at each end of a virtual circuit to communicate, their IP addresses are mapped to DLCIs. This is so that a multipoint device can point out the appropriate destination virtual circuit on the frame relay network to each packet sent over the single physical interface.

Each DLCI can have a local meaning. In other words, two DTE devices connected via a virtual circuit use different DLCI values when referring to the same connection.

Here is an example that shows how to configure a DLCI number to an interface:

```
RouterA(config-if)#frame-relay interface-dlci ?
<16-1007> Define a DLCI as part of the current
  subinterface
RouterA(config-if)#frame-relay interface-dlci 16
```

Local Management Interface (LMI)

The Local Management Interface (LMI) was developed in 1990 by Cisco Systems, StrataCom, Northern Telecom, and Digital Equipment Corporation. The protocol produced by this group became known as the "Gang-of-Four LMI," or "Cisco LMI." This "gang" took the basic frame relay protocol and added extensions to the protocol features that allowed internetworking devices to communicate easily with a frame relay network. LMI is only used between the router and the service provider's switch.

LMI messages provide information about the current DLCI values, the global or local significance of the DLCI values, and the status of virtual circuits. You will need to check with your frame relay provider to find out which LMI type to use. The default type is Cisco, but you may need to change to ANSI or Q.933a. You can display the three

LMI types on your screen using the command shown here:

```
RouterA(config-if)#frame-relay lmi-type ?
 cisco
 ansi
 q933a
```

All standard LMI signaling formats are supported by the following:

ANSI   Annex D, defined by ANSI standard T1.617.

ITU-T (Q.933a)   Annex A, defined by ITU-T Recommendation Q.933a.

Cisco   LMI, defined by the "Gang of Four" (default).

NOTE   With Cisco IOS version 11.2 and above, the LMI type is auto-detected.

Subinterfaces

You can have multiple virtual circuits on a single serial interface and treat each virtual circuit as a separate interface, called a subinterface. Think of a subinterface as a hardware interface defined by the IOS software.

The advantage to using subinterfaces is that you can assign different Network-layer characteristics to each subinterface and virtual circuit, such as IP routing on one virtual circuit and IPX on another. Define subinterfaces with the command interface s0.*subinterfacenumber*, as shown in this example:

```
RouterA(config)#int s0.?
 <0-4294967295> Serial interface number
RouterA(config)#int s0.16 ?
 multipoint     Treat as a multipoint link
 point-to-point Treat as a point-to-point link
```

You can define a limitless number of subinterfaces on a given physical interface, keeping router memory in mind. In the above example, we chose to use subinterface 16 because that is the DLCI number of that interface. You can choose any number between 0 and 4294967295.

The two types of subinterfaces are point-to-point and multipoint. Point-to-point subinterfaces are used when a single virtual circuit connects one router to another. Multipoint subinterfaces are used when the router is at the center of a star of virtual circuits.

Mapping Frame Relay

As we explained earlier, in order for IP devices at the ends of virtual circuits to communicate, their addresses must be mapped to the DLCIs. There are two ways to make this mapping happen:

- Use the frame relay map command.
- Use the inverse-arp function.

For each packet sent out of a physical interface, mappings allow a multipoint device to identify a virtual circuit on the frame relay network.

This is an example program that uses the frame relay map command:

```
RouterA(config)#int s0.16 point-to-point
RouterA(config-if)#encap frame-relay ietf
RouterA(config-if)#no inverse-arp
RouterA(config-if)#ip address 172.16.30.1
255.255.255.0
RouterA(config-if)#frame-relay map ip 172.16.30.17 20
↪cisco broadcast
RouterA(config-if)#frame-relay map ip 172.16.30.18 30
↪broadcast
RouterA(config-if)#frame-relay map ip 172.16.30.19 40
```

Here's what we did: First we chose our subinterface and set the encapsulation to IETF. We then turned off inverse-arp (IARP) and mapped three virtual circuits and their corresponding DLCI numbers. (IARP would map our DLCIs to IP addresses dynamically, as demonstrated below.) Notice that we specified Cisco encapsulation on the first virtual circuit. The other two virtual circuits will use the encapsulation type specified in the interface command (IETF). The frame relay map command is the only way to mix both Cisco and IETF encapsulation types. The broadcast keyword at the end of the map command tells the router to forward broadcasts for this interface to this specific virtual circuit.

Instead of putting in map commands for each virtual circuit, you can use the inverse-arp (IARP) function to perform dynamic mapping of the IP address to the DLCI number. In that case, your configuration program would look like this:

```
RouterA(config)#int s0.16 multipoint
RouterA(config-if)#encap frame-relay ietf
RouterA(config-if)#ip address 172.16.30.1 255.255.255.0
```

Yes, this is a whole lot easier, but it's not as stable as using the map command. Why? Sometimes when you use the inverse-arp function, configuration errors occur, because virtual circuits can be insidiously and dynamically mapped to unknown devices.

Frame relay mapping isn't something an administrator would typically do. This process is usually performed at the switching office. Check with your provider before doing any frame relay configurations.

Monitoring Frame Relay Operation in the Router

When you are working in a production environment that uses frame relay and while you are studying for the CCNA exam, this topic is an important one. You must have a fundamental understanding not only of how to configure frame relay but also of the commands to monitor and troubleshoot frame relay.

Cisco frame relay support is stable and popular. If you want to work in a production environment, the ability to configure and maintain frame relay networks is sometimes a prerequisite to landing such a job. Knowing how to monitor and troubleshoot this protocol is a big part of that skill.

There are several ways to check the status of your interfaces and PVCs once you have frame relay encapsulation set up and running. Use the show frame-relay ? command at the router prompt to display all the commands you can use to view frame relay specifications:

```
Router#sh frame-relay ?
  ip       show frame relay IP statistics
  lapf     show frame relay lapf status/statistics
  lmi      show frame relay lmi statistics
  map      Frame-Relay map table
  pvc      show frame relay pvc statistics
  route    show frame relay route
  svc      show frame relay SVC stuff
  traffic  Frame-Relay protocol statistics
```

For monitoring purposes, the commands you'll be using are show frame-relay pvc, show frame-relay lmi, show frame-relay traffic, and show interface. Here's how to use each command:

show frame pvc   Gives the statistics of your PVCs on all configured frame relay interfaces.

show frame lmi   Displays the LMI statistics and the LMI type used on your frame relay network.

show frame-relay traffic   Shows you the global frame relay statistics since the last time the router was booted.

show interface s0   Displays your LMI information and DLCI type (local or switched) but not the DLCI number.

Exam Essentials

Understand where each of the terms is used in a frame relay network.   Remember that a DTE is typically the router; the DCE is typically the CSU/DSU and switch located at the provider.

Understand how to configure frame relay on a Cisco router. It is crucial that you understand the difference between encapsulation, DLCI, LMI, and mappings.

Know how many encapsulation and LMI types Cisco supports. Cisco supports two encapsulation methods (Cisco and IETF) and three LMI types (Cisco, ANSI, and Q.933a).

Remember which commands display your DLCI number and LMI type. The commands `show frame pvc` and `show running-config` display your DCLI number. The `show interface` and `show frame-relay lmi` commands give you the router's LMI and bandwidth information.

Key Terms and Concepts

central office (CO)   Point at which the local loop gains access to the service provider's high-speed trunk lines. This is often referred to as a POP (point of presence).

customer premise equipment (CPE)   All wiring and equipment on the customer's side of the demarc.

data circuit-terminating equipment (DCE)   Specific communications equipment, such as packet switches, that interface between a packet switching exchange (PSE) and DTE devices. DCEs are typically found in carrier facilities.

Data Link Connection Identifiers (DLCIs)   Used to identify a frame relay virtual circuit. A frame relay service provider, like a telephone company, typically assigns DLCI values that are used by the frame relay protocol to distinguish between different virtual circuits on the network.

data terminal equipment (DTE)   End systems that communicate over an X.25 network (such as host systems, terminals, and PCs that belong to the individual subscriber) and that are present at the same site.

demarcation point (demarc)   The boundary between the customer's in-house wiring and the service provider's wiring. This is the end of responsibility for the service provider.

encapsulation A method of encasing or wrapping data (packets) within a protocol that is understood on the link.

Local Management Interface (LMI) LMI messages are used to provide three types of information—the current DLCI values, the global or local significance of the DLCI values, and the status of virtual circuits—to routers participating in the frame relay network.

local loop Wiring running from the demarc to the CO.

packet switching exchange (PSE) Switches that constitute the majority of a carrier's network and handle the transfer of data between DTE devices via the X.25 packet-switched network.

permanent virtual circuit (PVC) An established connection used for recurrent, steady data transfer. PVC sessions are continuously active, so DTEs can transmit data whenever necessary.

switched virtual circuit (SVC) A temporary connection used for intermittent data transfers. When using an SVC, DTE devices must establish, maintain, and then terminate a session every time they need to communicate.

Sample Questions

1. Which of the following is a valid command syntax to create a frame relay subinterface?

   A. int s0.43569 point-to-point

   B. int s0.16

   C. int 16.s0 point-to-point

   D. int s0 sub 16

   Answer: A. The way to configure a subinterface on your serial interface is with this syntax:

   ```
   interface [serial number] [point-to-point or
   multipoint]
   ```

2. What are the LMI types supported by Cisco? (Choose all that apply.)

A. IETF

B. ANSI

C. Cisco

D. Q.933a

Answer: B, C, D. Cisco supports three different LMI types: Cisco, ANSI, and Q.933a.

3. What are the frame relay encapsulation types that Cisco supports? (Choose all that apply.)

A. ANSI

B. Q.933a

C. Cisco

D. IETF

Answer: C, D. Cisco supports two encapsulation methods when running frame relay. Cisco is the default, and IETF is used to connect Cisco equipment to other brands of routers.

4. Which two commands show the LMI type configured on your router?

A. `sh frame-relay dlci`

B. `sh frame pvc`

C. `sh frame lmi`

D. `show interface`

Answer: C, D. To see the LMI type configured on your router, use the `show frame lmi` and `show interface` commands.

5. Which command displays the DLCI number set on an interface?

A. `sh int s0`

B. `sh frame-relay dlci`

C. sh frame pvc

D. sh frame-relay lmi

Answer: C. The show interface command will *not* show your DLCI number. show frame pvc and sh run give you the DLCI numbers for each interface.

High-Level Data-Link Control (HDLC)

The High-Level Data-Link Control protocol (HDLC) is a popular ISO-standard, bit-oriented, Data Link–layer protocol. It specifies an encapsulation method for data on synchronous serial data links using frame characters and checksums. HDLC is a point-to-point protocol used on leased lines. No authentication can be used with HDLC.

HDLC is the default encapsulation used by Cisco routers over synchronous serial links. Cisco's HDLC is proprietary—it won't communicate with any other vendor's HDLC implementation. Figure 5.2 shows the Cisco HDLC format.

FIGURE 5.2: Cisco HDLC frame format

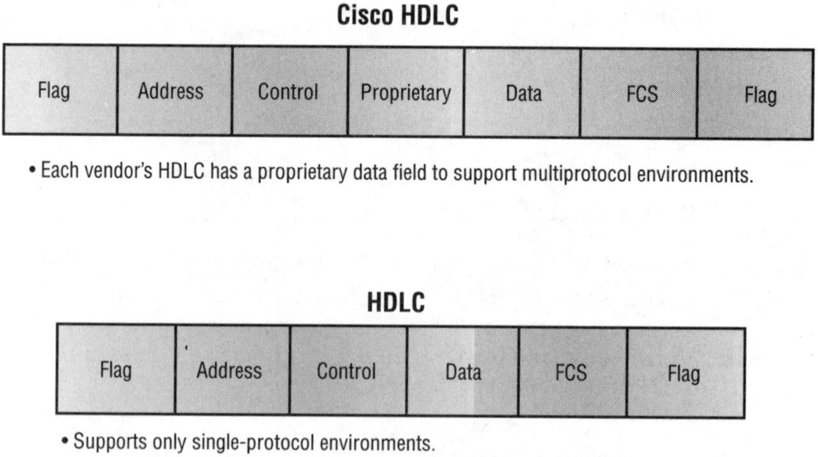

Cisco HDLC

Flag	Address	Control	Proprietary	Data	FCS	Flag

• Each vendor's HDLC has a proprietary data field to support multiprotocol environments.

HDLC

Flag	Address	Control	Data	FCS	Flag

• Supports only single-protocol environments.

The reason that every vendor has a proprietary HDLC encapsulation method is that each vendor has a different way for the HDLC protocol to communicate with the Network-layer protocols. If the vendors didn't have a way for HDLC to communicate with the different Layer 3 protocols, then HDLC would only be able to carry one protocol. This proprietary header is placed in the data field of the HDLC encapsulation.

If you had only one Cisco router and you needed to connect to, say, a Bay router because you had your other Cisco router on order, then you couldn't use the default HDLC serial encapsulation. You would use something like PPP, as discussed in Chapter 1.

Exam Essentials

Remember that the Cisco implementation of HDLC is proprietary. Cisco has created their own version of HDLC that is not compatible with other vendors' HDLC implementation.

Key Terms and Concepts

High-Level Data Link Control (HDLC) An encapsulation method used on serial links.

Sample Questions

1. Which of the following is/are true regarding HDLC? (Choose all that apply.)

   A. It works on all LAN and WAN interfaces.

   B. It is a synchronous and asynchronous encapsulation method.

   C. It is only used on Cisco routers.

   D. Cisco routers use a proprietary version of HDLC.

Answer: D. Cisco routers use HDLC, which is Cisco proprietary encapsulation method, by default on configured serial links.

Asynchronous Transfer Mode (ATM)

Asynchronous transfer mode (ATM) can be used both as a LAN and WAN protocol. However, ATM is not a broadcast media like Ethernet, so what we need is a way to resolve the difference between ATM's connection-oriented, point-to-point protocol and the connectionless, broadcast domains of a LAN medium that Ethernet uses. This is called LAN emulation (LANE).

Cisco designed LANE to hide ATM and look like 802.3 Ethernet and 802.5 Token Ring networks to end users on a LAN. LANE works by making the ATM network emulate a Media Access Control (MAC) broadcast network. Before LANE, a proprietary conversion device was needed to convert from LAN to ATM.

This objective will provide you with far more information than you need for the CCNA exam.

NOTE You must know that dedicated WAN protocols are PPP, HDLC, and SLIP. Circuit-switched protocols are PPP and SLIP. Packet-switched protocols are X.25, frame relay, and ATM.

Critical Information

LAN emulation (LANE) is an ATM service defined by the ATM Forum specification *LAN Emulation over ATM, ATM Forum 94-0035*. The ATM Forum sat down together and devised a specification for LANE services across ATM to include three important characteristics:

- Connectionless service between LANs
- The ability to carry multicast services
- Media Access Control driver service

LANE services must provide connectivity between all ATM devices and all LAN devices. This connectivity extends to devices that are attached ATM stations as well as attached LAN devices that are crossing the ATM network. Connectivity between ATM devices and all other LAN devices is done through emulated LANs (ELANs).

ELANs are also used to create independent broadcast domains that are similar in concept to Ethernet segments or Token Ring networks. ELANs also allow ATM to work with existing older equipment.

ELANs have some similarities to virtual LANs. ELAN workstations are independent of physical location, and ELANs must be connected to a router in order to communicate with each other. You can create an unlimited number of ELANs in an ATM network, and a router can participate in any number of these emulated LANs.

Connectivity begins at the MAC sublayer of the Data Link layer, allowing Windows upper-level NDIS/ODI driver interfaces to transmit Layer 3 protocols like TCP/IP, IPX, AppleTalk, and APPN, as well as allowing existing applications to continue operating without disturbance.

LANE provides a conversion process that allows you to take the connectionless environment of a LAN and change it into the connection-oriented world of ATM. The LANE converter receives LAN packets, places a 5-byte ATM-specific identification header on the front of the cell, and removes the checksum (frame check sequence) from the packet. It then fragments the packets into a 48-byte payload with a 5-byte header, creating a 53-byte cell. After the packet has traveled the ATM network, the ATM information is removed and the packet is reassembled and returned to the LAN environment.

Exam Essentials

Remember that LANE is used to run ATM on a LAN.   LAN emulation allows ATM to run on a broadcast LAN like Ethernet.

Key Terms and Concepts

asynchronous transfer mode (ATM) A cell-based, time-sensitive LAN and WAN technology.

LAN emulation (LANE) Allows ATM cells to be transmitted on a broadcast medium.

Sample Questions

1. What type of transport does ATM use?

A. Cell

B. Token

C. Packet

D. A combination of tokens and packets

Answer: A. ATM uses cells to transport data. The LANE converter operating at Layer 2 receives LAN packets, places a 5-byte ATM-specific identification header on the front of the cell, and removes the checksum (frame check sequence) from the packet. It then fragments the packets into a 48-byte payload with a 5-byte header, creating a 53-byte cell.

2. What does ATM use to communicate on an Ethernet network?

A. Contention

B. Packets

C. LANE

D. ELAN

Answer: C. ATM uses LANE (LAN emulation) at Layer 2 to translate Layer 2 packets into cells and vice versa to communicate in LAN environments.

Chapter

6

Network Management

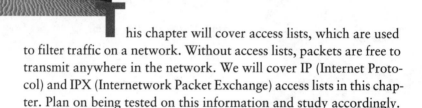

This chapter will cover access lists, which are used to filter traffic on a network. Without access lists, packets are free to transmit anywhere in the network. We will cover IP (Internet Protocol) and IPX (Internetwork Packet Exchange) access lists in this chapter. Plan on being tested on this information and study accordingly.

Telnet is an IP program that works at the Application layer and allows terminal emulation. This chapter will show you how to use Telnet, access multiple devices simultaneously using Telnet, and also how to resolve host names so you can telnet without using an IP address. Testing and verifying an internetwork using Telnet, `ping`, and `trace` is also covered.

This chapter will finish by showing you how to configure your router to resolve names using Domain Name System (DNS).

Access Lists

Access lists are essentially lists of conditions; they're powerful tools that control access both to and from network segments. They can filter unwanted packets and can be used to implement security policies. With the right combination of access lists, network managers are armed with the power to enforce nearly any access policy they can invent.

To be successful on the CCNA exam, you need a complete understanding of IP and IPX access lists.

Critical Information

IP and IPX access lists work similarly—they're both packet filters that packets are compared with, categorized by, and acted upon. Once the lists are built, they can be applied to either inbound or outbound traffic on any interface. Applying an access list will then cause the router to analyze every packet crossing that interface in the specified direction and to take action accordingly.

There are a few important rules a packet follows when it's being compared with an access list:

- A packet is always compared with each line of the access list in sequential order (i.e., it'll always start with line 1, then go to line 2, then line 3, and so on).

- A packet is compared with lines of the access list only until a match is made. Once the packet matches a line of the access list, it's acted upon, and no further comparisons take place.

- There is an implicit "deny" at the end of each access list. This means that if a packet doesn't match up to any lines in the access list, it'll be discarded.

Each of these rules has some powerful implications when filtering IP and IPX packets with access lists.

There are two types of access lists used with IP and IPX:

Standard Access Lists   These use only the source IP address in an IP packet to filter the network. This basically permits or denies all messages from that address. IPX standards can filter on both source and destination IPX address.

Extended Access Lists   These check for both source and destination IP address, protocol field in the Network-layer header, and port number at the Transport-layer header. IPX extended access lists use source and destination IPX address, Network-layer protocol field, and socket numbers in the Transport-layer header.

Once you create an access list, you apply it to an interface with either an inbound or outbound list:

Inbound Access Lists   Packets are processed through the access list before being routed to the outbound interface.

Outbound Access Lists   Packets are routed to the outbound interface and then processed through the access list.

There are also some guidelines that should be followed when creating and implementing access lists on a router:

- You can only assign one access list per interface, per protocol, and per direction. This means that if you are creating IP access lists, you can only have one inbound access list and one outbound access list per interface.

- Organize your access lists so that the more specific tests are at the top of the access list.

- Any time a new test is added to the access list, it will be placed at the bottom of the list.

- You cannot remove one line from an access list. If you try to do this, you will remove the entire list. It is best to copy the access list to a text editor before trying to edit the list. The only exception is when using named access lists.

- Unless your access list ends with a `permit any` command, all packets will be discarded if they do not meet any of the list's tests. Every list should have at least one `permit` statement, or you might as well shut the interface down.

- Create access lists and *then* apply them to an interface. It's possible to issue a command to apply an access list to an interface before the list has been created; obviously, if you do that, you will not filter any traffic on that interface until the access list has been created.

- Access lists are designed to filter traffic going through the router. They will not filter traffic originating from the router.

- Place IP standard access lists as close to the destination as possible.

- Place IP extended access lists as close to the source as possible.

IP Access Lists

IP access lists are configured in global configuration mode. The access lists are identified by the number assigned to the access list. The numbers 0 through 99 represent a standard IP access list, and the numbers 100 to 199 represent an extended IP access list. Let's take a look at both of these types of access lists in the next section.

Standard IP Access Lists

Standard IP access lists can analyze the source IP addresses of TCP/IP packets and then take action based upon that analysis. Each line of a standard IP access list is created with a command in the following format:

```
access-list [number] [permit or deny] [source address]
```

To define access lists, use the access-list command in configuration mode. Each access list is assigned a unique number to distinguish it from the other lists. IP standard access lists are given numbers between 1 and 99, but other access-list types require different number ranges. Here is an example command:

```
access-list 10 permit 172.16.30.2
```

This command adds a line to access list 10. The permit or deny keyword indicates whether to allow or discard matching packets, and the [source address] is used to define which source IP addresses should be acted upon.

Applying an IP Access List to an Interface

Even though you configure an access list, it won't filter anything until you apply it to an interface. First, enter configuration mode and select the Ethernet 0 interface. Then, we'll use the ip access-group command to specify 10 out. Here is an example:

```
(config-int)ip access-group 10 out
```

Wildcard Masking

Wildcard masking allows you to specify either an entire network or a specific host. You can use wildcard masking in both standard and extended access lists.

In this example, we've used a wildcard mask to specify the source address:

Address	172.	16.	30.	0
Mask	0.	0.	0.	255

It consists of a 32-bit binary string of 0s followed by 1s, broken into octets and written in decimal. Ones are considered *throwaway bits,* meaning that their corresponding positions in the address are irrelevant. By specifying the source address and mask as shown above, we're saying that the 172, 16, and 30 are required to match up, but the last octet of the IP address can be any value (remember that 255 is decimal format for binary 11111111). Likewise, when you specify a mask as follows:

Address	172.	16.	30.	2
Mask	0.	0.	0.	0

you're requiring 172, 16, 30, and 2 all to match up exactly, because you've set all mask values to 0.

Extended IP Access Lists

The function of extended access lists is pretty much the same as that of standard access lists. The difference centers on what can be filtered. In standard IP access lists, your decisions to permit or deny packets are limited to comparisons with the packets' source address information. But with extended IP access lists, you can act on any of the following:

- Source address
- Destination address
- IP protocol (TCP, UDP, ICMP, etc.)
- Port information (WWW, DNS, FTP, etc.)

So with extended access lists, your abilities are extended. You can make much more detailed lists than you can with the standard type. The syntax for each line on extended access lists is similar to that of standard access lists. The first three fields—access-list, *number*, and permit or deny–are exactly the same. But you can additionally specify a protocol before the source and create destination and port fields after the source address. Here's a template for each part of an extended IP access list; detailed examples of how to use this command are in the Necessary Procedures section later:

```
access-list [number] [permit or deny] [protocol]
↳[source] [destination] [port]
```

IPX Access Lists

This section covers the IPX access list commands featured in the CCNA exam. It is important that you pay close attention to the fine details of the output that a command provides. In this section you will learn how IPX access lists are used to control IPX traffic. We will cover standard IPX access lists, extended IPX access lists, and IPX SAP filters.

You should have a basic understanding of how access lists are created and how they are applied to an interface.

Standard IPX Access Lists

Standard IPX access lists allow or deny packets based on source and destination IPX addresses. With standard IP access lists, you can only use a source IP address. The syntax for each line of an IPX standard access list is as follows:

```
access-list [number] [permit or deny] [source]
↳[destination]
```

The second argument is a list number. This tells the router what type of access list is being used. Below is an example of the types of access lists that can be used:

```
RouterA(config)#access-list ?
  <1-99>      IP standard access list
  <100-199>   IP extended access list
  <1000-1099> IPX SAP access list
  <1100-1199> Extended 48-bit MAC address access list
```

```
<1200-1299>   IPX summary address access list
<200-299>     Protocol type-code access list
<300-399>     DECnet access list
<600-699>     Appletalk access list
<700-799>     48-bit MAC address access list
<800-899>     IPX standard access list
<900-999>     IPX extended access list
```

Notice that standard IPX access lists use any number from 800 to 899.

Extended IPX Access Lists

Standard IPX access lists only filter on source or destination access lists. Extended IPX access lists can filter based on any of the following:

- Source network/node

- Destination network/node

- IPX protocol (SAP, SPX, etc.)

- IPX socket

Extended access lists are in the range 900–999 and are configured just like standard access lists, with the addition of protocol and socket information. Here's a template for building lines in an IPX extended access list:

```
access-list [number] [permit or deny] [protocol]
 [source] [socket] [destination] [socket]
```

When you move from standard into extended access lists, you're simply adding the ability to filter based on protocol, socket (or port, for IP), and destination node/network.

NOTE It is important to note that if you create an access list (regardless of protocol), the Cisco router will apply an implicit deny any at the end of the list. For example, if you apply a deny statement for IP and you do not add any permit statements, you will effectively shut down the interface to which you applied the list.

IPX SAP Filters

IPX SAP filters are implemented using the same tools discussed above. They have an important place in controlling IPX SAP traffic. Why is this important? Because if you can control the SAPs, you can control the access to IPX devices. Access lists in the 1000–1099 range are used to specify IPX SAP filters. Here's the template for each line of an IPX SAP filter:

```
access-list [number] [permit or deny] [source]
↳[service type]
```

Applying an IPX Access List to an Interface

After you build an access list, it won't do anything until you apply it to an interface. You do this with the `ipx access-group` command. Your only options are to choose whether the access list will filter on incoming or outgoing packets. Here is an example:

```
config t
int s0
ipx access-group 110 out
```

Necessary Procedures

This section will provide you with configuration examples of IP and IPX access lists.

Configuring an IP Standard Access List

Here is an example of configuring with standard access lists:

```
RouterA#config t
RouterA(config)#access-list ?
  <1-99>       IP standard access list
  <100-199>    IP extended access list
  <1000-1099>  IPX SAP access list
  <1100-1199>  Extended 48-bit MAC address access list
  <1200-1299>  IPX summary address access list
  <200-299>    Protocol type-code access list
```

```
<300-399>    DECnet access list
<600-699>    Appletalk access list
<700-799>    48-bit MAC address access list
<800-899>    IPX standard access list
<900-999>    IPX extended access list
```

To apply this configuration to an Ethernet interface, you could use this example:

```
RouterA#config t
Enter configuration commands, one per line. nd with
CNTL/Z.
RouterA(config)#int e0
RouterA(config-if)#ip access-group 10 out
RouterA(config-if)#^Z
RouterA#
```

Wildcards can be used in a standard access list as follows:

```
RouterA#config t
RouterA(config)#access-list 10 permit 172.16.50.2
0.0.0.0
RouterA(config)#access-list 10 permit 172.16.30.0
0.0.0.255
RouterA(config)#int e0
RouterA(config-if)#ip access-group 11 out
RouterA(config-if)#^Z
RouterA#
```

Configuring an IP Extended Access Lists

Here is an example program that could be used to configure an extended access list:

```
RouterA#config t
RouterA(config)#access-list 110 permit tcp host
⤷172.16.50.2 host 172.16.10.2 eq 8080
RouterA(config)#access-list 110 permit tcp
⤷172.16.30.0 0.0.0.255 host 172.16.10.2 eq 8080
```

```
RouterA(config)#access-list 110 permit tcp any any
↳eq www
RouterA(config)#int e0
RouterA(config-if)#ip access-group 110 out
RouterA(config-if)#^Z
```

Here's how the three access-list lines above map to our new template for extended IP access lists:

Protocol	Source	Destination	Port
tcp	host 172.16.50.2	host 172.16.10.2	eq 8080
tcp	172.16.30.0 0.0.0.255	host 172.16.10.2	eq 8080
tcp	any	any	eq www

The new field is for the protocol, and it's specified as TCP. In this case, you chose to allow TCP connections to your proxy on port 8080.

Earlier we presented three different methods of specifying source and destination addresses and an example of wildcard masking, but there are two new methods presented here; in reality, we're just using some keywords to save ourselves the effort of typing in the masks:

- host 172.16.10.2 is the same as specifying 172.16.10.2 0.0.0.0 with wildcard masking. Setting all the bits in the wildcard mask to zeros basically says there are no wildcards, so you can be referring to only a single machine or host. This means you can use the host keyword instead of the mask of 0.0.0.0.

- any is equivalent to specifying 0.0.0.0 255.255.255.255 with wildcard masking. When you set all bits in a wildcard mask to ones, you get 255.255.255.255, so you're saying that none of the bits really matter. You can use this when you don't care about source or destination addresses because you're filtering based on some other parameter. In this example, you're filtering based upon the port.

Finally, you can specify the port to be acted upon. How well do you remember your TCP ports? You can press question mark to get the list of available ports, as shown below. At this point, you could just end the command without specifying any port information, in which case all ports would be allowed. We chose to use the eq operator, but there are other numeric comparisons available that can be selected to specify more than one port. Once you select eq, you again have many options available:

```
RouterA#config t
RouterA(config)#access-list 110 permit tcp host
↳172.16.50.2 host 172.16.10.2 eq ?
  <0-65535>    Port number
  bgp          Border Gateway Protocol (179)
  chargen      Character generator (19)
  cmd          Remote commands (rcmd, 514)
  daytime      Daytime (13)
  discard      Discard (9)
  domain       Domain Name Service (53)
  echo         Echo (7)
  exec         Exec (rsh, 512)
  finger       Finger (79)
  ftp          File Transfer Protocol (21)
  ftp-data     FTP data connections (used
  ↳infrequently, 20)
  gopher       Gopher (70)
  hostname     NIC hostname server (101)
  ident        Ident Protocol (113)
  irc          Internet Relay Chat (194)
  klogin       Kerberos login (543)
  kshell       Kerberos shell (544)
  login        Login (rlogin, 513)
  lpd          Printer service (515)
  nntp         Network News Transport Protocol (119)
  pim-auto-rp  PIM Auto-RP (496)
  pop2         Post Office Protocol v2 (109)
  pop3         Post Office Protocol v3 (110)
  smtp         Simple Mail Transport Protocol (25)
```

sunrpc	Sun Remote Procedure Call (111)
syslog	Syslog (514)
tacacs	TAC Access Control System (49)
talk	Talk (517)
telnet	Telnet (23)
time	Time (37)
uucp	Unix-to-Unix Copy Program (540)
whois	Nicname (43)
www	World Wide Web (HTTP, 80)

You can either specify the number of the port or use one of the keywords listed above. Notice that in the description, the port that's actually filtered is listed. If you can't remember that Simple Mail Transfer Protocol (SMTP) uses port 25, just enter **smtp**. This can make reading long access lists a whole lot easier.

Verifying IP Access Lists

Here are some specific access-list commands for monitoring and verifying the lists and descriptions of the functions they provide:

show access-lists   This command lists all of the access lists running on the router. It also lists each line of the access list and reports the number of packets that matched each line. This information is priceless when you are troubleshooting access lists. If you configure an access list and then use this command, you should be able to see the counter increments change as packets hit the access list.

show ip access-list   This command shows you only the IP access lists, whereas the show access-list command displays all lists.

sh log   If you add this log syntax at the end of your extended access list, a log will be generated with the following information:

Access list number

Source address

Source port

Destination address

Destination port

Number of packets

All of this log information could be redirected to the syslog server and stored for security purposes.

clear access-list counter This command clears the counters for the show access-list commands.

TIP You can use the show ip interfaces and the show run commands to see which interfaces have IP access lists set.

Configuring an IPX Standard Access List

To configure IPX standard access lists, use the same commands as IP standard access lists, but with list numbers 800–899 in the configuration (instead of the numbers 1–99 for IP lists). Here is an example:

```
RouterA#config t
RouterA(config)#access-list 810 permit 30 10
RouterA(config)#access-list 810 deny 50 10
RouterA(config)#int e0
RouterA(config-if)#ipx access-group 810 out
RouterA(config-if)#^Z
RouterA#
```

The number 810 corresponds to the range 800–899 that's reserved for IPX standard access lists. The permit/deny parameter is the same as it is with IP packets. Here the specified source and destination are based on IPX network addresses. No wildcard masking is required to specify an entire IPX network—just list the network address and you are done!

Configuring an IPX Extended Access List

Use the online help to wade through the syntax of creating an extended IPX access list.

```
RouterA(config)#access-list ?
  <1-99>        IP standard access list
```

```
<100-199>    IP extended access list
<1000-1099>  IPX SAP access list
<1100-1199>  Extended 48-bit MAC address access list
<1200-1299>  IPX summary address access list
<200-299>    Protocol type-code access list
<300-399>    DECnet access list
<600-699>    Appletalk access list
<700-799>    48-bit MAC address access list
<800-899>    IPX standard access list
<900-999>    IPX extended access list
```

```
RouterA(config)#access-list 910 ?
  deny     Specify packets to reject
  permit   Specify packets to permit
```

```
RouterA(config)#access-list 910 permit ?
  -1       Any IPX protocol type
  <0-255>  Protocol type number (DECIMAL)
  <cr>
```

```
RouterA(config)#access-list 910 permit -1 ?
  -1           Any IPX net
  <0-FFFFFFFF> Source net
  N.H.H.H      Source net.host address
  <cr>
```

```
RouterA(config)#access-list 910 permit -1 -1 ?
  <0-FFFFFFFF> Source Socket (0 for all sockets)
 ↳HEXIDECIMAL
  <cr>
```

```
RouterA(config)#access-list 910 permit -1 -1 0 ?
  -1           Any IPX net
  <0-FFFFFFFF> Destination net
  N.H.H.H      Destination net.host address
  <cr>
```

```
RouterA(config)#access-list 910 permit -1 -1 0 -1 ?
  <0-FFFFFFFF>  Destination Socket (0 for all
  ⤷sockets) HEXIDECIMAL
  <cr>
RouterA(config)#access-list 910 permit -1 -1 0 -1 0 log
```

The log command could be used to log any attempts from, say, network 50 to access network 10 and record the following information:

- Source address

- Source socket

- Destination address

- Destination socket

- Protocol type

IPX SAP Filters

Now practice creating an IPX SAP filter. Assume that on your Admin LAN network, you have three NetWare servers, but you want only the one with internal IPX network address 11.0000.0000.0001 to be seen by the outside world. To accomplish that, you'd configure and apply an access list as follows:

```
RouterA#config t
RouterA(config)#access-list 1010 permit
⤷11.0000.0000.0001 0
RouterA(config)#int e0
RouterA(config-if)#ipx input-sap-filter 1010
RouterA(config-if)#^Z
RouterA#
```

Here's how the above access list command maps to the template:

Access List	Number	Permit or Deny	Source	Service Type
access-list	1010	permit	11.0000.0000.0001	0

The number 1010 falls into the range 1000–1099, reserved for IPX SAP filters. The source network is the network/node address of the server. The resulting access list allows packets from 11.0000.0000.0001 to enter the Ethernet interface and be included in SAP updates across the network. As with other access lists, there's an implicit deny any that blocks all other SAP updates arriving at the router on the Ethernet interface. Finally, the 0 entered for service type indicates that all services should be allowed:

```
RouterA#config t
RouterA(config)#access-list 1010 permit
%11.0000.0000.0001 ?
  <0-FFFF>  Service type-code (0 matches all services)
  N.H.H.H   Source net.host mask
  <cr>
```

To add the IPX SAP filter to an interface, use one of the following commands:

```
RouterA(config-if)#ipx input-sap-filter 1010
```
or

```
RouterA(config-if)#ipx output-sap-filter 1010
```

Exam Essentials

Practice setting IP extended access lists. The only way to select the right answer for access-list questions is to understand the command syntax.

Know the commands to view access lists. You must remember the commands for viewing access lists set on both global configurations and interfaces.

Know the difference between standard and extended access lists. Standard access lists can only filter by source address. Also, standard access lists cannot filter by protocol or port. Extended access lists can filter by source and destination address, protocol, and port. IP standard access lists use number 1–99; IP extended access lists use 100–199. IPX standard lists use 800–899; and IP extended use 900–999.

Know the difference between the types of IPX access lists. It is important to understand what each type of list can filter on.

Remember how to apply an IPX list to an interface. By using the ipx access-group command, you can apply access lists to an interface.

Key Terms and Concepts

access list Used in routers to filter packets either trying to enter or leave an interface.

extended access list Security used in Cisco routers that can filter by source and destination address as well as by protocol and port.

standard access list Security used in Cisco routers that can filter only by source address.

Sample Questions

1. Which of the following commands allow traffic from network 172.16.30.0 to enter interface Ethernet 0?

   A. access-list 10 permit 0.0.0.255 172.16.30.0 in

   B. access-list 10 permit 172.16.30.0 0.0.0.0, access-group 10 out

   C. access-list 10 permit 172.16.30.0 0.0.0.255, int e0, access-group 10 in

   D. access-list 10 permit 172.16.30.0 0.0.0.255, int e0, ip access-group 10 in

   Answer: D. To create a standard IP access list, you must use numbers between 1 and 99. You can only filter by source IP address. You apply that list by going to an interface and using the ip access-group command.

2. Which of the following are valid IP extended access lists?

A. `access-list 99 permit tcp any 172.16.30.0`
   `255.255.255.0 eq ftp`

B. `access-list 199 permit ip any 172.16.30.0 0.0.0.255`
   `eq ftp`

C. `access-list 199 permit tcp any 172.16.30.0 0.0.0.255`
   `eq ftp`

D. `access-list 109 permit ip any host 172.16.30.5 eq ftp`

Answer: C. On an extended access list, you can permit or deny based on the source, destination, and protocol. You can only filter by port number or well-known port name when using TCP, UDP, or ICMP.

3. Which of the following commands will show you which interfaces have IP access lists set? (Choose all that apply.)

A. `sh int`

B. `sh run`

C. `sh ip int`

D. `sh access-list`

Answer: B, C. You can use the `show ip interfaces` and the `show run` commands to see which interfaces have IP access lists set.

4. Which of the following commands will show only extended access list 187?

A. `sh int`

B. `sh ip int`

C. `sh access-list 187`

D. `sh access-lists`

Answer: C. Answer D will show access list 187, but only answer C will show only the *extended* access list 187.

5. If you create the following IPX access list, what will happen?

```
access-list 873 permit 30 4d
int e0
  ipx network 4d
  ipx access-group 873 out
int e1
  ipx network 30
int e2
  ipx network 50
```

A. Interface e1 can send packets out e0.

B. Interface e0 can send packets out e1.

C. Interface e1 can send packets out e2

D. Network 50 can send packets out to network 4d.

Answer: A. The access list 873 is a standard IPX access list that can only filter on source and destination network/node. This list permits network 30 out network 4d. This is applied to an interface with the `ipx access-group` command. Remember that an implicit deny any is attached to the end of any list so that with this list, only network 30 will be allowed out network 4d; everything else is denied.

Telnet

Telnet is a virtual terminal protocol that is part of the TCP/IP protocol suite. Telnet allows you to make connections to remote devices and gather information and run programs. Before describing Telnet, in this objective we will show you how to create a hosts table to resolve hostnames and how to use Cisco Discovery Protocol (CDP) to gather information about neighbor routers and switches.

Cisco Discovery Protocol (CDP)

Cisco Discovery Protocol (CDP) is a Cisco proprietary protocol that uses a SNAP frame at the Data Link layer to gather information about neighbor Cisco devices like routers and switches.

CDP starts by default on any router version 10.3 or later, and discovers neighboring Cisco routers running CDP by doing a Data Link multicast. It doesn't matter which protocol is running at the Network layer, since it does not contain Network-layer information.

Once CDP has discovered a router, it can then display information about the upper-layer protocols, such as IP and IPX. A router caches the information it receives from its CDP neighbors. Anytime a router receives updated information that a CDP neighbor has changed, it discards the old information in favor of the new broadcast.

From a router prompt, type sh cdp to see the CDP timers.

```
RouterB#show cdp ?
  entry      Information for specific neighbor entry
  interface  CDP interface status and configuration
  neighbors  CDP neighbor entries
  traffic    CDP statistics
  <cr>
RouterB#show cdp
Global CDP information:
          Sending CDP packets every 60 seconds
          Sending a holdtime value of 180 second
```

This shows the defaults for CDP. The interfaces send CDP packets every 60 seconds by default and will hold any information obtained from CDP packets sent by neighboring Cisco devices for a maximum of 180 seconds. If no packets are received from a neighbor device within 180 seconds, that neighbor's information will be discarded. You can change the packet update frequency as well as the holdtime with the global configuration commands cdp timer and cdp holdtime.

```
RouterB#config t
Enter configuration commands, one per line.  End
↳with CNTL/Z.
RouterB(config)#cdp ?
 holdtime  Specify the holdtime (in sec) to be sent
↳in packets
 timer     Specify the rate at which CDP packets are
↳sent(in sec)
 run

RouterB(config)#cdp timer 90
RouterB(config)#cdp holdtime 240
RouterB(config)#^Z
RouterB#
00:47:54: %SYS-5-CONFIG_I: Configured from console
↳by console
RouterB#sh cdp
Global CDP information:
        Sending CDP packets every 90 seconds
        Sending a holdtime value of 240 seconds
```

CDP protocol can be disabled on a Cisco device or just on a certain
interfaces. To disable CDP completely, use the no cdp run global
configuration command as shown below.

```
RouterB#config t
Enter configuration commands, one per line.  End
↳with CNTL/Z.
RouterB(config)#no cdp ?
 holdtime  Specify the holdtime (in sec) to be sent
↳in packets
 timer     Specify the rate at which CDP packets are
↳sent(in sec)
 run

RouterB(config)#no cdp run
RouterB(config)#^Z
RouterB#
```

```
00:57:05: %SYS-5-CONFIG_I: Configured from console
↳by console
RouterB#sh cdp
% CDP is not enabled
```

To disable CDP on a single interface, use the no cdp enable from interface configuration mode.

```
RouterB#config terminal
Enter configuration commands, one per line.   End
↳with CNTL/Z.
RouterB(config)#int e0
RouterB(config-if)#no cdp ?
  enable  Enable CDP on interface
RouterB(config-if)#no cdp enable
RouterB(config-if)#^Z
```

By typing **sh cdp interface**, we can see the interface information. Notice our timers are set to 90 and 240 instead of the default of 60 and 180. Also missing is the Ethernet 0 interface, which we disabled CDP on.

```
RouterB#show cdp interface
Serial0 is up, line protocol is up
  Encapsulation HDLC
  Sending CDP packets every 90 seconds
  Holdtime is 180 seconds
Serial1 is up, line protocol is up
  Encapsulation HDLC
  Sending CDP packets every 90 seconds
  Holdtime is 180 seconds
```

Let's turn Ethernet 0 back on.

```
RouterB#config t
Enter configuration commands, one per line.   End
↳with CNTL/Z.
RouterB(Bconfig)#interface ethernet 0
RouterB(config-if)#cdp enable
```

```
RouterB(config-if)#^Z
RouterB#show cdp interface
Ethernet0 is up, line protocol is up
  Encapsulation ARPA
  Sending CDP packets every 90 seconds
  Holdtime is 180 seconds
Serial0 is up, line protocol is up
  Encapsulation HDLC
  Sending CDP packets every 90 seconds
  Holdtime is 180 seconds
Serial1 is up, line protocol is up
  Encapsulation HDLC
  Sending CDP packets every 90 seconds
  Holdtime is 180 seconds
RouterB#
```

The show cdp entry command can give you the CDP information received from all routers by typing an asterisk (*) or a specific router by typing the router name. Note this is case-sensitive.

```
RouterB#show cdp entry *
-------------------------
Device ID: RouterA
Entry address(es):
  IP address: 172.16.40.2
Platform: cisco 2500,  Capabilities: Router
Interface: Serial1,  Port ID (outgoing port): Serial0
Holdtime : 137 sec

Version :
Cisco Internetwork Operating System Software
IOS (tm) 2500 Software (C2500-JS40-L),
↻Version 11.2(13), RELEASE SOFTWARE (fc1)
Copyright (c) 1986-1998 by cisco Systems, Inc.
Compiled Tue 31-Mar-98 20:06 by tlane

-------------------------
```

```
Device ID: NOR2500
Entry address(es):
  IP address: 172.16.30.1
  IP address: 172.16.30.1
Interface: Serial0,  Port ID (outgoing port): Serial1
Holdtime : 176 sec

Version :
Cisco Internetwork Operating System Software
IOS (tm) 2500 Software (C2500-JS-L),
↳Version 12.0(8), RELEASE SOFTWARE (fc1)
Copyright (c) 1986-1999 by cisco Systems, Inc.
Compiled Mon 29-Nov-99 14:52 by kpma


-------------------------
Device ID: den2600
Entry address(es):
  IP address: 172.16.60.2
Platform: cisco 2621,  Capabilities: Router
Interface: Ethernet0,  Port ID (outgoing port):
↳FastEthernet0/0
Holdtime : 166 sec

Version :
Cisco Internetwork Operating System Software
IOS (tm) C2600 Software (C2600-DOS-M),
↳Version 12.0(4)T,  RELEASE SOFTWARE (fc1)
Copyright (c) 1986-1999 by cisco Systems, Inc.
Compiled Wed 28-Apr-99 17:29 by kpma
```

The show cdp neighbors command gives you information about directly attached Cisco devices.

```
RouterB#show cdp neighbors
Capability Codes: R - Router, T - Trans Bridge,
                  B - Source Route Bridge, S - Switch,
                  H - Host, I - IGMP, r - Repeater
```

```
Device ID  Local Intrfce  Holdtme  Capability  Platform  Port ID
RouterA    Ser 1          158      R           2500      Ser 0
NOR2500    Ser 0          138      R           2500      Ser 1
den2600    Eth 0          133      R           2621      Fas 0/0
```

For each neighbor, this command displays the following:

Neighbor Device ID   The hostname of the neighbor router that this router exchanges CDP information with.

Local Interface   The local interface of the router running the command. Notice everything is being heard from Ethernet 0.

Holdtime   How much longer the device will hold the neighbor information before discarding.

Capability   Router's capability code—R for router, S for switch, etc.

Platform   Which type of Cisco device the neighbor is.

Port ID   The neighbor interface that the CDP information is broadcast out from.

The sh cdp neighbors detail command will give you the same information as the sh cdp entry * command.

```
RouterB#show cdp neighbors detail
--------------------------
Device ID: RouterA
Entry address(es):
  IP address: 172.16.40.2
Platform: cisco 2500,  Capabilities: Router
Interface: Serial1,  Port ID (outgoing port): Serial0
Holdtime : 151 sec

Version :
Cisco Internetwork Operating System Software
IOS (tm) 2500 Software (C2500-JS40-L),
↳Version 11.2(13), RELEASE SOFTWARE (fc1)
```

```
Copyright (c) 1986-1998 by cisco Systems, Inc.
Compiled Tue 31-Mar-98 20:06 by tlane


-------------------------
Device ID: NOR2500
Entry address(es):
  IP address: 172.16.30.1
Platform: cisco 2500,  Capabilities: Router
Interface: Serial0,  Port ID (outgoing port): Serial1
Holdtime : 130 sec

Version :
Cisco Internetwork Operating System Software
IOS (tm) 2500 Software (C2500-JS-L),
 ⮑Version 12.0(8), RELEASE SOFTWARE (fc1)
Copyright (c) 1986-1999 by cisco Systems, Inc.
Compiled Mon 29-Nov-99 14:52 by kpma


-------------------------
Device ID: den2600
Entry address(es):
  IP address: 172.16.60.2
Platform: cisco 2621,  Capabilities: Router
Interface: Ethernet0,  Port ID (outgoing port):
 ⮑FastEthernet0/0
Holdtime : 123 sec

Version :
Cisco Internetwork Operating System Software
IOS (tm) C2600 Software (C2600-DOS-M),
 ⮑Version 12.0(4)T,  RELEASE SOFTWARE (fc1)
Copyright (c) 1986-1999 by cisco Systems, Inc.
Compiled Wed 28-Apr-99 17:29 by kpma


RouterB#
```

This is an important objective for the CCNA exam; make sure you understand everything here before you attempt your exam.

Critical Information

After your router or switch has at least one IP address configured, you can use the Telnet program to finish configuring the device and also to verify its configuration instead of needing to use a console cable. You use the Telnet program by typing `telnet` from any command prompt (DOS or Cisco). VTY passwords must be set on the routers for this to work.

Cisco Discovery Protocol (CDP) can be used to gather information about routers and switches that are directly connected to your device. To gather information about device not directly connected, use the Telnet application to connect to your neighbor devices and then run CDP on those remote devices to gather CDP information about remote devices.

You can issue the `telnet` command from any router prompt, as in the following example:

```
Todd2509#telnet 172.16.10.2
Trying 172.16.10.2 ... Open

Password required, but none set

[Connection to 172.16.10.2 closed by foreign host]
Todd2509#
```

Remember that the VTY ports on a router are configured as `login`, which means that you must either set the VTY passwords or use the `no login` command. (See Chapter 9 for details on setting passwords.)

On a Cisco router, you do not need to use the `telnet` command. If you just type in an IP address from a command prompt, the router will assume you want to telnet to the device, as shown below:

```
Todd2509#172.16.10.2
Trying 172.16.10.2 ... Open

Password required, but none set

[Connection to 172.16.10.2 closed by foreign host]
Todd2509#
```

Remember that the VTY password is the user-mode password, not the enable password. Watch what happens when we try to go into privileged mode after telnetting to router 2501B:

```
2501B>en
% No password set
2501B>
```

This is a good security feature. You don't want just anyone telnetting to your device and then being able to just type the command `enable` to get into privileged mode. You must set your enable password or enable secret password to use Telnet to configure remote devices.

Telnetting to Multiple Devices Simultaneously

If you telnet to a router or switch, you can end the connection by typing `exit` at any time. However, what if you want to keep your connection to a remote device but still come back to your original router console? To keep the connection, you can press the Ctrl+Shift+6 key combination, release it, and then press X.

Here's an example of connecting to multiple devices from our Todd2509 router console after the VTY password has been set:

```
RouterB#telnet 172.16.10.2
Trying 172.16.10.2 ... Open
```

```
User Access Verification

Password:
2501B>
Todd2509#
```

In the example above, we telnetted to the 2501B router, then typed the password to enter user mode. We then pressed Ctrl+Shift+6, then X (this doesn't show on the screen output), something like this:

```
Password:[******]
2501B>[Ctrl+Shift+6][X]
Todd2509#
```

Now, the bold items in brackets don't show up in the screen output (and you don't type the brackets, of course), and the password does not show on the screen, but we'll sometimes include the keys used so you can see what's going on.

You can also telnet to a 1900 switch. However, you must set the enable password level 15 on the switch before you can gain access via the Telnet application. (See Chapter 9 for information about how to set the 1900 switch passwords.)

In the following example, we telnet to a 1900 switch, which then gives us the console output of the switch.

```
Todd2509#telnet 192.168.0.148
Trying 192.168.0.148 ... Open

Catalyst 1900 Management Console
Copyright (c) Cisco Systems, Inc.  1993-1999
All rights reserved.
Enterprise Edition Software
Ethernet Address:       00-B0-64-75-6B-C0

PCA Number:             73-3122-04
PCA Serial Number:      FAB040131E2
```

```
Model Number:           WS-C1912-A
System Serial Number:   FAB0401U0JQ
Power Supply S/N:       PHI033108SD
PCB Serial Number:      FAB040131E2,73-3122-04
--------------------------------------------------

1 user(s) now active on Management Console.


        User Interface Menu

    [M] Menus
    [K] Command Line

Enter Selection:
```

At this point, we press Ctrl+Shift+6, then X, which takes us back to the Todd2509 router console:

```
Todd2509#
```

Checking Telnet Connections

To see the connections made from your router to a remote device, use the show sessions command, as shown here:

```
Todd2509#sh sessions
Conn Host           Address         Byte  Idle Conn Name
   1 172.16.10.2    172.16.10.2       0     0   172.16.10.2
*  2 192.168.0.148  192.168.0.148     0     0   192.168.0.148
Todd2509#
```

Notice the asterisk (*) next to connection 2. This means that session 2 was the last session. You can return to your last session by pressing Enter twice. You can also return to any session by typing the number of the connection and pressing Enter twice.

Checking Telnet Users

You can list all active consoles and VTY ports in use on your router with the show users command, as shown below:

```
Todd2509#sh users
    Line    User    Host(s)         Idle Location
*   0 con 0         172.16.10.2     00:07:52
                    192.168.0.148   00:07:18
```

In the command's output, the con represents the local console. In this example, the console is connected to two remote IP addresses, or devices.

In the next example, we type show users on the 2501B router, which the Todd2509 router had telnetted to:

```
2501B>sh users
    Line    User    Host(s)         Idle Location
    0 con 0         idle            9
*   2 vty 0
```

This output shows that the console is active and that VTY port 2 is being used. The asterisk represents the current terminal session user.

Closing Telnet Sessions

You can end Telnet sessions a few different ways. Typing exit or disconnect is probably the easiest and quickest.

To end a session from a remote device, use the exit command, as shown below:

```
2509# [Press Enter twice here.]
[Resuming connection 2 to 192.168.0.148 ... ]

switch>exit

[Connection to 192.168.0.148 closed by foreign host]
Todd2509#
```

To end a session from a local device, use the disconnect command, as shown below:

```
Todd2509#disconnect ?
  <1-2>  The number of an active network connection
  WORD   The name of an active network connection
  <cr>
```

```
Todd2509#disconnect 1
Closing connection to 172.16.10.2 [confirm]
Todd2509#
```

In this example, we used the session number 1 because that was the connection to the 2501B router that we wanted to end. As explained earlier, you can use the show sessions command to see the connection number.

If you want to end a session of a device attached to your router through Telnet, you might want to first check if any devices are attached to your router. Use the show users command to get that information, as shown below:

```
2501B#show users
      Line      User      Host(s)           Idle Location
*   0 con 0               idle              0
    1 aux 0               idle              0
    2 vty 0               idle              0 172.16.10.1
```

This output shows that VTY 2 has IP address 172.16.10.1 connected. That is the Todd2509 router.

To clear the connection, use the clear line # command, as follows:

```
2501B#clear line 2
[confirm]
  [OK]
```

Verify that the user has been disconnected with the show users command.

```
2501B#sh users
    Line      User      Host(s)         Idle Location
*   0 con 0             idle            0
    1 aux 0             idle            1

2501B#
```

This output shows that the line has been cleared.

Resolving Hostnames

In order to use a hostname rather than an IP address to connect to a remote device, the device that you are using to make the connection must be able to translate the hostname to an IP address. There are two ways to resolve hostnames to IP addresses: building a host table on each router, or building a Domain Name System (DNS) server, which is like a dynamic host table.

A host table provides name resolution only on the router on which it was built. The command to build a host table on a router is:

```
ip host name tcp_port_number ip_address
```

The default is TCP port number is 23. You can create a session using Telnet with a different TCP port number, if needed, and you can assign up to eight IP addresses to a hostname.

Here is an example of configuring a host table with two entries to resolve the names for the 2501B router and the switch:

```
Todd2509#config t
Enter configuration commands, one per line.  End
↳with CNTL/Z.
Todd2509(config)#ip host ?
  WORD  Name of host

Todd2509(config)#ip host 2501B ?
  <0-65535>  Default telnet port number
  A.B.C.D    Host IP address (maximum of 8)
```

```
Todd2509(config)#ip host 2501B 172.16.10.2 ?
  A.B.C.D  Host IP address (maximum of 8)
  <cr>
Todd2509(config)#ip host 2501B 172.16.10.2
Todd2509(config)#ip host switch 192.168.0.148
Todd2509(config)#^Z
```

To see the host table, use the show hosts command, as shown below:

```
Todd2509#sh hosts
Default domain is not set
Name/address lookup uses domain service
Name servers are 255.255.255.255


Host            Flags      Age Type    Address(es)
2501B           (perm, OK) 0   IP      172.16.10.2
switch          (perm, OK) 0   IP      192.168.0.148
Todd2509#
```

In the router output above, you can see the two hostnames and their associated IP addresses. The perm in the Flags column means the entry is manually configured. If it said temp, it would be an entry resolved by DNS.

To verify that the host table resolves names, try typing the hostnames at a router prompt. Remember that if you don't specify the command, the router assumes you want to telnet. In the following example, we use the hostnames to telnet to the remote devices and then press Ctrl+Shift+6, then X to return to the main console of the Todd2509 router:

```
Todd2509#2501b
Trying 2501B (172.16.10.2)... Open

User Access Verification

Password:
2501B>[Ctrl+Shift+6,then x]
Todd2509#
```

```
Todd2509#switch
Trying switch (192.168.0.148)... Open

Catalyst 1900 Management Console
Copyright (c) Cisco Systems, Inc.  1993-1999
All rights reserved.
Enterprise Edition Software
Ethernet Address:        00-B0-64-75-6B-C0

PCA Number:              73-3122-04
PCA Serial Number:       FAB040131E2
Model Number:            WS-C1912-A
System Serial Number:    FAB0401U0JQ
Power Supply S/N:        PHI033108SD
PCB Serial Number:       FAB040131E2,73-3122-04
--------------------------------------------------

1 user(s) now active on Management Console.

          User Interface Menu

     [M] Menus
     [K] Command Line

 Enter Selection:[Ctrl+Shift+6,then x]
 Todd2509#
```

We successfully used the host table to create a session to two devices and used the names to telnet to both devices. Notice in the entries in the show session output below that the hostname now shows up instead of the IP address:

```
Todd2509#show session
Conn Host            Address              Byte    Idle Conn Name
   1 switch          192.168.0.148          0       0 switch
*  2 2501b           172.16.10.2            0       0 2501b
Todd2509#
```

You can remove a hostname from the table by using the `no ip host` command, as in the following example:

```
RouterA(config)#no ip host routerb
```

The problem with the host table method is that you would need to create a host table on each router to be able to resolve names. If you have many routers and want to resolve names, using DNS is a better choice; DNS just happens to be covered in the next objective.

Checking Network Connectivity

You can use the `ping` and `trace` commands to test connectivity to remote devices. Both commands can be used with many protocols, not just IP.

To see all the different protocols that you can use with `ping`, use the `ping ?` command, as shown below.

```
RouterB#ping ?
  WORD       Ping destination address or hostname
  apollo     Apollo echo
  appletalk  Appletalk echo
  clns       CLNS echo
  decnet     DECnet echo
  ip         IP echo
  ipx        Novell/IPX echo
  srb        srb echo
  tag        Tag encapsulated IP echo
  vines      Vines echo
  xns        XNS echo
  <cr>
RouterB#ping 172.16.50.2
Type escape sequence to abort.
Sending 5, 100-byte ICMP Echos to 172.16.50.2,
↳timeout is 2 seconds:
!!!!!
Success rate is 100 percent (5/5), round-trip min/
↳avg/max = 32/32/32 ms
RouterB#
```

The ping output displays the minimum, average, and maximum times it takes for a ping packet to find a specified system and return.

The trace command allows you to see all the hops a ping takes. This can be a good command to use to troubleshoot a failed ping since it shows where the ping was lost. Here is an example:

```
RouterB#trace ?
  WORD        Trace route to destination address or
  ♦hostname
  appletalk  AppleTalk Trace
  clns       ISO CLNS Trace
  ip         IP Trace
  ipx        IPX Trace
  oldvines   Vines Trace (Cisco)
  vines      Vines Trace (Banyan)
  <cr>
RouterB#trace 172.16.50.2

Type escape sequence to abort.
Tracing the route to 172.16.50.2

  1 172.16.40.2 16 msec 16 msec 16 msec
  2 172.16.50.2 16 msec 16 msec 16 msec
RouterB#
```

The trace command shows the hop or hops that a packet traverses on its way to a remote device.

Exam Essentials

Understand how you can telnet simultaneously to multiple hosts.
By using the keystrokes Ctrl+Shift+6, then X, you can telnet to multiple sessions from a router.

Understand how to configure and verify the hosts table. To create a hosts table use the global configuration command `ip host` *hostname ip_address*. Verify this with the `show hosts` command.

Key Terms and Concepts

Telnet   Telnet comes from the words "telephone network," since that is how most Telnet sessions used to occur. Telnet is used to provide a terminal emulation.

host table   Table on a device that resolves hostnames to IP addresses

ping   Packet Internet Groper is used to test IP connectivity by using ICMP echo requests and echo replies.

trace   Traceroute is the full command name, and it is used to find the path a packet takes as it traverses through an internetwork. `trace` uses ICMP timeouts.

Sample Questions

1. What keystroke sequence is used for multiple Telnet sessions from a router simultaneously?

A. Ctrl+Shift+6 key, then X

B. Ctrl+P

C. Ctrl+A+6

D. Shift+Tab, then X

Answer: A. The keystroke sequence that toggles between Telnet sessions is Ctrl+Shift+6 key, then X.

2. If you are telnetted to a remote router, what can you type to clear the session?

A. `finish`

B. `disconnect`

C. connect

D. ftp

Answer: B. You can use the disconnect command to end a Telnet session with a remote router.

Domain Name System (DNS)

If you have many devices and don't want to create a host table in each device, you can use a DNS server to resolve hostnames. This objective will show you how to configure your router to resolve names using DNS.

This subject isn't heavily tested, but you should be aware of DNS configuration in case the exam does ask questions about it.

Critical Information

Anytime a Cisco device receives a command it doesn't understand, it tries to resolve this through DNS by default. Watch what happens when we type the special command todd at a Cisco router prompt:

```
Todd2509#todd
Translating "todd"...domain server (255.255.255.255)
% Unknown command or computer name, or unable to
find computer address
Todd2509#
```

It doesn't know the name, or what command we are trying to type, so it tries to resolve this through DNS. This is annoying for two reasons: first, because it doesn't know our name, and second, because we need to wait for the name lookup to time out. You can avoid this and prevent the default DNS lookup by using the no ip domain-lookup command on your router from global configuration mode.

If you have a DNS server on your network, you need to add a few commands to make DNS name resolution work:

- The first command is `ip domain-lookup`, which is turned on by default. It only needs to be entered if you previously turned it off (with the `no ip domain-lookup` command).

- The second command is `ip name-server`. This sets the IP address of the DNS server. You can enter the IP addresses of up to six servers.

- The last command is `ip domain-name`. Although this command is optional, it should be set. It appends the domain name to the hostname you type in. Since DNS uses a fully qualified domain name (FQDN) system, you must have a full DNS name, in the form *domain.com*.

Here is an example of using these three commands:

```
Todd2509#config t
Enter configuration commands, one per line.  End
↳with CNTL/Z.
Todd2509(config)#ip domain-lookup
Todd2509(config)#ip name-server ?
  A.B.C.D  Domain server IP address (maximum of 6)
Todd2509(config)#ip name-server 192.168.0.70
Todd2509(config)#ip domain-name lammle.com
Todd2509(config)#^Z
Todd2509#
```

After the DNS configurations are set, you can test the DNS server by using a hostname to `ping` or telnet to a device, as shown below:

```
Todd2509#ping 2501b
Translating "2501b"...domain server (192.168.0.70) [OK]
Type escape sequence to abort.
Sending 5, 100-byte ICMP Echos to 172.16.10.2, timeout
↳is 2 seconds:
!!!!!
Success rate is 100 percent (5/5), round-trip min/avg/
↳max = 28/31/32 ms
```

Notice that the DNS server is used by the router to resolve the name.

After a name is resolved using DNS, use the show hosts command to see that the device cached this information in the host table, as shown below:

```
Todd2509#sh hosts
Default domain is lammle.com
Name/address lookup uses domain service
Name servers are 192.168.0.70

Host                Flags       Age Type   Address(es)
2501b.lammle.com    (temp, OK)  0   IP     172.16.10.2
switch              (perm, OK)  0   IP     192.168.0.148
Todd2509#
```

The entry that was resolved is shown as temp, but the switch device is still perm, which means it is a static entry. Notice that the hostname is a full domain name. If we hadn't used the ip domain-name lammle.com command, we would have needed to type in ping 2501b.lammle.com, which is a pain.

Exam Essentials

Remember the command to turn on DNS if it has been disabled. The command ip domain-lookup enables DNS name lookup on a router. It is turned on by default.

Key Terms and Concepts

Domain Name System (DNS)   Used to resolve hostnames on an internetwork.

host table   Table on a device that resolves hostnames to IP addresses.

Sample Questions

1. What command is used to view the hosts table on a router?

A. show ip hosts

B. show hosts

C. show host table

D. sho ip host table

Answer: B. The show hosts command is used to see the host table on a router.

2. Which of the following commands is used to turn on DNS resolution if it was disabled?

A. ip dns on

B. domain lookup

C. ip domain-lookup

D. ip-domain lookup

Answer: C. The ip domain-lookup command is used to turn on DNS resolution on a router if it has been disabled.

Chapter 7

LAN Design

his chapter will cover the Ethernet standard for LANs; 10 Mbps Ethernet as well as Fast Ethernet and Gigabit Ethernet will be discussed. The IEEE standards for these and other technologies will be covered in Chapter 8.

This chapter will finish with a short discussion on Token Ring, a short discussion being more than needed for the CCNA exam.

This is an important chapter, and it works directly with Chapter 8. You must understand the Ethernet standards to pass the CCNA exam.

Ethernet

Ethernet is a contention media access method that allows all hosts on a network to share the same bandwidth of a link. Ethernet is popular because it is easy to implement, easy to troubleshoot, and easy to add new technologies (like Fast Ethernet and Gigabit Ethernet) to existing network infrastructures. Ethernet uses the Data Link and Physical layer specifications, and this section of the book will give you both the Data Link and Physical layer information you need to effectively implement, troubleshoot, and maintain an Ethernet network.

Ethernet networking uses a protocol called Carrier Sense Multiple Access with Collision Detection (CSMA/CD), which helps devices share bandwidth evenly without having two devices transmit at the same time on the network media.

CSMA/CD was created to overcome the problem of collisions that occur when packets are transmitted simultaneously from different nodes. Good collision management is important, because when a node transmits in a CSMA/CD network, all the other nodes on the network receive and examine that transmission. Only bridges and routers effectively prevent a transmission from propagating through the entire network.

The CSMA/CD protocol works like this: When a host wants to transmit over the network, it first checks for the presence of a digital signal on the wire. If all is clear (if no other host is transmitting), the host will then proceed with its transmission. And it doesn't stop there. The transmitting host constantly monitors the wire to make sure no other hosts begin transmitting. If the host detects another signal on the wire, it sends out an extended jam signal that causes all nodes on the segment to stop sending data. Other nodes respond to that jam signal by waiting a bit before attempting to transmit again. If, after 15 tries, collisions keep occurring, the nodes attempting to transmit will then time out.

Ethernet at the Data Link Layer

Ethernet at the Data Link layer is responsible for Ethernet addressing, which is typically called hardware addressing or MAC (Media Access Control) addressing. Ethernet is also responsible for framing packets received from the Network layer and preparing them for transmission on the local network through the Ethernet contention media access method. There are four different types of Ethernet frames available, and we will discuss all four in later sections.

Ethernet Addressing

Ethernet addressing uses the Media Access Control (MAC) address burned into each and every Ethernet network interface card (NIC). The MAC address, sometimes referred to as a hardware address, is a 48-bit address written in a canonical format to ensure that addresses are at least written in the same format, even if different LAN technologies are used.

Figure 7.1 shows the 48 MAC address and how the bits are divided up.

FIGURE 7.1: Ethernet addressing using MAC addresses

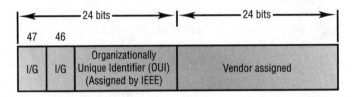

The Organizationally Unique Identifier (OUI) is assigned by the IEEE to an organization (24 bits or 3 bytes). That organization, in turn, assigns a globally administered address (24 bits or 3 bytes) that is unique (supposedly) to each and every adapter they manufacture. Notice bit 46. Bit 46 must be 0 if it is a globally assigned bit from the manufacturer, and it must be 1 if it is locally administered from the network administrator.

Address Resolution Protocol

Address Resolution Protocol (ARP) is used by the IP to provide dynamic mapping of 32-bit IP addresses to 48-bit MAC addresses. The ARP cache is a table of these listings and is checked every time communication is initiated between machines in an IP network. If the required hardware address cannot be found in the cache, a broadcast is send out to resolve it. The broadcast address of (FFFFFFFF) is already stored, but not visible in the table. If a reply to an ARP broadcast is received by the router, the previously unknown address is entered in the cache. The next time the IP address needs to be resoved to an IP address, no broadcast will be necessary. Every listing in the cache has a timestamp and a TTL (time to live). When this time expires, the entry is deleted from the table to make room for new address resolutions. Should the cache become full and no TTLs have expired yet, then the oldest entry or entries are purged.

Ethernet Frames

The Data Link layer is responsible for combining bits into bytes and bytes into frames. Frames are used at the Data Link layer to encapsulate packets handed down from the Network layer for transmission on a type of media access. There are three types of media access methods: contention (Ethernet), token passing (Token Ring and FDDI), and polling (IBM Mainframes and 100VG-Anylan). This CCNA exam covers primarily Ethernet (contention) media access.

The function of Ethernet stations is to pass data frames between each other by using a group of bits known as a MAC frame format. This provides error detection from a cyclic redundancy check (CRC). However, remember that this is error detection, not error correction. The 802.3 and Ethernet frames is shown in Figure 7.2.

FIGURE 7.2: 802.3 and Ethernet frame formats

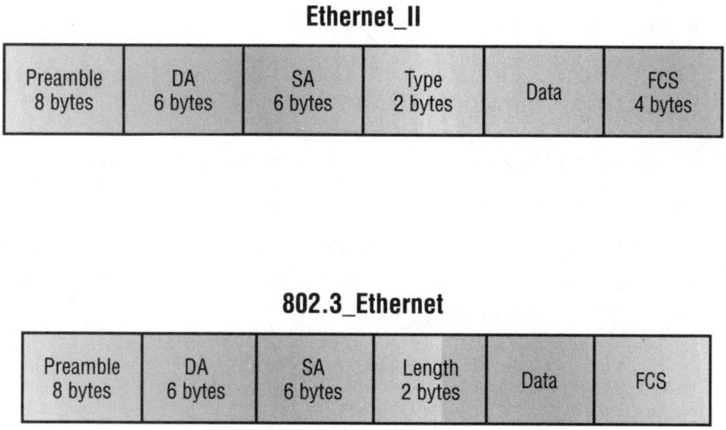

Ethernet_II

Preamble 8 bytes	DA 6 bytes	SA 6 bytes	Type 2 bytes	Data	FCS 4 bytes

802.3_Ethernet

Preamble 8 bytes	DA 6 bytes	SA 6 bytes	Length 2 bytes	Data	FCS

These are the fields in the 802.3 and Ethernet frame types:

Preamble   An alternating 1,0 pattern provides a 5 MHz clock at the start of each packet, which allows the receiving devices to lock the incoming bit stream. Uses either a SFD or Synch field to indicate to the receiving station that the data portion of the message will follow.

Start Frame Delimiter (SFD)/Synch The SFD field alternates 1,0,1,0,1,0, etc., and the Synch field is all 1s. The preamble and SFD/Synch field is 64 bits long.

Destination Address Transmits a 48-bit value using the least significant bit first. Used by each receiving station to determine whether incoming packet is addressed to its particular node. The destination address can be an individual address, broadcast or multicast MAC address. Remember that a broadcast is all ones, or Fs, in hex and is sent to all devices, where a multicast is sent to only a similar subset of nodes on a network.

Source Address 48-bit MAC address supplied by the transmitting device. It uses the least significant bit first. Broadcast and multicast address formats are illegal within the Source Address field.

Length or Type 802.3 uses a Length field, where the Ethernet frames uses a Type field, to identify the Network-layer protocol. 802.3 cannot identify the upper-layer protocol and must be used with a proprietary LAN; for example, IPX.

Data Packet sent down to the Data Link layer from the Network layer; 46 to 1500 bytes.

Frame Check Sequence (FCS) A field at the end of the frame, used to store the CRC.

Let's take a look at some frames caught on our trusty Etherpeek network analyzer. The frame below has only three fields: a destination, a source, and a type field:

```
Destination:   00:60:f5:00:1f:27
Source:        00:60:f5:00:1f:2c
Protocol Type:08-00   IP
```

This is an Ethernet_II frame. Notice the Type field is IP, or 08-00 in hexadecimal).

The next frame has the same fields, so it must also be an Ethernet_II frame. We put this one in so you could see that the frame can carry more than just IP. It can also carry IPX, or 81-37h. Notice that this frame was a broadcast:

```
Destination:  ff:ff:ff:ff:ff:ff Ethernet Broadcast
Source:       02:07:01:22:de:a4
Protocol Type:81-37  NetWare
```

You can tell because the destination hardware address is all 1s in binary, or all Fs in hexadecimal.

Notice the length field in the next frame:

```
Flags:        0x80  802.3
Status:       0x00
Packet Length:64
Timestamp:    12:45:45.192000 06/26/1998
Destination:  ff:ff:ff:ff:ff:ff Ethernet Broadcast
Source:       08:00:11:07:57:28
Length:       34
```

This must be an 802.3 frame. What protocol is this going to be handed to the Network layer? It doesn't say in the frame, so it must be IPX. Why? Because when Novell created the 802.3 frame type (before the IEEE did, and the IEEE called it 802.3 Raw), Novell was pretty much the only LAN server out there. So, Novell assumed that if you're running a LAN, it must be IPX.

802.2 and SNAP

Remember that the 802.3 Ethernet frame cannot by itself identify the upper-layer (Network) protocol. It needs help. The IEEE defined the 802.2 LLC specifications to provide this function and more. Figure 7.3 shows the IEEE 802.3 with LLC (802.2) and the Sub-Network Access Protocol (SNAP) frame types. This illustration shows how the LLC header information is added to the data portion of the frame.

FIGURE 7.3: 802.2 and SNAP frame types

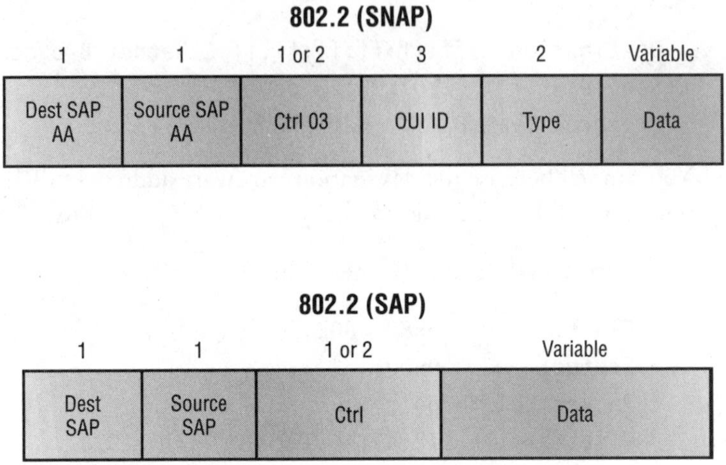

802.2 (SNAP)

1	1	1 or 2	3	2	Variable
Dest SAP AA	Source SAP AA	Ctrl 03	OUI ID	Type	Data

802.2 (SAP)

1	1	1 or 2	Variable
Dest SAP	Source SAP	Ctrl	Data

Now, let's take a look at an 802.2 frame and SNAP captured from our analyzer.

802.2 Frame

The following is an 802.2 frame captured with a protocol analyzer:

```
Flags:          0x80   802.3
Status:         0x02   Truncated
Packet Length:64
Slice Length:  51
Timestamp:      12:42:00.592000 03/26/1998
Destination:    ff:ff:ff:ff:ff:ff Ethernet Broadcast
Source:         00:80:c7:a8:f0:3d
LLC Length:     37
Dest. SAP:      0xe0   NetWare
Source SAP:     0xe0   NetWare  Individual LLC
↳Sublayer Management Function
Command:        0x03   Unnumbered Information
```

Notice the first frame has a length field, so it's probably an 802.3, right? But look again—it also has a DSAP and a SSAP, so it has to be an 802.2 frame. (Remember that an 802.2 frame is an 802.3 frame with the LLC information in the data field of the header, so we know what the upper-layer protocol is.)

SNAP Frame

The SNAP frame has its own Protocol field to identify the upper-layer protocol. This is really a way to allow an Ethernet_II frame to be used in an 802.3 frame. Even though the following network trace shows a protocol field, it is really an Ethernet_II type (Ether-Type) field. Here is a SNAP frame:

```
Flags:         0x80   802.3
  Status:         0x00
  Packet Length:78
  Timestamp:      09:32:48.264000 01/04/2000
802.3 Header
  Destination:  09:00:07:FF:FF:FF  AT Ph 2 Broadcast
  Source:       00:00:86:10:C1:6F
  LLC Length:   60
802.2 Logical Link Control (LLC) Header
  Dest. SAP:    0xAA   SNAP
  Source SAP:   0xAA   SNAP
  Command:      0x03   Unnumbered Information
  Protocol:     0x080007809B   AppleTalk
```

You can identify a SNAP frame, because the DSAP and SSAP fields are always AA, plus the command field is always 3. The reason this frame type was created is because not all protocols worked well with the 802.3 Ethernet frame that didn't have an Ether-Type field. To allow the proprietary protocols created by application developers to be used in the LLC frame, the IEEE then defined the SNAP format. It is not used that often, and it is mostly seen with AppleTalk and proprietary frames. Cisco uses a SNAP frame with their proprietary protocol CDP.

Ethernet at the Physical Layer

In a shared-hub Ethernet environment, if one station sends a frame, then all devices must synchronize to the digital signal being transmitted and extract the frame from the wire. All devices that use the same physical media and listen to each frame are considered in the same collision domain. This means that only one device can transmit at any given time, and any other device on the network segment must synchronize with the signal and extract the frame. If two stations try to transmit at the same time, a collision will occur. In 1984, the IEEE Ethernet committee released the CSMA/CD protocol. This basically tells all stations to constantly be listening for any other device trying to transmit at the same time they are and to stop and wait for a predetermined time if they do sense a collision.

Ethernet uses a bus topology, which means that whenever a device transmits, the signal must run from one end of the segment to the other. Ethernet also defined baseband technology, which means that when a station does transmit, it will use the entire bandwidth on the wire and will not share it.

Full-duplex Ethernet uses point-to-point connections and is typically referred to as collision-free because it doesn't share bandwidth with any other devices. Frames sent by two nodes cannot collide, because there are physically separate transmit and receive circuits between the nodes.

If you have a full-duplex 10 Mbps Ethernet operating bidirectionally on the same switch port, you can theoretically have aggregate throughput of 20 Mbps. Full-duplex can now be used in 10BaseT, 100BaseT, and 100BaseFL media, but only if all the other network devices (NICs, for example) can support full-duplex transmission.

Half-Duplex Ethernet Design

Half-duplex Ethernet has been around a long time. Ethernet_II came out in 1984 and is still the most popular of all LAN topologies. When a station is sending to another station, the transmitting circuitry is active at the transmitting station, and the receiving circuitry is active at the receiving station. This circuitry uses a single cable similar to a narrow, one-way bridge.

Full-Duplex Ethernet Design

Full-duplex Ethernet switch technology provides a point-to-point connection between the transmitter of the transmitting station and the receiver of the receiving station. With half-duplex circuitry, a standard Ethernet can usually provide only 50 to 60 percent of the bandwidth available. In contrast, full-duplex Ethernets can provide a full 100 percent, because they can transmit and receive simultaneously and because collisions don't occur.

In order to run a full-duplex Ethernet, you must have the following:

- Two 10 Mbps or 100 Mbps paths
- Full-duplex NICs
- Loopback and collision detection disabled
- Software drivers supporting two simultaneous data paths
- Adherence to Ethernet distance standards

Exam Essentials

Remember what is needed to run full-duplex.   You do not have to know the distance requirements, but it is important to understand the rest of the configuration requirements for running full-duplex.

Understand the definitions of half- and full-duplex.   Half-duplex uses a single cable similar to a narrow, one-way bridge. Full-duplex provides a point-to-point connection between the transmitter of the sending station and the receiver of the destination station. Full-duplex uses two cables—one to send and one to receive—so there should never be data collisions.

Key Terms and Concepts

Address Resolution Protocol (ARP)   Used to gain a hardware address from an IP address.

Ethernet   Contention media access method.

frame   A logical group of ones and zeros, defined at the Data Link layer, that is used to transmit packets over a LAN.

packet   Defined at the Network layer of the OSI Reference Model and used to route user data to remote networks.

full-duplex   Provides a point-to-point connection between the transmitter of the sending station and the receiver of the destination station.

half-duplex   Uses a single cable similar to a narrow, one-way bridge.

Sample Questions

1. Which of the following is true? (Choose all that apply.)

  A. Frames are defined at the Network layer.

  B. Frames are defined at the Data Link layer.

  C. Packets are defined at the Network layer.

  D. Packets are defined at the Data Link layer.

  Answer: B, C. Frames use hardware addressing, and packets use logical addressing.

2. Which statement is true about a MAC address?

  A. Routers use hardware addresses to find a network device on the remote side of another router.

  B. Routers use hardware addresses to find a network device on a LAN.

  C. MAC addresses are 8 bytes long.

  D. MAC addresses are only used in Ethernet networks.

Answer: B. Any network device, not just a router, uses a hardware address to find a network device on a local network, never a remote network.

3. Which of the following statements describes half-duplex?

A. It provides a point-to-point connection between the transmitter of the transmitting station and the receiver of the receiving station.

B. It is used in all Cisco switches.

C. It uses a single cable similar to a narrow one-way bridge.

D. It is no longer supported.

Answer: C. Half-duplex uses a single cable for both sending and receiving data. This allows data collisions and other bandwidth problems in Ethernet.

4. Which of the following statements describes full-duplex?

A. It provides a point-to-point connection between the transmitter of the sending station and the receiver of the destination station.

B. It uses a single cable similar to a narrow, one-way bridge.

C. It is used in all Cisco switches.

D. When you upgrade your servers to full-duplex, all clients must be upgraded at the same time.

Answer: A. Full-duplex uses separate cables for sending and receiving data. One transmits, the other sends, allowing for simultaneous two-way communication.

Fast Ethernet

Having a fundamental understanding of Fast Ethernet is useful for administrators working in a production environment. When you take the CCNA exam, this knowledge will help you answer questions regarding other exam objectives, although there may not be any questions specifically pertaining to Fast Ethernet. It is important not to skip any of the exam objectives as you study for the test, even if you do not expect to see test questions on all the objectives.

This section covers how Cisco views the features and benefits of Fast Ethernet.

Critical Information

In 1995, the IEEE approved the IEEE 802.3u, the 100BaseT Fast Ethernet standard. It defines the Physical and Data Link layers, uses the CSMA/CD (Carrier Sense Multiple Access with Collision Detection) protocol, and is 10 times faster than 10BaseT. These are some of the new technology stars:

100BaseFX Ethernet over fiber at 100 Mbps using 802.3 specs. It uses two-strand–, 50/125–, or 62.5/125–micron multimode fiber optic cable.

100BaseT4 Using 802.3 specs, carries 100 Mbps over Category 3, 4, or 5 UTP cabling with a standard RJ-45 connector. 100BaseT4 uses all eight wires on a RJ-45 connector.

100BaseTX Fast Ethernet over Category 5 UTP cabling. It's compatible with, and adheres to, 802.3 specifications. It can also use two-pair, 100-ohm shielded twisted-pair (STP) cable or Type 1 STP cable.

100BaseX This refers to either the 100BaseTX or 100BaseFX media. This standard was approved to ensure compatibility between the Ethernet CSMA/CD and the ANSI X3T9.5 standard.

100VG-AnyLAN An IEEE movement into Fast Ethernet and Token Ring that doesn't appear to be taking off, mostly because it's not compatible with the 802.3 standards and Cisco doesn't support it.

Advantages of Fast Ethernet

Migrating or upgrading your network to 100BaseT from 10BaseT can substantially improve throughput and overall performance. Because 100BaseT uses the same signaling techniques as 10BaseT, a gradual migration to 100BaseT doesn't have to be expensive or time-consuming. Partially converting a LAN is a viable alternative to converting all clients simultaneously. These are some of the advantages of 100BaseT over 10BaseT:

- 100BaseT has 10 times the performance of 10BaseT.

- Existing cabling and network equipment can be used.

- It can use 10 Mbps and 100 Mbps together.

- 100BaseT uses tried-and-true CSMA/CD technology.

- Migration is easy.

100BaseT networks use the same "time slots" as 10BaseT networks. What are time slots? They require a station to transmit all its bits before another station can transmit its packet. For 100BaseT networks to transmit in the same time slots, the distance must be reduced. This means that instead of the 5-4-3 rule that the standard Ethernet uses (five network segments, four repeaters, only three segments populated), you can use only two Class II repeaters in a 100BaseT network. The timing in Fast Ethernet is shorter (10 percent of Ethernet). The maximum frame size, or time slot, is 1518 bytes. The physical distance is reduced because both Fast and regular Ethernet specifications state that the round-trip time must not exceed 512 bit times. Since Fast Ethernet transmits faster, a signal of 512 bits covers a shorter distance.

Exam Essentials

Remember the advantages of Fast Ethernet.   It's much faster than 10BaseT, is easy to migrate, and uses CSMA/CD.

Key Terms and Concepts

100BaseFX   Ethernet over fiber at 100 Mbps using 802.3 specs. It uses two-strand, 50/125– or 62.5/125–micron multimode fiber optic cable.

100BaseTX   Fast Ethernet over Category 5 UTP cabling. It's compatible with, and adheres to, 802.3 specifications. It can also use two-pair, 100-ohm shielded twisted pair (STP) cable or Type 1 STP cable.

Carrier Sense Multiple Access with Collision Detection (CSMA/CD) Protocol designed to run with Ethernet networks. It helps nodes communicate on a physical medium.

repeater   Physical device used to extend the distance of a digital signal.

Sample Questions

1. What is an advantage of migrating to Fast Ethernet?

A. Easier to administrate

B. Less expensive than 10BaseT

C. Easy migration from 10 Mbps Ethernet

D. Makes servers faster

Answer: C. It is easy to migrate to Fast Ethernet because it uses the same signaling techniques as 10 Mbps Ethernet.

2. What is the specification for Ethernet over fiber at 100 Mbps using 802.3 specs?

A. 100BaseTX

B. 100BaseFX

C. 100BaseT

D. 100VG AnyLan

Answer: B. 100BaseFX is the Ethernet over fiber at 100 Mbps using 802.3 specs.

3. What does the *FX* in 100BaseFX represent?

A. Full-duplex

B. Fast UTP

C. Fiber optics

D. Finally Xerox specifications

Answer: C. 100BaseFX is Ethernet over fiber at 100 Mbps.

Gigabit Ethernet

Gigabit Ethernet is the newest member of the Ethernet family, and it's very welcome. It is still not very widely implemented, but that will change in the near future.

Not too much is needed to understand about Gigabit Ethernet for the new CCNA exam.

Critical Information

Understanding the difference between the different media access speeds that Ethernet provides is important. The Electronic Industries Association and the newer Telecommunications Industry Association (EIA/TIA) are the standards bodies that create the Physical-layer specifications for Ethernet. The EIA/TIA specifies that Ethernet use a registered jack connector with a 45 wiring sequence (RJ-45) on unshielded twisted-pair (UTP) cabling. The following points outline the different Ethernet media requirements for Gigabit Ethernet:

- 1000BaseCX: Copper shielded twisted-pair that can only run up to 25 meters

- 1000BaseT: Category 5, 4-pair UTP wiring, up to 100 meters

- 1000BaseSX: Multimode fiber using 62.5- and 50-micron core, uses a 780-nanometer laser, and can go up to 260 meters

- 1000BaseLX: Single-mode fiber that uses a 9-micron core, 1300-nanometer laser, and can go up to 10 km.

Exam Essentials

Remember the distance of 1000BaseSX. This is multimode fiber using 62.5- and 50-micron core; it uses a 780-nanometer laser and can go up to 260 meters.

Key Terms and Concepts

Ethernet Contention media access method.

Gigabit Ethernet Contention media access method running at gigabit speed.

Sample Questions

1. What is the maximum cable distance of 1000BaseCX?

A. 25 meters

B. 260 meters

C. 100 meters

D. 328 feet

Answer: A. The maximum cable distance for 100BaseCX (copper cabling) is 25 meters.

2. What is the maximum cable distance for 1000BaseSX?

A. 25 meters

B. 260 meters

C. 100 meters

D. 328 feet

Answer: B. The maximum cable distance for 1000BaseSX cabling is 260 meters.

Token Ring

Token Ring is a LAN token-passing media access method that runs at 4 or 16 Mbps. This objective covers far more than you need to know for the CCNA exam.

Critical Information

IBM created Token Ring in the 1970s; it was popular with true-blue customers needing to migrate from a mainframe environment. It lost to Ethernet in the popularity polls because it's pricey by comparison. However, depending on what you're looking for, Token Ring is a more resilient network, especially under heavy loads. Sometimes you actually do get what you pay for.

Like Ethernet, the IEEE came out with its own standard for Token Ring, designated 802.5. This standard was so close to the IBM standard that the IEEE is now responsible for administrating both specifications.

At the Physical layer, Token Ring runs as a star topology using shielded twisted-pair (STP) wiring. Each station connects to a central hub called a multistation access unit (MSAU). Logically, it runs in a ring where each station receives signals from its nearest active upstream neighbor (NAUN) and repeats these signals to its downstream neighbors.

Token Ring uses MAC addresses like Ethernet does, but that's where the similarities end. Token Ring media access is described point by point below:

- Stations can't transmit whenever they want like Ethernet stations can. Instead, they have to wait to be given a special frame called a token. When a station receives a token, it does one of two things:

  - It appends the data it wants to send onto the end of the frame, then changes the T bit in the frame. Doing that alerts the receiving station that data is attached.

  - If the station that gets a token doesn't need to send any data, it simply passes the token on to the next station in the ring.

- The information frame circles the ring until it gets to the destination station. The destination station copies the frame and then tags the frame as being copied. The frame continues around until it reaches the originating station, which then removes the tag.

- Typically, only one frame can be on a ring at any given time. However, by using early token release, a station can transmit a new token onto the ring after transmitting its first frame.

- Collisions don't happen, because stations can't transmit unless they have a token.

Active Monitor

One station on a Token Ring network is always an active monitor. The active monitor makes sure that there isn't more than one token on the ring at any given time. Also, if a transmitting station fails, that station isn't able to remove the token as it makes it way back through the ring. Should this occur, the active monitor would step in, remove the token, and then generate a new one. In addition, many stations on the ring will be designated as standby monitors (to act as backups) in case the active monitor goes offline.

Exam Essentials

Remember that Token Ring uses an active monitor. The active monitor makes sure that there isn't more than one token on the Ring at any given time.

Key Terms and Concepts

Token Ring Token-passing media access method that has no collisons.

active monitor Machine that makes sure there is only one token on the ring at any given time.

Sample Question

1. What is the active monitor used for in a Token Ring network?

   A. Makes sure that there isn't more than one token on the ATM ring network at any given time

   B. Makes sure that there isn't more than one token on the Ethernet ring at any given time

   C. Makes sure that there isn't more than one token on the ring at any given time

   D. Makes sure that there is more than one token on the ring at any given time

   Answer: C. The active monitor for Token Ring monitors the ring to make sure that there is only one token circulating through the virtual ring of nodes.

Chapter

8

Physical Connectivity

CISCO EXAM OBJECTIVES COVERED IN THIS CHAPTER:

► **IEEE Standards** *(pages 234 – 240)*

► **ANSI Standards** *(pages 241 – 244)*

his chapter will cover the Institute of Electrical and Electronics Engineers (IEEE) and American National Standards Institute (ANSI) standards that are covered on the CCNA exam.

There are quite a few different standards created by these groups, and a whole book could be written on each set. We will shorten this down to what you need to know for the CCNA exam only.

IEEE Standards

The IEEE has created what is called the 802 series of standards. The "802" comes from the date they were introduced (February of 1980). We will discuss the different IEEE standards, but we'll really focus on the IEEE standards for Ethernet, which is what you are tested on for the CCNA exam.

Critical Information

Table 8.1 describes the different IEEE standards. The CCNA exam is concerned only with the 802.3 specifications.

TABLE 8.1: IEEE Standards

Standard	Description
802.1	Specification for Spanning-Tree Protocol (STP)
802.2	Specification for the LLC sublayer of the Data Link layer

TABLE 8.1: IEEE Standards *(continued)*

Standard	Description
802.3	Data Link and Physical layer specifications for CSMA/CD access method
802.3u	Specifications for CSMA/CD Fast Ethernet
802.3z	Specifications for CSMA/CD Gigabit Ethernet
802.4	Token Bus specification
802.5	Token Ring Specification
802.6	Metropolitan area network (MAN) specifications based on Distributed Queue Dual Bus (DQDB) technology
802.12	Demand Priority access method

IEEE 802.3

In 1980, Digital, Intel, and Xerox created the original Ethernet_I. Predictably, Ethernet_II followed, in 1982. Ethernet_II is also described as Carrier Sense Multiple Access with Collision Detection (CSMA/CD). In response, the IEEE created the 802.3 subcommittee to come up with an Ethernet standard that happens to be almost identical to the Ethernet_II version of Ethernet. The two differ only in their descriptions of the Data Link layer. Ethernet_II has a Type field, whereas 802.3 has a Length field. Even so, they're both common in their Physical-layer specifications, MAC addressing, and understanding of the LLC sublayer's responsibilities.

Ethernet_II and 802.3 both define a bus-topology LAN at 10 Mbps with baseband technology, and the cabling defined in these standards is identical:

The original IEEE 802.3 standards are the following:

10Base2 10 Mbps, baseband technology, up to 185 meters in length. Known as thinnet, it can support up to 30 workstations on a single segment.

10Base5   10 Mbps, baseband technology, up to 500 meters in length. Known as thicknet, it can support up to 208 workstations per segment.

10BaseT   10 Mbps using Category 3 twisted-pair wiring. Unlike 10Base2 and 10Base5 networks, each device must connect into a hub or switch, and you can only have one host per segment or wire.

Each of the 802.3 standards defines an Attachment Unit Interface (AUI), which allows a one-bit-at-a-time transfer to the Physical layer from the Data Link media access method. This allowed the MAC to remain constant while the Physical layer can support any existing and new technologies The original AUI interface was a 15-pin connector, which allowed a transceiver (transmitter/receiver) that provides a 15-pin to twisted-pair conversion. Typically, the AUI has a transceiver built in, and the connections are now usually just RJ-45 connections; however, AUI ports can support BNC and fiber connectors using specialized tranceivers.

However, the AUI interface cannot support 100 Mbps Ethernet because of the high frequencies involved. 100BaseT needed a new interface, and the 802.3u specifications created a new interface called the Media Independent Interface (MII), which provides 100 Mbps throughput. The MII transfers in units known as nibbles, that is, 4 bits at a time. Gigabit Ethernet uses a Gigabit Media Independent Interface (GMII), which is 8 bits at a time.

Ethernet is a media access method that is specified at the Data Link layer and uses specific Physical-layer cabling and signaling techniques. It is important to be able to differentiate between the types of connectors that can be used to connect an Ethernet network together. We'll discuss the various unshielded twisted-pair (UTP) cablings used today in an Ethernet LAN.

Cabling the Ethernet Local Area Network

The first Ethernet LAN specification was created and implemented by Digital, Intel, and Xerox. The IEEE used this specification to create the IEEE 802.3 committee. This was a 10 Mbps network that ran on coax, twisted-pair, and fiber physical media.

The IEEE extended the 802.3 committee to two new committees known as 802.3u (Fast Ethernet) and 802.3z (Gigabit Ethernet). These are both specified on twisted-pair and fiber physical media. Figure 8.1 shows the IEEE 802.3 and original Ethernet Physical-layer specifications.

FIGURE 8.1: Ethernet Physical-layer specifications

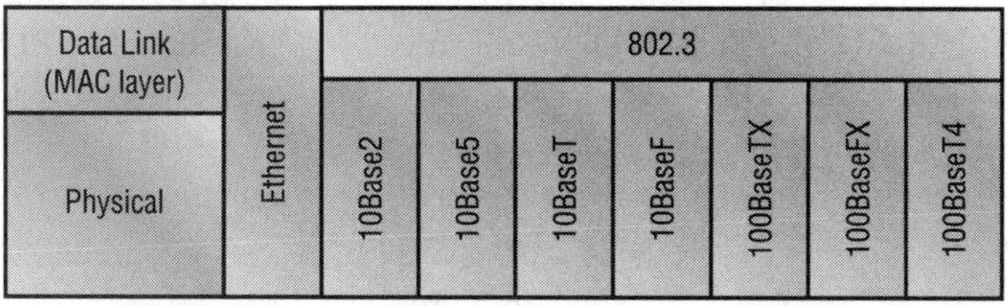

When designing your LAN, it is important to be able to understand the different types of Ethernet media available. It would certainly be great to run Gigabit Ethernet to each desktop and 10 Gbps between switches, and this might happen one day, but it is unrealistic to think you can cost-justify that network today. By mixing and matching the different types of Ethernet media methods today, you can create a cost-justifying network that works great.

The following points give a general understanding of where to use the different Ethernet media in your hierarchical network:

- 10 Mbps switches can be used at the Access layer to provide good performance at a low price. 100 Mbps links can be used for high-bandwidth-consuming clients or servers. No servers should be at 10 Mbps if possible.

- Use Fast Ethernet between Access-layer switches and Distribution-layer switches. 10 Mbps links would create a bottleneck.

- Use Fast Ethernet (or Gigabit if applicable) between Distribution-layer switches and the Core. Also, links between the Core switches should be implementing the fastest media you can afford. Dual links between Distribution and Core switches are recommend for redundancy and load balancing.

Ethernet Media and Connector Requirements

Understanding the differences between the various media access speeds that Ethernet provides is important. However, understanding the connector requirements for each implementation is also a consideration before making any decision.

The Electronic Industries Association and the newer Telecommunications Industry Association (EIA/TIA) are the standards bodies that creates the Physical-layer specifications for Ethernet. The EIA/TIA specifies that Ethernet use a registered jack connector with a 45 wiring sequence (RJ-45) on unshielded twisted-pair (UTP) cabling. Table 8.2 outlines the Ethernet media requirements:

TABLE 8.2: Ethernet Media Requirements

Cable Type	Requirements
10Base2	50-ohm coax, called thinnet. Up to 185 meters and 30 hosts per segment. Uses a physical and logical bus with AUI connectors.
10Base5	50-ohm coax, called thicknet. Up to 500 meters and 208 users per segment. Uses a physical and logical bus with AUI connectors.
10BaseT	EIA/TIA Category 3, 4, or 5 two-pair UTP wiring. One user per segment, up to 100 meters. Uses RJ-45 connectors with a physical star topology and a logical bus.
100BaseTX	EIA/TIA Category 5, 6, or 7 two-pair UTP wiring. One user per segment, up to 100 meters. Uses RJ-45 MII connectors with a physical star topology and a logical bus.
100BaseFX	Uses fiber cabling 62.5/125–micron multimode fiber. Point-to-point topology, up to 400 meters in length. Uses ST or SC connectors, which are duplex media-interface connectors.
1000BaseCX	Copper shielded twisted-pair (STP) that can only run up to 25 meters.
1000BaseT	Category 5, 4-pair UTP wiring, up to 100 meters.

TABLE 8.2: Ethernet Media Requirements *(continued)*

Cable Type	Requirements
1000BaseSX	Multimode fiber using 62.5- and 50-micron core, uses a 780-nanometer laser, and can go up to 260 meters.
1000BaseLX	Single-mode fiber that uses a 9-micron core, uses 1300-nanometer laser, and can go up to 10 km.

Exam Essentials

Remember the different 802.3 Ethernet specifications. 802.3 is 10 Mbps Ethernet, 802.3u is Fast Ethernet, and 802.3z is Gigabit Ethernet.

Remember the distance for the various standards. 10BaseT has a maximum distance of 100 meters. 100BaseT has a maximum of 100 meters. 100BaseSX can go up to 260 meters.

Understand baseband technology. Baseband technology, in contrast to broadband technology, uses the entire bandwidth for one digital signal. All LANs are baseband technology.

Key Terms

802   IEEE body overseeing the standards for LANs.

802.3   IEEE LAN protocol that defines the MAC sublayer of the Data Link layer and Physical layer using CSMA/CD.

802.3u   Fast Ethernet implementation of CSMA/CD.

802.3z   Gigabit Ethernet implementation of CSMA/CD.

Sample Questions

1. What is the IEEE standard for Fast Ethernet?

A. 802.2

B. 802.3

C. 802.3u

D. 802.3z

Answer: C. The IEEE standard for Fast Ethernet cabling is the IEEE 802.3u standard.

2. What does the "base" in 10BaseT mean?

A. Basement technology

B. Backbone technology

C. Baseband technology

D. Broadband technology

Answer: C. The "base" in 10BaseT stands for baseband technology.

3. What is the maximum distance of 100BaseT?

A. 100 feet

B. 100 meters

C. 400 feet

D. 100 feet

Answer: B. The maximum distance for both 100BaseT and 10BaseT is 100 meters, or approximately 300 feet.

ANSI Standards

The ANSI (American National Standards Institute) standard that you need to be aware of for the CCNA exam is Fiber Distributed Data Interface (FDDI). We will cover more than you need to know for the CCNA exam.

Critical Information

FDDI, as shown in Figure 8.2, is a token-passing media access topology. ANSI X3T9.5 defines the standard for a dual Token Ring LAN operating at 100 Mbps over fiber optics. Copper Distributed Data Interface (CDDI) can be used with UTP cable to connect servers or other stations directly into the ring (see Figure 8.2).

FIGURE 8.2: FDDI

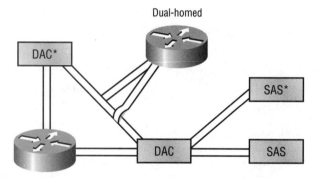

* Dual Attached Connection
* Single Attached Station

The advantages of FDDI include the following:

- FDDI can run very long distances and can do so in electronically hostile environments where a lot of electromagnetic, radio, or frequency interference is present.

- It runs at a high speed compared with 10 Mbps Ethernet and 4/16 Mbps Token Ring LANs. FDDI can run at 200 Mbps if dual rings are active.

- FDDI employs a token-passing media access with dual counter-rotating rings, as shown in Figure 8.3. Typically, only one ring is active at any given time. That way, if a break or outage occurs, the FDDI ring will wrap back the other direction, keeping the ring intact. Some stations can be attached to both rings for redundancy reasons; these are known as dual attachment stations and would be used mostly for high-availability stations like servers.

- Cisco routers can attach with a technique called dual-homing. This provides fault tolerance by providing a primary and backup path to the FDDI ring.

- FDDI is both a logical and physical ring—the only LAN that is an actual, physical ring. Like Token Ring, FDDI provides predictable deterministic delays and priorities.

- FDDI uses MAC addresses like other LANs do, but it uses a different numbering scheme. Instead of the eight-bit bytes that Ethernet and Token Ring uses, it applies four-bit symbols. FDDI has 12 four-bit symbols that make up its MAC addresses.

- Token Ring allows only one token on the ring at any given time, whereas FDDI permits several tokens to be present on the ring concurrently.

Some drawbacks of migrating to FDDI include the following:

- Relatively high latency occurs when Ethernet-to-FDDI and FDDI-to-Ethernet translation is performed between LANs.

- Capacity is still shared because FDDI dual ring is a shared LAN.

- There's no full duplex capability in shared networks.

- It's expensive—very expensive! FDDI components—i.e., hubs and NICs—aren't exactly bargain equipment.

Figure 8.3 shows how an FDDI LAN would wrap the primary ring back to the standby, secondary ring if a failure occurred.

FIGURE 8.3: Dual-ring reliability

Primary and secondary
rings will wrap to maintain
network reliability.

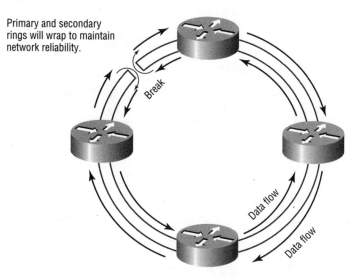

When a station realizes that no tokens have been received from its
nearest active upstream neighbor (NAUN) for a predetermined
period, it sends out a beacon as an alert and as an attempt to locate
the failure. Once it starts to receive its own beacons, it assumes the
ring is up and running. If it doesn't receive its beacon back in a predetermined amount of time, the primary ring will wrap to the secondary ring as shown.

Exam Essentials

Know the top speed of FDDI.   You can get 200 Mbps on a FDDI if
dual rings are used

Key Terms and Concepts

Fiber Distributed Data Interface (FDDI)   A token-passing, physical
ring technology.

token passing Media access method that allows workstations to transmit when they receive a token.

Sample Questions

1. What is the most throughput possible for FDDI?

   A. 100 Mbps

   B. 200 Mbps

   C. 500 Mbps

   D. 1000 Mbps

   Answer: B. The top throughput for FDDI is 200 Mbps using 100 Mbps on each of the two rings.

2. What type of media access does FDDI use?

   A. Contention

   B. Token-passing

   C. Polling

   D. Demand access

   Answer: B. Token passing is used in both FDDI and Token Ring environments. A token is passed, and the interface that holds the token is allowed to transmit data. The rest of the nodes must wait until it is their turn to transmit when they get the token.

Chapter

9

Cisco Basics, IOS, and Network Basics

ou can use all of the commands we review in this objective in your production network. To truly learn and understand these commands, you need hands-on experience. Practice the commands over and over again before you take the CCNA exam and before trying them on a real network. As you practice, pay close attention to the details of what a command is really doing and the information it can provide.

This chapter starts with the basics: how to log in to a router and the two different modes that a router provides. You will then learn how to use the question mark to access help when using Cisco commands. The command history and editing features will be talked about in detail, as well as the different types of memory a Cisco router uses.

After that, we'll cover what happens when a router boots up and which files it uses to boot. You will learn how to view these files and copy them. One of the most useful topics we'll discuss is how to set your router passwords, banners, and identification.

Cisco routers can be configured manually or with a setup routine. We will go through both methods in this chapter. You will also learn how to copy and restore a Cisco IOS.

The commands to troubleshoot an internetwork are included in this chapter; using Cisco router IOS and the different switching modes within a router will be discussed as well.

This chapter will end with a discussion on the Cisco IOS that is used on the 1900 switch. You'll learn how to log in, set your passwords, and configure an IP address.

IOS CLI Router

This objective is dedicated to the Cisco IOS (Internetworking Operating System). It will help you learn hands-on techniques for configuring a command-line interface (CLI) router and switch.

This is obviously important for production networks, but it is essential to understand for the CCNA exam.

Critical Information

You first log in to user mode and then can change to privileged mode. It is important to remember how to log in to both modes and the different commands that can be run in each.

Cisco routers are configured from the user interface, which you can run either from the console port on the router or by telnetting to the router from another host through any router interface. You can also connect a modem to the auxiliary port and dial into the router for console access.

The Exec Command Interpreter

Cisco IOS software has a command interpreter called the Exec. The Exec first interprets the command you type and then executes the operation you've commanded. (You have to log in to the router before an Exec command can be entered.)

The Exec has two levels of access: user and privileged. These two levels, sometimes referred to as modes, serve as security for access into the different levels of commands.

User mode is for ordinary tasks like checking a router's status, connecting to remote devices, making temporary changes to terminal settings, and viewing basic system information. But in this mode, your view of the router's configuration and your troubleshooting capabilities are very limited.

Privileged mode is used to change the configuration of the router. (From here, you can access the configuration mode discussed next.) The commands in privileged mode include all those in user mode, plus those used to set operating system parameters, get detailed information on a router's status, test and run debug operations, and access global configuration modes.

Very few procedures are involved in logging in, but they are important to know both when you configure a Cisco router and when you take the CCNA exam.

Logging In to User Mode

You can connect to a router and log in by attaching a console cable to the console port of the router. The other end of the console cable should be connected to a PC or terminal. If you are using a PC, you must use a terminal emulation program such as Hyperterminal. When using Hyperterminal, you should set the settings to the following:

Setting	Option
Bits Per Second	9600
Data Bits	8
Parity	None
Stop Bits	1
Flow Control	None

Once this is done, you will be asked to press Enter to continue.

If a user-mode password is configured on the console line, you will have to enter this password before gaining access to user mode. If no password is assigned, you will be greeted with a Router> prompt. The > prompt indicates that you are in user mode. Here is an example:

```
Bob con0 is now available
Press RETURN to get started.
User Access Verification
Password:
Bob>
```

Logging In to Privileged Mode

Once you are in user mode, you can enter privileged mode by typing **enable** and then providing the password when prompted. Type **disable** to return to user mode, as in this example (note that the password does not appear on the screen):

```
Bob>enable
Password:
Bob#disable
Bob>
```

Initial Configuration Using the Setup Command

If you use the commands write erase or erase startup-config and then either reload your router or power it off and on, you'll see the system configuration dialog screen. You can also type **setup** within privileged mode to get the dialog screen at any time, which can be helpful in configuring your router.

For this section of the exam, you'll need to know how to configure a router using the setup command. The setup command can be helpful, but it is not necessarily one you'll use in a production environment. It may prompt you for commands that you don't use in your internetwork, which can be tedious. When going through this section, notice the difference between configuring your router using the initial setup and the setup command, including which management prompts you are using.

Using the Initial Setup or the Setup Command

If you erase the startup-config file and reboot your router, you will see the following dialog upon bootup:

```
Notice: NVRAM invalid, possibly due to write erase.
       --- System Configuration Dialog ---
At any point you may enter a question mark '?' for
↳help.
Use CTRL-c to abort configuration dialog at any
↳prompt.
Default settings are in square brackets '[]'.
```

```
Would you like to enter the initial configuration
⤷dialog? [yes][Enter]
```

Press Enter at the [yes] prompt to continue with the configuration and see how the router responds:

```
First, would you like to see the current interface
⤷summary? [yes][Enter]

Any interface listed with OK? value "NO" does not have
a valid configuration
Interface   IP-Address   OK?  Method   Status  Protocol
Ethernet0   unassigned   NO   not set  up      down
Serial0     unassigned   NO   not set  up      down
Serial1     unassigned   NO   not set  up      down
Configuring global parameters:
```

By pressing Enter at the [yes] prompt to view the current interface summary, you're assured that the power-on self-test (POST) has found all the interfaces.

In this case, you have two serial ports and one Ethernet port. They aren't okay (see the NO not set next to them?), because they aren't set up yet. They're designated as unassigned. The router now wants the name of the router you're trying to configure, which is RouterA in this example. Type that now and then press Enter. The router responds with this dialog (we'll show the passwords from here on, but remember that they won't be seen on screen):

```
Enter host name [Router]:RouterA
The enable secret is a one-way cryptographic secret used
instead of the enable password when it exists.
Enter enable secret:sean
The enable password is used when there is no enable
secret and when using older software and some boot
images.
Enter enable password:seanx
  Enter virtual terminal password:seanvty
  Configure SNMP Network Management? [yes]:n
```

```
  Configure IP? [yes][Enter]
Configure IP? [yes][Enter]
    Configure IGRP routing? [yes]:n
    Configure RIP routing? [no]:[Enter]

Configuring interface parameters:

Configuring interface Ethernet0:
  Is this interface in use? [yes][Enter]
  Configure IP on this interface? [yes][Enter]
    IP address for this interface:172.16.10.1
    Number of bits in subnet field [0]:8
    Class B network is 172.16.0.0, 8 subnet bits;
↳mask is 255.255.255.0

Configuring interface Serial0:
  Is this interface in use? [yes]:[Enter]
  Configure IP on this interface? [yes]:[Enter]
  Configure IP unnumbered on this interface?
↳[no]:[Enter]
    IP address for this interface:172.16.20.1
    Number of bits in subnet field [8]:[Enter]
    Class B network is 172.16.0.0, 8 subnet bits;
↳mask is 255.255.255.0

Configuring interface Serial1:
  Is this interface in use? [yes]:n
```

Notice that we had you reply *no* to the routing commands like RIP and IGRP. Also notice that for the subnet mask, you were to enter **8** for the number of bits. The router doesn't count the default masks in the number of bits, so even though you set the number of bits to 8, the subnet mask will still be realized as 255.255.255.0. The third byte is the only one used for subnetting.

After you answer no to configuring Serial1, the router shows the configuration it created. It then asks whether you want to save the configuration:

```
Use this configuration? [yes/no]:y
```

Type **y** for *yes*, and then press Enter. The router saves the configuration to nonvolatile RAM (which is explained in the section "Router Memory" below).

Context-Sensitive Help

Some of the commands used to configure and administer a Cisco router can be hard to remember. By using the context-sensitive help facility, you can get either the next possible command or a list of commands that start with a certain letter.

You can access a help screen for any command by typing a question mark (?) after the command. This will give you a list of the commands available. You can then choose the next command in the command string and type a question mark again to get the next command, and so on until you have the complete command string.

For example, if you need to set the clock on your router, but you don't know what the commands are, you could type **clock ?**. You must leave one space between the command **clock** (or another command) and the question mark, or your query won't work. In this example, the next command is **set**; you would type **clock set** and then a space and a question mark to get the next command, and so on until you have the complete command string.

Suppose you need to know all the commands that start with *cl* because you can't remember the command you need. You can type **cl?** to see all the commands that start with *cl*. Notice that there is no space between the letters and the question mark. This tells the Exec to give you all the commands that start with *cl*.

To master the help features Cisco provides, you need to practice using question-mark commands on a Cisco router. The following example shows how to set the router time using the help screens. Notice the difference between typing **clock** ? and **cl**?:

```
Router#cl?
clear  clock
Router#clock ?
set  Set the time and date
```

Notice the space between clock and ?. You could also type **clo** ?.

Look at the last line of the previous example. This tells you the next command is set and that this command is used to set the date and time. This form of help is called command syntax help, because it tells you which keywords or arguments are required to continue with a command.

Next, type **clock set** ? as follows:

```
Router#clock set ?
  hh:mm:ss  Current Time (hh:mm:ss)
```

Doing this has given you even more information on how to set the clock. Now type **clock set 10:29:30** ? like this:

```
Router#clock set 10:29:30 ?
  <1-31>  Day of the month
  MONTH  Month of the year
```

The router responds by giving you a message that it wants information about the day and month. So you need to type in more information, as in this example:

```
RouterB#clock set 10:29:30 23 5
                               ^
% Invalid input detected at '^' marker
```

Notice that if you type a number (5, in this case) instead of the name of the month (May), you receive a % Invalid input message. The router is very clear about what it considers invalid input—it includes a caret symbol (^) to indicate where the error is in the command.

To continue, type in **clock set 10:29:30 23 May ?** as seen here:

```
Router#clock set 10:29:30 23 May ?
  <1993-2035>  Year
```

Okay, the router accepted May and now wants you to specify the year. So, to finish this command, type in **clock set 10:29:30 23 May 2001.**

Command History and Editing Features

The user interface comes with an advanced editing feature that can help you type repetitive commands. This feature helps administrators configure routers efficiently. The command history and editing features do not change the configuration in any way; their only purpose is to make things easier for the administrator.

First of all, you can turn off the advanced editing features at any time by typing the command **terminal no editing**; you can re-enable them by entering **terminal editing**.

Using the advanced editing features is completely up to the administrator configuring the router. None of the advanced editing feature commands are mandatory in any configuration—unless you are taking the CCNA exam, of course!

Table 9.1 describes the different commands used to edit and review the command history.

TABLE 9.1: Router-Command History

Command	Purpose
Ctrl+A	Move to the beginning of the command line
Ctrl+E	Move to the end of the command line
Ctrl+F (or right arrow)	Move forward one character
Ctrl+B (or left arrow)	Move back one character

TABLE 9.1: Router-Command History *(continued)*

Command	Purpose
Ctrl+P (or up arrow)	Repeat previous command
Ctrl+N (or down arrow)	Repeat most recent command
Esc+B	Move backward one word
Esc+F	Move forward one word
Router>**show history**	Show command buffer
Router>**terminal history size**	Set command buffer size .
Router>**terminal no editing**	Disable advanced editing features
Router>**terminal editing**	Re-enable advanced editing

Another helpful editing feature is Tab, which completes an entry for you. For example, you could type in **sh run** and then press the Tab key:

```
Router#sh run[Tab]
Router#sh running-config
```

The router finishes typing in sh running-config for you. Remember to use Tab for those long commands.

Router Memory

These are the different types of memory used in a Cisco router:

ROM   is used by the router to store the bootstrap startup program, operating system software, and power-on self-test (POST). ROM chips are installed in sockets on the router's motherboard so that they can be replaced or upgraded. The IOS included in the ROM is a scaled-down, and usually older, version.

Flash   is basically an erasable, reprogrammable ROM that holds the operating system image and microcode. It allows you to "flash" the router and perform upgrades without removing and replacing chips on the motherboard. Flash is retained even when the router is turned off.

RAM provides caching and packet buffering, plus information like routing tables. RAM is used to hold the running operating system when the router is powered on; it is cleared when the router is reset or powered off.

Nonvolatile RAM (NVRAM) stores the router's startup configuration file. NVRAM retains its information even when the router is rebooted or shut down.

Files Stored in Memory

These are the files stored in the different types of memory defined above:

- startup-config
- running-config
- Cisco IOS

startup-config

The startup configuration file (startup-config) is held in NVRAM. When the router is started, the file is accessed and placed into DRAM (sometimes just referred to as RAM). Type **show startup-config** to see the configuration, as in this example:

```
RouterB#sh startup-config
Using 661 out of 32762 bytes
!
version 11.0
service udp-small-servers
service tcp-small-servers
!
hostname RouterB
!
enable secret 5 $1$jMYk$21eDXo8XXwrBiVm5RR9wN.
```

```
enable password password
!
!
interface Ethernet0
 ip address 172.16.30.1 255.255.255.0
!
interface Serial0
 ip address 172.16.20.2 255.255.255.0
 no fair-queue
 clockrate 56000
!
interface Serial1
 ip address 172.16.40.1 255.255.255.0
 clockrate 56000
```

running-config

The running configuration file is the configuration from NVRAM placed in RAM at startup. By typing **config terminal** (**config t** will also work), you open the file for updating; any changes you make will amend the running-config file. When you're happy with the new configuration, copy it to startup-config, as shown here:

```
Router#copy running-config startup-config
Building configuration...
[OK]
```

You can also view the running configuration file at any time by typing **show running-config**. However, you do not have to type in the full commands. You can abbreviate commands, as long as they are unique. For example, to carry out the command show running-config, you can type simply **sh run**. For show startup-config, you can type **sh start**. For copy running-config startup-config, you can type **copy run start**.

Cisco IOS

The flash memory holds the router's Internetworking Operating System (IOS). You can see the IOS currently stored in flash with the show flash command (or **sh flash**), which displays your flash memory and reveals both the size of your files and the amount of free flash memory. Here is an example:

```
Router#sh flash

System flash directory:
File  Length     Name/status
  1   3612396   igs-i-1.110-16
[3612460 bytes used, 4776148 available, 8388608
↳total]
8192K bytes of processor board System flash (Read ONLY)
```

Cisco has new commands to help administrators manage configuration files from privileged Exec mode. Table 9.2 is a list of the commands used to start and save configurations on Cisco routers.

TABLE 9.2: Router Configuration

Command	Purpose
show startup-config	Shows the configuration that will be loaded when the router boots.
show running-config	Shows the configuration that's currently loaded into RAM and running.
copy running-config startup-config	Copies the configuration stored in running RAM to backup or NVRAM.
copy startup-config running-config	Copies the configuration stored in NVRAM to running RAM.

TABLE 9.2: Router Configuration *(continued)*

Command	Purpose
`erase startup-config`	Erases the configuration in the router's NVRAM and lands it right back into the initial configuration dialog. (Don't try this one at work!)
`reload`	Reboots the router and reloads the startup configuration into memory.
`setup`	Starts the initial configuration dialog.

It is time to run through all of the commands that can help you manage the configuration files. One of the things you should notice when running these commands is that none of them is run from configuration mode (`config t`); all are run from the privileged-mode prompt (Router#).

show startup-config

Below is the output of the command **sh start** (show startup-config) when no configuration has been saved to NVRAM:

```
Router#sh start
%% Non-volatile configuration memory has not been
↪set up or has bad checksum
```

show running-config

This command will show you the router configuration that is currently loaded in RAM and running. If you typed **config t**, you would be changing this file. The output below was cut for brevity.

```
Router#sh run
Building configuration...
```

```
Current configuration:
!
version 11.2
```

copy running-config startup-config

This command copies the running configuration file into NVRAM or startup-config. This will completely erase the existing startup-config file and replace it with the running-config file. Here is an example:

```
Router#copy run start
Building configuration...
[OK]
```

copy startup-config running-config

This command is used to copy the configuration from NVRAM into running RAM. You can use this if you changed your configuration but had problems with the new setup. Note that this command just appends anything in the startup-config that is not in the running-config—it doesn't overwrite anything. Here's an example:

```
Router#copy start run
Building configuration...
[OK]
```

erase startup-config

This command is used to erase the configuration in NVRAM:

```
Router#erase start
[OK]
```

If you used the command **sh start** after erasing the NVRAM configuration, you would get an error message, as shown earlier in this chapter. You also would be put into setup mode when you rebooted your router.

reload

This command reboots the router. Take a look at this example:

```
Router#reload
```

```
Proceed with reload?[Enter]
```

setup

This command puts you into setup mode regardless of what your configuration is set at, as seen here:

```
Router#setup

        --- System Configuration Dialog ---

At any point you may enter a question mark '?' for
↳help.
Use ctrl-c to abort configuration dialog at any
↳prompt.
Default settings are in square brackets '[]'.
Continue with configuration dialog? [yes/no]:
```

Router Passwords

There are five different types of passwords used in securing Cisco routers: enable secret, enable, virtual terminal, auxiliary, and console. These are their functions:

Enable Secret Password   This password is a one-way cryptographic secret password used in versions 10.3 and up. It takes precedence over the enable password. You can configure the enable secret password either when setting up your router or at any time after that.

Enable Password   This password is used when there is no enable secret and when you are using older software and some boot images. It's manually encrypted by the administrator. You can define this within setup mode or anytime after that.

Virtual Terminal (VTY) Password   This password is used for Telnet sessions to the router. You can change the VTY password at any time, but it must be specified or you won't be able to telnet to the router. You can specify this type of password during setup or anytime after that.

Auxiliary Password   This password is used for the auxiliary port. This port is used to connect a modem to a router for remote console connections. This can only be set up manually.

Console Password   This password is used for the console port. It can only be set up manually. This sets up a password for anyone who connects directly to your router's console port.

MOTD Banner

The MOTD (message of the day) banner, configured with the `banner motd` command, is the first message displayed when any user connects to the router.

Router Identification

A router's identifying information consists of two things: its hostname and its interface. You can set an interface description by using the `description` command.

Hostname

You can change the name your router displays by using the `hostname` command. For example, to change the name of a router to RouterC, you would type **hostname RouterC**.

Interfaces

The interfaces, also known as ports, on Cisco 2500 routers are referred to as Serial0, Serial1, and Ethernet0, and are considered fixed configurations. When you are in configuration mode, you can type **s0, s1,** and **e0** to reference these ports. If you were using Token Ring, you would use **t0**; if you used FDDI, you would use **f0**.

If the device is modular, like a Catalyst 5000 switch, the interfaces are numbered using the syntax *type slot/port*. For example, to configure a port on a 5000 switch for Ethernet card 4, port 2, you would use **e 4/2**.

Cisco 7000 and 7500 series routers have cards called Versatile Interface Processors (VIPs). These can have one or two slots for each port adapter, and each port adapter can have multiple interfaces.

The numbering syntax is *type slot/port number adapter/port*. For example, if you wanted to configure a port on the third Ethernet VIP card, first port (0), second Ethernet interface, you would type **e 2/0/1**. (Yes, the 5000 uses module numbers starting with 1, and the 7200 uses slot numbers starting with 0.)

These are some other commands that can be used within an interface configuration:

shutdown   To change the administrative state of a router interface, use the shutdown command. By itself, it will turn the administrative state of the interface down. The no shutdown command turns the administrative state of an interface up.

description   You can also add a description or text line to an interface by using the description command. This lets you document your interfaces for administrative purposes. For example, you can add circuit numbers to your serial links.

Manipulating Configuration Files

As an administrator, and to pass the CCNA exam, you need to know how to back up configuration files in places other than NVRAM. Whenever you are going to make a configuration change, it is good practice to copy the original configuration first to a TFTP host before making any changes.

Earlier in this chapter, we reviewed how to use the copy startup-config running-config and copy running-config startup-config commands. Those commands are used for manipulating and copying configuration files, which is the focus of this section.

However, since those commands were demonstrated previously, here we will talk only about copying and manipulating configuration files between Cisco routers and a TFTP host and back again. There are a couple ways of doing this. The first command is config net. This is used to copy a configuration from a TFTP host into running RAM. You cannot use this command to copy the configuration into NVRAM.

The second command for copying a configuration file is simply copy. You can use this a few different ways. First, you can use it to copy a configuration file from a TFTP host into running RAM, or you can use it to copy files from a TFTP host into NVRAM. These commands are copy tftp run or copy tftp start.

You can also use the copy command to copy the configuration from either running-config or startup-config to a TFTP host by using the commands copy run tftp or copy start tftp.

Using *config net*

The config net command is not as useful in production networks as the copy tftp run command (discussed below). Basically, all config net does is copy a configuration file stored on a TFTP host into running RAM. When using config net, you must supply the IP address or hostname of the network TFTP host. Here is an example:

```
Router#config net
Host or network configuration file [host]?[Enter]
Address of remote host [255.255.255.255]?172.16.10.1
Name of configuration file [router-confg]?RouterA-
↳confg
Configure using RouterA-confg from 172.16.10.1?
↳[confirm][Enter]
Loading RouterA-confg
```

Using *copy run tftp*

You can copy the router's current configuration from a router to a TFTP server by typing **copy running-config tftp**. Doing this gives you a backup of the router configuration and allows you to run the configuration from this server. You can also configure the router by making your changes to the configuration file stored on the TFTP server; when you're happy with the new configuration, copy the file to the router by using the copy tftp running-config command (the short form is copy run tftp). Take a look at this example:

```
RouterC#copy run tftp
Remote host []?172.16.10.1
```

```
Name of configuration file to write [routerc-
%confg]?[Enter]
Write file routerc-confg on host 172.16.10.1?
%[confirm][Enter]
Building configuration...
OK
```

By default, Cisco adds –confg to the end of the router's hostname to create a default filename. When configuring an IOS device from a TFTP server, the device's default method is to try to load a file with the name of the device followed by the string –confg.

Using *copy tftp run*

To copy a configuration from a TFTP host to a router, use the copy tftp run or copy tftp start commands, as seen here:

```
Router#copy tftp run
Host or network configuration file [host]?[Enter]
Address of remote host [255.255.255.255]?172.16.10.1
Name of configuration file []? detroit-confg[Enter]
Configure using detroit-confg from 172.16.10.1?
%[confirm][Enter]
Loading detroit-confg ..from 172.16.10.1 (via
%Ethernet0): !
[OK - 717/32723 bytes]
Detroit#
```

Notice in this example that the hostname of the router changed immediately after the configuration file was loaded; this happened because the configuration file was loaded directly into DRAM. You would need to use a copy run start command at this point.

Copying the IOS to a TFTP Host

You can copy the contents of flash (the Cisco IOS) to a TFTP server by typing **copy flash tftp**. This copy can serve as a backup version of the Cisco IOS; it can also be used to verify that the copy in flash is the same as the original file. You can restore the Cisco IOS, or upgrade it, by typing **copy tftp flash**.

The router Exec will understand what you are trying to do by the way you word the command. For example, if you type **copy tftp run**, it will look for a Cisco configuration on a TFTP host to copy a configuration into running RAM. If you include the word flash in the command, the router knows you are referring to a Cisco IOS and not a configuration.

Configuring Serial Interfaces

If you have connected a Cisco DTE/DCE (data terminal equipment/data communication equipment) cable, and you are simulating a WAN link between routers, you need to add a clock source.

By default, Cisco routers are DTE devices, but when you have routers connected to simulate a WAN link, you can define a serial interface as a DCE device. Because Cisco routers use synchronous communications—which means a clock is required and is usually supplied from an external source—you need to add the clock rate command to the DCE serial ports on your routers. Why? Because you don't have a CSU/DSU that would normally handle the clocking on the line for you. You must specify the clock rate command on the DCE interfaces to simulate a clocking source. You should also specify the bandwidth command, because it's used by some routing protocols like IGRP to make routing decisions. If you are using RIP or static routing, the bandwidth command will not help.

To configure your router to enable clocking, you would type in the following commands:

```
RouterB#config t
Enter configuration commands, one per line.  End
↳with CNTL/Z.
RouterB(config)#int s0
RouterB(config-if)#clock rate ?
        Speed (bits per second)
   1200
   2400
   4800
   9600
   19200
```

```
        38400
        56000
        64000
        72000
        125000
        148000
        250000
        500000
        800000
        1000000
        1300000
        2000000
        4000000
<300-8000000>    Choose clock rate from list above

RouterB(config-if)#clock rate 56000
RouterB(config-if)#bandwidth ?
  <1-10000000>  Bandwidth in kilobits
RouterB(config-if)#bandwidth 56
RouterB(config-if)#int s1
RouterB(config-if)#clock rate 56000
RouterB(config-if)#bandwidth 56
RouterB(config-if)#^Z
```

Necessary Procedures

You need to practice some commands. This section reviews the processes for setting passwords, the MOTD banner, and the hostname, and for setting the identification of an interface using the description command.

Setting Passwords

The following examples show how to set Cisco router passwords. Of course, you should choose your own passwords in place of the ones used in the examples.

Enable Secret Password

To set the enable secret password, type the following commands:

```
Router#config t
Enter configuration commands, one per line.  End
↳with CNTL/Z.
Router(config)#enable secret sean
Router(config)#^Z
```

Enable Password

To set the enable password, type the following commands:

```
Router#config t
Enter configuration commands, one per line.  End
↳with CNTL/Z.
Router(config)#enable password sean
The enable password you have chosen is the same as
↳your enable secret.
This is not recommended.  Re-enter the enable
↳password.
Router(config)#enable password sean
Router(config)#^Z
```

Notice that if you type the same password as the enable secret, you get a warning message. If, despite the warning, you choose the same password again, the router would accept it—but neither the secret nor enable passwords would work. Can you say password recovery?

Virtual Terminal Password

To set your VTY password, type the following commands:

```
Router#config t
Enter configuration commands, one per line.  End
↳with CNTL/Z.
Router(config)#line vty 0 4
Router(config-line)#login
Router(config-line)#password sean1
Router(config-line)#^Z
```

The command **line vty 0 4** specifies the number of Telnet sessions allowed in the router. You can also set up a different password for each line by typing **line vty** *port number*. The login command tells the router to prompt for a password. If no login command is used, users can gain access via the VTY port without being prompted for a password.

Auxiliary Password

To set the auxiliary password, use the following commands:

```
Router#config t
Enter configuration commands, one per line.  End
↳with CNTL/Z.
Router(config)#line aux 0
Router(config-line)#login
Router(config-line)#password sean2
Router(config-line)#^Z
```

Console Password

Finally, to set the console password, use these commands:

```
Router#config t
Enter configuration commands, one per line.  End
↳with CNTL/Z.
Router(config)#line con 0
Router(config-line)#login
Router(config-line)#password sean3
Router(config-line)#^Z
```

Configuring Banners

You can add a message of the day (MOTD) banner that will be displayed whenever anyone logs in to your Cisco router. The command is banner motd *delimiter*. You must start the banner with a delimiting character of your choice. Here's an example using the octothorp (#) as a delimiter:

```
RouterC(config)#banner motd #
Enter TEXT message.  End with the character '#'.
```

```
If you are not authorized to be in Acme's router,
↳log out immediately! Violators will be prosecuted!
#[Enter]
RouterC(config)#end
```

The output for this example will look like this when users either telnet to the router or connect to a console port:

```
Router con0 is now available

Press ENTER to get started.

If you are not authorized to be in Acme.com router,
↳log out immediately!

User Access Verification
Password:
```

This output shows an example of what you'd see when connecting to your router's console port. It tells you that the router is available, and then to press Enter to get started. You will see the MOTD banner and then be asked for the user-mode password, if one is configured.

Changing Router Identification

You can change the name your router displays by using the hostname command. For example, to change the name of a router to RouterC, type the following commands:

```
Router#config t
Enter configuration commands, one per line.  End
↳with CNTL/Z.
Router(config)#hostname RouterC
RouterC(config-line)#^Z
```

Notice that there is no space in the command hostname.

Using *copy flash tftp*

Start with a ping from your router to your TFTP server to ensure that IP connectivity is working from the router that is targeted to copy the flash over to your TFTP host. After you've verified connectivity, the flash can be copied to your TFTP server, as shown in this example:

```
RouterC#ping 172.16.10.2
Type escape sequence to abort.
Sending 5, 100-byte ICMP Echos to 172.16.10.2,
↳timeout is 2 seconds:
.!!!!
Success rate is 80 percent (4/5), round-trip min/
↳avg/max = 1/2/4 ms
RouterC#copy flash tftp
System flash directory:
File  Length   Name/status
  1   3621884  igs-i-1.110-18.bin
[3621948 bytes used, 572356 available, 4194304 total]
Address or name of remote host
↳[255.255.255.255]?172.16.10.2
Source file name?igs-i-1.110-18.bin
Destination file name [igs-i-1.110-18.bin]?[Enter]
Verifying checksum for 'igs-i-1.110-18.bin' (file #
↳1)... OK
Copy 'igs-i-1.110-18.bin' from Flash to server
  as 'igs-i-1.110-18.bin'? [yes/no]y
!!!!!!!!!!!!!!!!!!!!!!!!!!!!!!!!!!!!!!!!!!!!!!!!!!!!!!!
!!!!!!!!!!!!!!!!!!!!!!!!!!!!!!!!!!!!!!!!!!!!!!!!!!!!!!!
!!!!!!!!!!!!!!!!!!!!!!!!!!!!!!!!!!!!!!!!!!!!!!!!!!!!!!!
!!!!!!!!!!!!!!!!!!!!!!!!!!!!!!!!!!!!!!!!!!!!!!!!!!!!!!!
!!!!!!!!!!!!!!!!!!!!!!!!!!!!!!!!!!!!!!!!!!!!!!!!!!!!!!!
!!!!!!!!!!!!!!!!!!!!!!!!!!!!!!!!!!!!!!!!!!!!!!!!!!!!!!!
!!!!!!!!!!!!!!!!!!!!!!!!!!!!!!!!!!!!!!!!!!!!!!!!!!!!!!!
!!!!!!!!!!!!!!!!!!!!!!!!!!!!!!!!!!!!!!!!!!!!!!!!!!!!!!!
!!!!!!!!!!!!!!!!!!!!!!!!!!!!!!!!!!!!!!!!!!!!!!!!!!!!!!!
!!!!!!!!!!!!!!!!!!!!!!!!!!!!!!!!!!!!!!!!!!!!!!!!!!!!!!!
!!!!!!!!!!!!!!!!!!!!!!!!!!!!!!!!!!!!!!!!!!!!!!!!!!!!!!!
!!!!!!!!!!!!!!!!!!!!!!!!!!!!!!!!!!!!!!!!!!!!!!!!!!!!!!!
```

```
!!!!!!!!!!!!!!!!!!!!!!!!!!!!!!!!!!!!!!!!!!!!!!!!!!!!!!!!!
!!!!!!!!!!!!!!!!!!!!!!!!!!!!!!
Upload to server done
Flash copy took 0:21:53 [hh:mm:ss]
RouterC#
```

If you tried this example, you probably noticed that it took almost 22 minutes to download the flash through a simulated WAN network. Keep this in mind when backing up your files from remote locations.

Using *copy tftp flash*

You can copy from a TFTP server to flash anytime by typing **copy tftp flash**. This command is very useful for downloading new versions of the Cisco IOS to your router. Here's an example:

```
RouterC#copy tftp flash

                    ****  NOTICE  ****
Flash load helper v1.0
This process will accept the copy options and then
↳terminate
the current system image to use the ROM based image
↳for the copy.
Routing functionality will not be available during
↳that time.
If you are logged in via telnet, this connection
↳will terminate.
Users with console access can see the results of the
↳copy operation.
                    ---- ******** ----
Proceed? [confirm][Enter]


System flash directory:
File  Length   Name/status
  1   3621884  igs-i-1.110-18.bin
[3621948 bytes used, 572356 available, 4194304 total]
Address or name of remote host [172.16.10.1]?[Enter]
Source file name?igs-i-1.110-18.bin
```

```
Destination file name [igs-i-1.110-18.bin]?[Enter]
Accessing file 'igs-i-1.110-18.bin' on 172.16.10.2...
Loading igs-i-1.110-18.bin from 172.16.10.2 (via
↳Serial0): ! [OK]


Erase flash device before writing? [confirm][Enter]
Flash contains files. Are you sure you want to
↳erase? [confirm][Enter]


Copy 'igs-i-1.110-18.bin' from server
 as 'igs-i-1.110-18.bin' into Flash WITH erase?
↳[yes/no]y


%SYS-5-RELOAD: Reload requested
%FLH: igs-i-1.110-18.bin from 172.16.10.2 to flash ...
System flash directory:
File  Length    Name/status
  1   3621884   igs-i-1.110-18.bin
[3621948 bytes used, 572356 available, 4194304 total]
Accessing file 'igs-i-1.110-18.bin' on 172.16.10.2...
Loading igs-i-1.110-18.bin from 172.16.10.2 (via
↳Serial0): ! [OK]
Erasing device... eeeeeeeeeeeeeeee ...erased
Loading igs-i-1.110-18.bin from 172.16.10.2 (via
↳Serial0):
!!!!!!!!!!!!!!!!!!!!!!!!!!!!!!!!!!!!!!!!!!!!!!!!!!!!!!!!!
!!!!!!!!!!!!!!!!!!!!!!!!!!!!!!!!!!!!!!!!!!!!!!!!!!!!!!!!!
!!!!!!!!!!!!!!!!!!!!!!!!!!!!!!!!!!!!!!!!!!!!!!!!!!!!!!!!!
!!!!!!!!!!!!!!!!!!!!!!!!!!!!!!!!!!!!!!!!!!!!!!!!!!!!!!!!!
!!!!!!!!!!!!!!!!!!!!!!!!!!!!!!!!!!!!!!!!!!!!!!!!!!!!!!!!!
!!!!!!!!!!!!!!!!!!!!!!!!!!!!!!!!!!!!!!!!!!!!!!!!!!!!!!!!!
!!!!!!!!!!!!!!!!!!!!!!!!!!!!!!!!!!!!!!!!!!!!!!!!!!!!!!!!!
!!!!!!!!!!!!!!!!!!!!!!!!!!!!!!!!!!!!!!!!!!!!!!!!!!!!!!!!!
!!!!!!!!!!!!!!!!!!!!!!!!!!!!!!!!!!!!!!!!!!!!!!!!!!!!!!!!!
!!!!!!!!!!!!!!!!!!!!!!!!!!!!!!!!!!!!!!!!!!!!!!!!!!!!!!!!!
!!!!!!!!!!!!!!!!!!!!!!!!!!!!!!!!!!!!!!!!!!!!!!!!!!!!!!!!!
!!!!!!!!!!!!!!!!!!!!!!!!!!!!!!!!!!!!!!!!!!!!!!!!!!!!!!!!!
!!!!!!!!!!!!!!!!!!!!!!!!!!!!!!!!!!!!!!!!!!!!!!!!!!!!!!!!!
!!!!!!!!!!!!!!!!!!!!!!!!!!!!!!!!
```

```
[OK - 3621884/4194304 bytes]

Verifying checksum... OK (0xC248)
Flash copy took 0:21:34 [hh:mm:ss]
%FLH: Re-booting system after download
```

After confirming a few entries, you're asked if it's okay to erase the entire contents of flash memory. The program asks the question because there's rarely room for more than one flash file. However, if there is room, you can have many different versions loaded in flash.

Each e in the output stands for *erase*, and each exclamation point (!) indicates that one UDP segment has been successfully transferred. The router must be rebooted to load the new image on a 2500 series router, because the currently running IOS image is in flash memory. Use show flash to verify that the size matches that of the original file.

Exam Essentials

Know the difference between user and privileged modes.   You cannot see the router configuration in user mode. You can both view and change the router configuration in privileged mode.

Remember how to log in to a router in both modes.   When you connect a console cable to a router, you are prompted with this message: Press Return to continue. At this point, you must enter a user-mode password if one is assigned. You can then type **enable** to enter privileged mode. You will be prompted for a password if one is assigned.

Remember how to set your passwords.   Make sure you know the difference between enable, enable secret, virtual terminal (VTY), console, and auxiliary passwords.

Know the different ways to use the question mark.   There are two different ways to use the question mark to gain help when administrating your router. You can type it without a space, as in **cl?** for example, to get all the commands that start with *cl*. Another option is to type a space before the question mark, as in **clock ?**, to get the next argument or command available.

Know how to configure a MOTD banner.   Practice setting banners and notice where they show up when you log in to the router.

Read about and memorize the identification terms and commands. Routers use interface terms s0 and e0 for Serial0 and Ethernet0. Switches have many physical ports on one card. To configure a 7000 router with a VIP card, use the *type slot/port number adapter/port* syntax.

Set your router name.   Be sure you know how to set a hostname. Remember that the command **hostname** is one word.

Know how to copy a configuration file from a TFTP host.   The commands to copy a configuration file from a TFTP host to a router are **config net**, **copy tftp run**, and **copy tftp start**.

Know how to copy a configuration file to a TFTP host.   The commands to copy a configuration file from a router to a TFTP host are **copy run tftp** and **copy start tftp**.

Practice copying a Cisco IOS to a TFTP server and back again. You need to understand the output of backing up and restoring a Cisco IOS. The only way to do this is to practice and look closely at the output of the commands.

Remember the commands to configure your router.   Practice going to different interfaces and setting IP addresses. Remember that the IP address and mask are configured on the same line. Also set your passwords, banner, and hostname. Set your router to do name resolution with the **ip host** command.

Remember when to use the clock rate command and how to set your clock rate.   The **clock rate** command is two words. Practice setting the clock rate on your DCE interfaces.

Key Terms and Concepts

advanced editing Cisco's way of creating shortcuts. These key combinations are mostly old Unix commands.

bandwidth A command used in Cisco routers to set the amount of availability of a link. This command only works if a dynamic routing protocol (EIGRP, for example) is running that can use the bandwidth of a link to help make routing decisions.

clock rate A command used in Cisco routers to set the clocking used on a line. Typically the clock will be provided by the provider or CDU/DSU.

context-sensitive help This form of help can also be called *command syntax help,* because it tells you which keywords or arguments are required to continue with a command.

Exec Cisco IOS software command interpreter.

flash Basically an erasable, reprogrammable ROM that holds the operating system image and microcode. It allows you to "flash" the router and perform upgrades without removing and replacing chips on the motherboard. Flash is retained even when the router is turned off.

nonvolatile RAM (NVRAM) Memory that stores the router's startup configuration file. NVRAM retains its information even when the router is rebooted or shut down.

privileged mode Used to view and change the configuration of the router.

RAM Provides caching and packet buffering, plus information like routing tables. RAM is used to hold the running operating system when the router is powered on; it is cleared when the router is reset or powered off.

ROM Used by the router to store the bootstrap startup program, operating system software, and power-on self-test (POST). ROM chips are installed in sockets on the router's motherboard so that they can be replaced or upgraded.

show   Command used from the Cisco command prompt to display configurations and statistics.

terminal   Another term for the console used in Cisco routers.

user mode   Used for ordinary tasks like checking the router's status.

virtual terminal (VTY)   A term from the old IBM days. It referred to a dumb terminal that connected into a mainframe network and asked the mainframe to process data.

Sample Questions

1. To change the name on a router, what command should you use?

A. config t, change name SF

B. config t, host name SF

C. config t, prompt SF

D. config t, hostname SF

Answer: D. The hostname command is one word.

2. To set a MOTD, which of the following is correct?

A. config t, motd banner #

B. banner motd $

C. config t, banner motd &

D. config t, banner #

Answer: C. Only answer C is correct. You can use any delimiting character you choose. Here is another example:

```
RouterB(config)#banner motd #
Enter TEXT message.  End with the character '#'.
If you are not authorized to be using Acme's
↳router, log out immediately! Violators will be
↳prosecuted!
#[Enter]
RouterB(config)#end
```

3. Which of the following commands will change your console password?

   A. config t, enable password bob

   B. config t, line console password bob

   C. config t, line console 0, login, password bob

   D. config t, line con 0, password login bob

   Answer: C. The login command is not required, but it is used to tell the router to ask for a console password.

4. Which of the following syntax examples is correct to configure a 7000 router with a VIP card?

   A. port adapter/card slot/port

   B. type slot/port number adapter/port

   C. slot type/port port/adapter

   D. type port/card

   Answer: B. To configure a 7000 router with a VIP card, use the syntax *type slot/port number adapter/port*.

5. Which of the following will change your enable secret password?

   A. config t, enable password bob

   B. config t, enable secret password bob

   C. config t, enable secret, login, password bob

   D. config t, enable secret bob

   Answer: D. Do not use the word *password* in the argument.

6. When you are in privileged mode, which of the following statements is true?

   A. You can do a reload to enter setup mode.

B. You can type **erase running-config** and then do a reload to enter setup mode.

C. You can type **setup** to enter setup mode.

D. If you type **erase start**, you will automatically be prompted with setup commands.

Answer: C. There are two ways to enter setup commands. You can type **erase start** and then reboot the router or you can type setup at any time at the privileged mode prompt.

7. To copy a configuration stored on a TFTP host and make it a startup-config file, what command should you use?

A. copy tftp flash

B. config net

C. copy start run

D. copy tftp start

E. copy tftp run

Answer: D. The only command that copies the configuration from a TFTP host to NVRAM is copy tftp startup-config (copy tftp start).

8. If you want to back up your running-config, what two commands are valid?

A. copy run start

B. copy run tftp

C. copy start tftp

D. config net

Answer: A, B. Copying the configuration into NVRAM (startup) and to a TFTP host are both considered backing up the running-config.

9. To copy a Cisco IOS to your router, what command should you use?

A. copy tftp flash

B. copy flash tftp

C. copy tftp run

D. copy run tftp

Answer: A. The correct command for copying a Cisco IOS to a router is copy tftp flash.

10. What is the command used to simulate a CSU/DSU device connected to your router?

A. clockrate

B. bandwidth

C. clock rate

D. band width

Answer: C. On an interface connected with a DCE cable, use the clock rate command.

Troubleshooting

As with the other topics covered in this chapter, be sure to get the hands-on experience that you can only get when sitting in front of a router. The CCNA exam will test you on the output of the different commands and what happens when the router is booted.

Critical Information

The commands copy running-config startup-config, copy startup-config running-config, show running-config, etc., covered in the previous objective, are all part of this objective as well. In addition to those commands, there are a few others that are important to understand both for the test and for configuring routers in a production environment:

show interface Provides general information about an interface, including the IP address and subnet mask.

show ip interface Gives you a look at the IP parameters on an interface.

show protocol Displays the protocols and addresses running on your router.

show ip protocol Gives you information about which routing protocols are running on your router (RIP, IGRP, etc.) and what their parameters are.

Necessary Procedures

This section covers the following commands:

- show interface
- show ip interface
- show protocol
- show ip protocol

Using *show interface*

The show interface (**sh int**) command displays the hardware interfaces installed on a router as well as their status. It begins with the first interface and continues through the rest. You can specify just one interface to view; for example, you can type **sh int e0** to see the status of that particular interface:

```
Router#sh int e0
Ethernet0 is up, line protocol is down
```

The lines that follow show the hardware address and other information about the connection (the output shown here was cut for brevity):

```
    Hardware is Lance, address is 00e0.1ea9.c418 (bia
✎00e0.1ea9.c418)
    Internet address is 172.16.30.1 255.255.255.0
    MTU 1500 bytes, BW 10000 Kbit, DLY 1000 usec, rely
✎128/255, load 1/255
    Encapsulation ARPA, loopback not set, keepalive
✎set (10 sec)
    ARP type: ARPA, ARP Timeout 4:00:00
    Last input never, output 0:00:01, output hang never
    Last clearing of "show interface" counters never
    Output queue 0/40, 0 drops; input queue 0/75, 0 drops
    5 minute input rate 0 bits/sec, 0 packets/sec
    5 minute output rate 0 bits/sec, 0 packets/sec
        0 packets input, 0 bytes, 0 no buffer
        Received 0 broadcasts, 0 runts, 0 giants
        0 input errors, 0 CRC, 0 frame, 0 overrun, 0
✎ignored, 0 abort
        0 input packets with dribble condition detected
        384 packets output, 23049 bytes, 0 underruns
        384 output errors, 0 collisions, 1 interface
✎resets, 0 restarts
        0 output buffer failures, 0 output buffers
✎swapped out
```

Using *show ip interface*

This command (the short form is **sh ip int**) displays the usability status of interfaces configured with IP. The usability status, as defined by Cisco, is an interface through which the software can send and receive packets. If the interface hardware is usable, it is then marked as up. If both ends of the communication link are up, then the line protocol will display up. Here is an example:

```
Router#sh ip int
Ethernet0 is up, line protocol is up
    Internet address is 172.16.10.1/24
```

```
Broadcast address is 255.255.255.255
Address determined by setup command
MTU is 1500 bytes
Helper address is not set
Directed broadcast forwarding is enabled
Outgoing access list is not set
Inbound  access list is not set
```

The command output was cut for brevity.

Using *show protocol*

The show protocol command (**sh prot**) details which protocols are configured on the router. In the sample output below, you can see that only the IP protocol is configured on interfaces e0, s0, and s1:

```
Router#sh prot
Global values:
  Internet Protocol routing is enabled
Ethernet0 is up, line protocol is down
  Internet address is 172.16.30.1 255.255.255.0
Serial0 is down, line protocol is up
  Internet address is 172.16.20.2 255.255.255.0
Serial1 is down, line protocol is up
  Internet address is 172.16.40.1 255.255.255.0
```

Using *show ip protocol*

To see more detail on the protocols on your system, use the show ip protocol command (**sh ip prot**). Notice in the sample output below that the routing protocol RIP is being used:

```
RouterC#sh ip prot
Routing Protocol is "rip"
  Sending updates every 30 seconds, next due in 22
↳seconds
  Invalid after 180 seconds, hold down 180, flushed
↳after 240
  Outgoing update filter list for all interfaces is
↳not set
```

```
    Incoming update filter list for all interfaces is
↳not set
    Redistributing: rip
    Routing for Networks:
      172.16.0.0
    Routing Information Sources:
      Gateway         Distance      Last Update
      172.16.40.1          120      0:00:02
    Distance: (default is 120)
```

The show ip protocol command also displays the current state of the active routing protocols. This is a helpful command to use when you are troubleshooting routers that are sending or receiving bad routing information.

Exam Essentials

Understand the output of each command.   Study the output carefully and be able to explain the output each command provides.

Understand when you would use each command.   Study the output and understand when you would use one command over another.

Key Terms and Concepts

interface   Port on a router that provides routing services to a LAN or WAN.

Sample Questions

1. Which of the following commands would you use to see the routed information configured on your router?

   A. show interface

   B. show ip interface

   C. show protocol

D. show ip protocol

Answer: C. The show protocol command displays the Layer 3 protocol information for those protocols configured on the router, as well as the addressing assigned to the router's interfaces.

2. Which of the following commands would you use to see the routing protocols configured on your router?

A. show interface

B. show ip interface

C. show protocol

D. show ip protocol

Answer: D. The show ip protocol command displays the routing protocols configured on the router, such as EIGRP, IGRP, IP RIP, and OSPF (Open Shortest Path First).

3. Which of the following commands would you use to see the usability status of interfaces configured with IP?

A. show interface

B. show ip interface

C. show protocol

D. show ip protocol

Answer: B. The show ip interface command displays much of the troubleshooting and configuration information regarding the routers interfaces.

Router Packet Switching Modes

This objective will teach you the different modes of how a packet is switched within a router. This is not a heavily tested objective, but you should go through it anyway as it doesn't hurt to know this information and you want to be prepared for anything.

Critical Information

The switching modes that can be used within a router are:

- Process switching
- Fast switching
- Autonomous switching
- Silicon switching
- Optimum switching
- Distributed switching
- Netflow switching
- Cisco Express Forwarding

Process Switching

As a packet arrives on a router to be forwarded, it's copied to the router's process buffer, and the router performs a lookup on the Layer 3 address. Using the routing table, an exit interface is associated with the destination address. The processor forwards the packet with the added new information to the exit interface, while the router initializes the fast-switching cache. Subsequent packets bound for the same destination address follow the same path as the first packet.

Overhead ensues because the processor is occupied with Layer 3 lookups, determining which interface the packet should exit from and calculating the CRC for the packets. If every packet required all of that to be routed, the processor could get really bogged down. The answer is to use fast switching whenever and wherever possible.

Fast Switching

Fast switching is the low-end architecture's enhancement from process switching. The first packet of a new session is copied to memory, then compared against the fast-switching cache to find the best interface through which to send it out to its destination. When this is completed, the packet is rewritten and forwarded to the chosen interface.

Instead of the route processor calculating the CRC, the individual interface processors do this, relieving the route processor of a great deal of work.

Fast switching is also on by default, and if it's been turned off, you can turn it back on by using the following command:

```
ip route-cache
```

So why would it be turned off? Sometimes it's necessary to turn fast switching off when troubleshooting network problems. Since packets don't move across the route processor after the first packet has been process-switched, you can't see them with packet-level tracing. It's also helpful to turn off fast switching if the interface card's memory is limited or consumed, or to alleviate congestion when low-speed interfaces become flooded with information from high-speed interfaces.

Autonomous Switching

Autonomous switching works by comparing packets against the autonomous-switching cache found on the interface processor, instead of the route or switch processor. Because the CiscoBus controller manages the switching job for autonomous switching, the route processor isn't interrupted. Thanks to the onboard processor cache, switching speed is increased. Instead of having to send the packet across the backplane of the router to the route processor, the needed cache is right there in the interface board processor.

Autonomous switching is available only on AGS+ and Cisco 7000 series routers that have high-speed controller interface cards. The command to enable autonomous switching is as follows:

```
ip route-cache autonomous
```

Silicon Switching

Silicon switching is available only on the Cisco 7000 with an Silicon Switch Processor (SSP). Silicon-switched packets are compared to the silicon-switching cache on the silicon switching engine (SSE). The SSP is a dedicated switch processor that offloads the switching process from the route processor, providing a fast-switching solution, but packets must still traverse the backplane of the router to get to the SSP and then back to the exit interface.

Optimum Switching

Optimum switching follows the same procedure as the other switching algorithms. When a new packet enters the interface, it is compared to the optimum-switching cache, rewritten, and sent to the chosen exit interface. Other packets associated with the same session will then follow the same path. All processing is carried out on the interface processor including the CRC. Optimum switching is faster than both fast switching and Netflow switching, unless you have implemented several access lists.

You need to enter the command for optimum switching on each individual interface—however, it's on by default on high-end routers, taking the place of fast switching. Its command syntax is as follows:

```
ip route-cache optimum
```

Optimum switching also needs to be turned off to view packets while troubleshooting a network problem.

Distributed Switching

Distributed switching happens on the Versatile Interface Processor (VIP) cards, which have a switching processor onboard, so it's very efficient. All required processing is done right on the VIP processor, which maintains a copy of the router's routing cache. With this arrangement, even the first packet doesn't need to be sent to the route processor to initialize the switching path as it does with the other switching algorithms. Router efficiency increases as more VIP cards are added.

Netflow Switching

Netflow switching is really more of an administration tool than a performance-enhancement tool. It collects detailed data for use in conjunction with circuit accounting and application utilization information. Due to all the additional data that Netflow collects (and may export), expect an increase in router overhead—possibly as much as a 5 percent increase in CPU utilization.

Netflow switching can be configured on most interface types and can be used in a switched environment. ATM, LAN, and VLAN technologies all support Netflow switching, and the Cisco 7200 and 7500 series routers provide its implementation.

Netflow gives you amenities such as the security flag in the cache that allows subsequent packets of an established flow to avoid access list processing. It's comparable to optimum and distributed switching, and is much better if access lists (especially long ones) will be placed in the switching path. However, the detailed information Netflow gathers and exports does load down the system, so plan carefully before implementing Netflow switching on a router.

Cisco Express Forwarding

Cisco Express Forwarding (CEF) is a switching function designed for high-end backbone routers. It functions on Layer 3 of the OSI model, and its biggest asset is the ability to remain stable in a large network. However, it's also more efficient than both the fast and optimum default switching paths.

CEF is wonderfully stable in large environments because it doesn't rely on cached information. Instead of using a CEF cache, it refers to two alternate resources. The forwarding information base (FIB) consists of information duplicated from the IP routing table. Every time routing information changes, the changes are propagated to the FIB, so instead of comparing old cache information, a packet looks to the FIB for its forwarding information. CEF stores the Layer 2 MAC addresses of connected routers (or next hop) in the other alternate resource, the adjacency table.

CEF was designed for large networks—if reliable and redundant switching paths are necessary, CEF is the way to go. However, keep in mind that its hardware requirements are really high, and it lacks support for many Cisco IOS features. CEF is definitely not the answer for all networks, at least not yet.

Exam Essentials

Read through this objective once. You don't need to study this more than once.

Key Terms and Concepts

packet switching mode   Method used by a Cisco router to handle a packet when it is received on an interface.

Sample Questions

1. What type of switching is the low-end architecture's enhancement from process switching?

   A. Process

   B. Fast

   C. Optimum

   D. Distributed

   Answer: B. Fast switching is the low-end architecture's enhancement from process switching. The first packet of a new session is copied to memory, then compared against the fast-switching cache to find the best interface through which to send it out to its destination.

▶ IOS CLI Switch

In this objective, we will show you how to configure the basics on the 1900 Catalyst switch. We will show you how to

- Set the passwords

- Set the hostname

- Configure the IP address and subnet mask

- Identify the interfaces

- Set a description on the interfaces

- Erase the switch configuration

The above list is more information than you need to know for your CCNA exam.

Critical Information

The first things that you should configure on a switch are the passwords. You don't want unauthorized users connecting to the switch. You can set both the user-mode and privileged-mode passwords, just like a router.

The login (user-mode) password can be used to verify authorization of the switch, including accessing any line and the console. The privileged-mode, or enable-mode, password is used to allow access to the switch so the configuration can be viewed or changed. This is the same as any Cisco router.

NOTE   Passwords on the 1900 cannot be fewer than four characters or more than eight. They are not case-sensitive.

Even though the 1900 switch uses a CLI running an IOS, the commands for the user-mode and enable-mode passwords are different than for a router. You use the command enable password, which is the same, but you choose different access levels, which are optional on a Cisco router but are not on the 1900 switch.

Setting the User-Mode and Enable-Mode Passwords

You use the same command to set the user-mode password and enable-mode password on the 1900 switch. However, you do use different level commands to control the type of access each password provides.

To configure the user-mode and enable-mode password, press **K** at the router console output. Enter enable mode by using the `enable` command and then enter global configuration mode by using the `config t` command. The following switch output shows an example of how to get into enable mode and then into global configuration mode:

```
1 user(s) now active on Management Console.

        User Interface Menu

    [M] Menus
    [K] Command Line
    [I] IP Configuration

Enter Selection:  K

        CLI session with the switch is open.
        To end the CLI session, enter [Exit].
```

>**enable**
#**config t**
```
Enter configuration commands, one per line.   End
↳with CNTL/Z
(config)#
```

Once you are in global configuration mode, you can set the user-mode and enable-mode passwords by using the `enable password` command. The switch output below shows the configuration of both passwords:

```
(config)#enable password ?
```

```
level  Set exec level password
(config)#enable password level ?
  <1-15>  Level number
```

To enter the user-mode password, use level 1. To enter the enable-mode password, use level 15. Remember the password must be at least four characters, but not longer than eight characters. The switch output below shows the user-mode password being denied because it is too long:

```
(config)#enable password level 1 seanodom
Error: Invalid password length.
Password must be between 4 and 8 characters
```

The following output is an example of how to set both the user-mode and enable-mode passwords on the 1900 switch:

```
(config)#enable password level 1 sean
(config)#enable password level 15 sean1
(config)#exit
#exit
CLI session with the switch is now closed.
Press any key to continue.
```

At this point, you can press Enter and test your passwords. You will be prompted for a user-mode password after you press **K** and then an enable-mode password after you type **enable**.

After we exit from configuration mode and then the privileged mode, the following console screen is displayed. Notice that when we press **K** this time, the switch prompts for a user-mode password:

```
Catalyst 1900 Management Console
Copyright (c) Cisco Systems, Inc.  1993-1998
All rights reserved.
Enterprise Edition Software
Ethernet Address:      00-30-80-CC-7D-00
PCA Number:            73-3122-04
PCA Serial Number:     FAB033725XG
```

```
Model Number:          WS-C1912-A
System Serial Number:  FAB0339T01M
Power Supply S/N:      PHI031801CF
PCB Serial Number:     FAB033725XG,73-3122-04
----------------------------------------------------
1 user(s) now active on Management Console.
        User Interface Menu
    [M] Menus
    [K] Command Line
Enter Selection:K
Enter password:****
        CLI session with the switch is open.
        To end the CLI session, enter [Exit].
>en
Enter password:****
#
```

After we entered user mode, we typed **en**, which is a shortcut for the enable command, and were prompted for the enable password. If you forget your password, unplug the 1900 switch and hold the Mode button in on the front of the switch while plugging the power cable back in. Choose the command for clearing the switch to factory defaults, which also clears all your passwords.

You have now set the user-mode and enable-mode passwords, but there still is one more password on a 1900 switch: the enable secret.

Setting the Enable Secret Password

The enable secret password is a more secure password and supersedes the enable password if set. You set this password the same way you set the enable secret password on a router. If you have an enable secret set, you don't even need to bother setting the enable-mode password. Here is an example:

```
(config)#enable secret sean2
```

You can make the enable password and enable secret commands the same on the 1900 switch, but on a router you are not allowed to

do this. You can use a show running-config (**sh run** for short) to see
the current configuration on the switch, as seen here:

```
#sh run
Building configuration...
Current configuration:

enable secret 5 $1$FMFQ$wFVYVLYn2aXscfB3J95.w.
enable password level 1 "SEAN"
enable password level 15 "SEAN1"
```

Notice the enable-mode passwords are not encrypted by default, but
the enable secret is. This is the same password configuration technique that you will find on a router.

One more thing to notice is that, even though we typed the passwords
as lowercase, the running-config shows them as uppercase. It
doesn't matter how you type them or how they show in the configuration, because the passwords are not case-sensitive.

Setting the Hostname

The 1900 switch command to set the hostname is exactly like any
router: hostname. Remember, it is one word. The switch output
below shows the console screen:

```
1 user(s) now active on Management Console.

        User Interface Menu

    [M] Menus
    [K] Command Line
    [I] IP Configuration
Enter Selection:K
Enter password:****
        CLI session with the switch is open.
        To end the CLI session, enter [Exit].
>en
```

```
Enter password:****
#config t
Enter configuration commands, one per line.  End
↳with CNTL/Z
(config)#hostname Seans1912
Seans1912(config)#
```

Press **K** to go into user mode, enter the password, use the **enable** command and enter the enable secret password. From global configuration mode, type the **hostname** command followed by the hostname you wish to give the switch.

Setting IP Information

The Catalyst 1900 switch has some default settings already configured on the switch from the factory. The default settings on the switch are as follows:

Setting	Value
IP address and default gateway	0.0.0.0
CDP	Enabled
Switching mode	FragmentFree
100BaseT ports	Auto-negotiate duplex mode
10BaseT ports	Half-duplex
Spanning-Tree	Enabled
Console password	Not set

By default, no IP address or default-gateway information is set. You would set both the IP address and the default gateway on a Layer 2 switch, just like any host. By typing the command show ip (or **sh ip**), you can see the default IP configuration of the switch, as seen here:

```
Sean21912#sh ip
IP Address: 0.0.0.0
Subnet Mask: 0.0.0.0
```

```
Default Gateway: 0.0.0.0
Management VLAN:  1
Domain name:
Name server 1: 0.0.0.0
Name server 2: 0.0.0.0
HTTP server : Enabled
HTTP port :  80
RIP : Enabled
```

Notice in the above switch output that no IP address, default gateway, or other IP parameters are configured. To set the IP configuration on a 1900 switch, use the command ip address. The default gateway should also be set using the ip default-gateway command.

The switch output below shows an example of how to set the IP address and default-gateway on a 1900 switch:

```
Seans1912#config t
Enter configuration commands, one per line.  End
↳with CNTL/Z
Seans1912(config)#ip address 172.16.10.16
↳255.255.255.0
Seans1912(config)#ip default-gateway 172.16.10.1
Seans1912(config)#
```

Once you have your IP information set, use the show ip command to verify your changes:

```
Seans1912#sh ip
IP Address: 172.16.10.16
Subnet Mask: 255.255.255.0
Default Gateway: 172.16.10.1
Management VLAN:  1
Domain name:
Name server 1: 0.0.0.0
Name server 2: 0.0.0.0
HTTP server : Enabled
HTTP port :  80
```

```
RIP : Enabled
Seans1912#
```

Configuring the 10BaseT Interfaces

It is important to understand how to access switch ports. The 1900 switch uses the *type slot/port* syntax. For example, Ethernet 0/3 is 10BaseT port 3. Another example would be Fast Ethernet 0/26. This is the first of the two Fast Ethernet ports available on the 1900 switch.

The 1900 switch *type slot/port* command can be used with either the interface command or the show command. The interface command allows you to set interface specific configurations. The 1900 switch has only one slot: zero (0).

To configure an interface on a 1900 switch, go to global configuration mode and use the interface command. The following help screens describe the *type slot/port* configuration method:

```
Seans1912#config t
Enter configuration commands, one per line.  End
↳with CNTL/Z
Seans1912(config)#int ethernet ?
  <0-0>  IEEE 802.3
```

From global configuration, use the interface command and the interface type, either ethernet or fastethernet (which can be abbreviated e or f, respectively).

The previous output asks for the slot. Since the 1900 switch is not modular, there is only one slot. The next output gives us a slash (/) to separate the slot/port configuration:

```
Seans1912(config)#int ethernet 0?
  /
Seans1912(config)#int ethernet 0/?
  <1-25>  IEEE 802.3
```

After the 0/ configuration command, the above output shows the number of ports you can configure. However, if you only have a 1912 switch, you really only have ports 1–12, 25 on the back of the switch, and 26 and 27 as the 100 Mbps uplinks. The Fast Ethernet ports did not show up on the above output, because we choose the Ethernet interface as our type and the ports are Fast Ethernet.

Here's the completed command:

```
Seans1912(config)#int ethernet 0/1
```

Fast Ethernet Interface Configuration

To configure the two Fast Ethernet ports, the command is still *type slot/port*, but the type is fastethernet instead of ethernet. An example would be: interface fastethernet 0/# (or, in short form, int f0/#).

The switch output below shows the configuration of a Fast Ethernet port on the 1900 switch:

```
Seans1912(config)#int fastethernet ?
  <0-0>  FastEthernet IEEE 802.3
Seans1912(config)#int fastethernet 0/?
  <26-27>  FastEthernet IEEE 802.3
Seans1912(config)#int fastethernet 0/26
Seans1912(config-if)#int fast 0/27
Seans1912(config-if)#^Z
```

Notice that the command is interface fastethernet, but the slot is still 0. The only ports available are 26 and 27.

Setting Descriptions

To set the descriptions, you need to be in interface configuration mode. From interface configuration mode, use the description command to describe each interface. You can make the descriptions more than one word, but you can't use spaces. You'll have to use the underscore, as shown below:

```
Seans1912#config t
Enter configuration commands, one per line.  End
↳with CNTL/Z
Seans1912(config)#int e0/1
```

```
Seans1912(config-if)#description Finance_VLAN
Seans1912(config-if)#int f0/26
Seans1912(config-if)#description trunk_to_Building_4
Seans1912(config-if)#^Z
```

In this configuration example, we set the description on both a
10 Mbps port and a 100 Mbps port.

Viewing Descriptions

Once you have configured the descriptions you want on each interface, you can then view the descriptions with either the show
interface or show running-config command. Here is an example:

```
Seans1912#sh int e0/1
Ethernet 0/1 is Suspended-no-linkbeat
Hardware is Built-in 10Base-T
Address is 0030.80CC.7D01
MTU 1500 bytes, BW 10000 Kbits
802.1d STP State:  Forwarding      Forward
↳Transitions:  1
Port monitoring: Disabled
Unknown unicast flooding: Enabled
Unregistered multicast flooding: Enabled
Description: Finance_VLAN
Duplex setting: Half duplex
Back pressure: Disabled

Seans1912#sh run
Building configuration...

Current configuration:
hostname " Seans1912"
!
ip address 172.16.10.16 255.255.255.0
ip default-gateway 172.16.10.1
!
interface Ethernet 0/1
```

```
    description "Finance_VLAN"
!
[output cut]
```

Notice in the above switch output that the sh int e0/1 command and the show run command both show the description set on an interface.

Configuring the Port Duplex

The 1900 switch has only 12 or 24 10BaseT ports and comes with one or two Fast Ethernet ports. You can only set the duplex on the 1900 switch, as the ports are all fixed speeds. Use the duplex command in interface configuration.

In the switch output below, notice the options available on the Fast Ethernet ports:

```
Seans1912(config)#int f0/26
Seans1912(config-if)#duplex ?
   auto                Enable auto duplex configuration
   full                Force full duplex operation
   full-flow-control   Force full duplex with flow
 ↳control
   half                Force half duplex operation
Seans1912(config-if)#duplex full
```

Verifying IP Connectivity

It is important to test the switch IP configuration. You can use the ping program, and you can telnet to the 1900 switch. However, you cannot telnet from the 1900 switch or use traceroute.

In the following example, we ping a host on the network from the 1900 CLI. Notice the output on a successful ping: exclamation points (!). If you receive periods (.) instead of exclamation points, that signifies a time-out:

```
Seans1912#ping 172.16.10.10
```

Sending 5, 100-byte ICMP Echos to 172.16.10.10, time
↳out is 2 seconds:

!!!!!

Success rate is 100 percent (5/5), round-trip min/
↳avg/max 0/2/10/ ms

Seans1912#**telnet 172.16.10.10**

                    ^

% Invalid input detected at '^' marker.

In the Telnet example above, notice the error when we tried to telnet from the 1900 switch. The command is not available on the 1900 switch. However, remember that you can telnet *to* a switch at any time, as long as IP is configured correctly.

Erasing the Switch Configuration

The switch configuration is stored in NVRAM just as any router. You cannot view the startup-config, or contents of NVRAM. You can only view the running-config. When you make a change to the switches' running-config, the switch automatically copies the configuration on the switch to NVRAM. This is a big difference from a router, where you have to type copy running-config startup-config. That option is not available on the 1900 switch.

You can delete the configuration in NVRAM on the 1900 switch if you want to start over and reconfigure the switch. To delete the contents of NVRAM on a 1900 switch, use the delete NVRAM command.

Notice in the switch output below that there are two options: nvram and vtp.

Seans1912#**delete ?**

  nvram NVRAM configuration

  vtp   Reset VTP configuration to defaults

Seans1912#**delete nvram**

This command resets the switch with factory
defaults. All system parameters will revert to
their default factory settings. All static and
dynamic addresses will be removed.

Reset system with factory defaults, [Y]es or [N]o?**y**

We want to delete the contents of NVRAM to the factory default settings. Notice the message received from the switch when the command delete NVRAM is used. Once you say yes, the configuration is gone.

Exam Essentials

Remember how to set the IP address on the 1900 switch. Use the global configuration command ip address.

Remember how to verify the IP address on the 1900 switch. Use the privileged-mode command show ip.

Key Terms and Concepts

1900 switch   Low-end switch from Cisco that runs the Cisco IOS.

duplex   Switch ports can either run half-duplex or full-duplex. Full-duplex provides twice the bandwidth that half-duplex provides.

nonvolatile RAM (NVRAM)   Keeps the switch configuration even if it is powered down.

Sample Questions

1. Which of the following is *not* true regarding the 1900 switch?

A. You can ping from a 1900 switch if configured.

B. You can ping to a 1900 switch if configured.

C. You can telnet to a 1900 switch if configured.

D. You can telnet from a 1900 switch if configured.

Answer: D. You cannot telnet from the 1900 switch CLI or Menu.

2. What command sets interface e0/10 on a 1900 switch to run full-duplex Ethernet?

   A. `full duplex on`

   B. `duplex on`

   C. `duplex full`

   D. `full-duplex`

   E. `set duplex on full`

   Answer: C. The interface command `duplex full` sets the interface to full-duplex communication.

3. If you wanted to verify the duplex on a 1900 switch, port 26, what command should you use?

   A. `sh port 26`

   B. `sh int 26`

   C. `sh int e0/26`

   D. `sh int f0/26`

   E. `sh int g0/26`

   F. `sh int h0/26`

   Answer: D. The 1900 switch uses the `show interface` *type slot/port* command to verify the duplex on a 1900 switch.

4. If you want to delete the `startup-config` on a 1900 switch, what command do you use?

   A. `erase startup-config`

   B. `delete startup-config`

   C. `delete nvram`

   D. `delete startup`

   Answer: C. The command `delete nvram` clears the configuration and restores the factory default configuration of the switch.

5. What commands would you use to identify port 3 on a 1900 switch and identify the switch as the Finance Server?

A. int e0/3, description Finance Server

B. int e0/3, description Finance_Server

C. set port name e0/3 Finance Server

D. set port name e0/3 Finance_Server

Answer: B. To configure the port 3 on the switch with a description, use the int e0/3 command in global configuration mode to enter the interface's configuration mode. Then assign a description using the description command, followed by the description you wish to assign to the port.

Index

Note to the Reader: Page numbers in **bold** indicate principle discussions of a topic or definitions of terms. Page numbers in *italic* indicate illustrations.

F

X

GET CISCO CERTIFIED WITH THE EXPERTS!

**CCNA™: Cisco®
Certified Network Associate®
Study Guide, 2nd Edition**
0-7821-2647-2

**CCDP™: Cisco®
Internetwork Design
Study Guide**
0-7821-2639-1

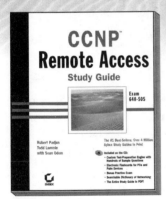

**CCNP: Remote Access
Study Guide**
0-7821-2710-X

CISCO STUDY GUIDES FROM SYBEX

- ◆ Written by renowned author Todd Lammle and his team of expert authors
- ◆ Up-to-date, comprehensive coverage of the revised Cisco exams
- ◆ Hands-on and written labs, plus hundreds of sample questions
- ◆ Assessment tests and practice exams
- ◆ Two technical edits ensure accuracy and relevance of information
- ◆ 700-800 pp; 7.5x9; Hardcover; $49.99

CUTTING-EDGE TEST PREP SOFTWARE ON THE CD

Electronic Flashcards help reinforce key information

Custom Testing Engine simulates Cisco's test format

Bonus Exam assesses knowledge retention

Searchable Ebook allows readers to study anytime, anywhere

CD Content: *CCNA Virtual Lab* e-trainer demo, *Dictionary of Networking* Ebook, and software utilities!

Also available:

CCNP™: Support Study Guide • 0-7821-2713-4
CCDA™: Cisco® Certified Design Associate Study Guide • 0-7821-2534-4
CCNP: Switching Study Guide • 0-7821-2711-8
CCNP: Routing Study Guide • 0-7821-2712-6
CCIE™: Cisco® Certified Internetwork Expert Study Guide
0-7821-2657-X

SYBEX®
www.sybex.com

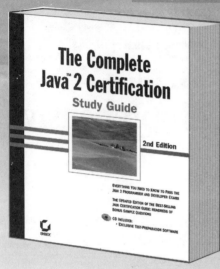

Visual JumpStart
Books from Sybex

The Fast and Easy Way to Learn!

AutoCAD 2000 — 0-7821-2777-0 · $19.99

Home Networking — 0-7821-2795-9 · $19.99

Dreamweaver Fireworks — 0-7821-2832-7 · $19.99 — Available soon

Photoshop — 0-7821-2866-1 · $19.99 — Available soon

Are you tired of wading through an ocean of text when you want to learn new software? If so, why not try *Visual JumpStart* books from Sybex? Just look at these features:

- Clear step-by-step explanations

- Concise coverage of essential features and tasks

- Easy-to-read screen shots reinforce your understanding

- Eye-pleasing illustrations to guide you through each task

- Real-world insights from expert trainers

www.sybex.com   SYBEX®

SYBEX BOOKS ON THE WEB

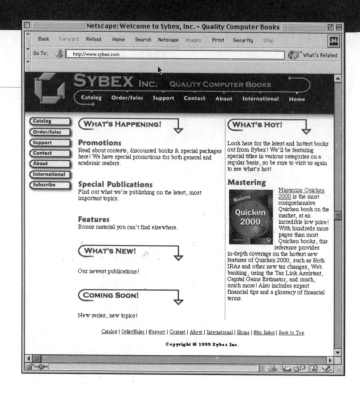

A t the dynamic and informative Sybex Web site, you can:

- view our complete online catalog
- preview a book you're interested in
- access special book content
- order books online at special discount prices
- learn about Sybex

www.sybex.com

SYBEX Inc. • 1151 Marina Village Parkway
Alameda, CA 94501 • 510-523-8233

SYBEX®